FAMILY
LAW

SECOND EDITION

DUNCAN J. BLOY, BA, LLM
Head of Law, Polytechnic of Wales

Series Editor C.J. CARR, MA, BCL

**BLACKSTONE
PRESS LIMITED**

This edition published in Great Britain 1989 by Blackstone Press Limited, Aldine Place, London W12 8AA

ISBN: 1 85431 031 3

Previously published by Financial Training Publications Limited
First edition, 1985

Typeset by LKM Typesetting Ltd, London EC1
Printed by Dotesios Printers Ltd, Bradford-on-Avon

Cartoons drawn by Anne Lee

CONTENTS

PREFACE

The second edition of this book seeks to reflect the major developments in family law over the last three years and suggests ways in which to approach the study of those issues which are currently under review, in particular changes to the law of divorce and new child care legislation. The chapters on children have been substantially rewritten and that on matrimonial jurisdiction has been sacrificed to allow for new material to be inserted.

I do hope that the second edition will enjoy as much support from students as did the first. The rapid changes in many areas of family law call for constant reassessment of the approach to study and I have endeavoured to give as much advice as possible on how to deal with laws which are subject to critical scrutiny and ultimately radical change.

I would again like to express my appreciation to Heather Saward at Blackstone Press for help in preparing the second edition and to wish her and her colleagues, Jonathan Harris and Alistair MacQueen every success with the new company. I would also like to express my grateful thanks to Mrs Glenys Williams for typing the new material for this edition and to Ann Cross for her assistance in tracing source material.

I would like to dedicate this edition to my parents who recently celebrated their golden wedding anniversary — which just goes to show that there are many people for whom this book, and the laws which it describes, is unnecessary!

The law is stated as at 1st August 1988.

INTRODUCTION: PASS FAMILY LAW

The examiners were not surprised when Timothy Woods failed the third year of his law degree, as they had been generally unimpressed by the standard of his work. However, they were amazed when they realised that he had achieved only 23% in family law. One commented in his report, 'I looked long and hard for any evidence which would have indicated that he had appreciated the purpose of the examination he had taken. There was no evidence of wider reading nor any sign that if there had been he would have known how to apply such knowledge to the questions set.'

Another said, 'I wanted to help but could find no reason whatsoever in the script before me, as to why I should have sympathy towards this candidate'.

The above story, essentially fact, is not untypical. Yet one finds that it is difficult to comprehend, as undergraduates reading family law, usually in their second or third year, confess that they find it an 'easy subject', although often they are unsure, when challenged, of what precisely they mean by the comment. My own feeling is that the depth of the subject is underestimated in the extreme and that students are often mentally unprepared for the rigours of the subject.

Some see it in a 'journalistic' context. Most of our daily newspapers, especially the tabloids, regale us with stories of divorce, adultery by the famous, or gargantuan claims for maintenance by the wives of the rich. We read about child kidnapping, child abuse, 'common-law wives', cohabitation contracts, inability to consummate, domestic violence and the like over our cornflakes and perhaps some are lulled into believing that the subject is not the academic equal of equity or land law. It is too easy to convince ourselves that because family law is often placed into a 'social context' then subjective opinion is an adequate substitute for informed comment. First-year undergraduates facing examinations the following week were told by their professor that they were 'all worms', their views worthless when compared to those of Lord Denning and his fellow judges. After all, he continued, 'You've studied law for 25 weeks; most of the judges have spent 25 years practising it'. They were suitably humbled but I believe remembered the moral behind the homily. Many students of family law, and other subjects as well, would do well to think of themselves as parasitic creatures, because to do well they must 'live' off the wisdom of others.

It might, of course, have helped Tim Woods and others who have failed family law examinations if their tutors had made it clear precisely what was expected of them when it came to the examinations – normally a three-hour, unseen paper covering a range of topics dealt with briefly during the academic year.

Is it enough to set one essay each term or to instruct the student to prepare a couple of tutorial papers? How does this help students to grasp, at an early stage, exactly what examiners will be looking for in those warm, balmy May days when they will be sweating it out in an examination room which only days before had been a sports hall or perhaps a dance studio. Can the student glean any assistance as to how to deal with examinations from the books which he is encouraged to buy at the beginning of each year? Ought they to be able to look to this medium for help? The latest textbook dealing with the subject runs to nearly 800 pages. It is a masterly work, well researched and up to date. It is both descriptive and analytical, it is questioning and incisive, not afraid to criticise. One would automatically consult it in order to appreciate the finer points of the subject, yet nowhere is any advice given to the student on how to deal with this impressive amount of information. Ought the undergraduate to seek to memorise and regurgitate at examination time? Or should it, perhaps, be used only to shed further light on topics covered in lectures, in other words, regarded as a reference work? Need the student think for himself about issues when the chances are the author has already stolen a march on him? I say this not as a criticism, but nevertheless it is a fact that students are not advised on how to use the knowledge they can readily glean from its many pages (P. M. Bromley and N. V. Lowe, *Family Law*, 7th ed.).

The preface to another recent family law book, *The Family, Law and Society: Cases and Materials* (2nd ed.) by B. M. Hoggett and D. S. Pearl, states its aim to be 'to introduce the student of family law to a far wider range of material than is to be found in the statutes and law reports'.

In this latter book the reader is faced with nearly 700 pages of material appertaining to family law. The other standard text, S. M. Cretney's *Principles of Family Law*, 4th ed., has over 1,000 pages and one feels it is legitimate to ask the question: How is the undergraduate meant to respond to this welter of information in the context of a 25 to 30-week course in family law with the inevitable examination at its conclusion? After all, the publishers of these texts all state that the books are aimed primarily at the student market.

It is incumbent upon me to attempt to justify why, in an already overcrowded academic market I am producing a text aimed once again at the undergraduate and, if we are to believe him, his dwindling grant provided from the public purse.

The first edition of this book attempted to identify from the vast range of materials in family law those which in the author's opinion deserved to be mentioned when a student was answering a question on a particular topic. So in that context much substantive law was discussed. Thus my aim was to identify and categorise those areas of family law which appeared to have most significance for the undergraduate.

The fact that a second edition has so quickly followed the first is some evidence that students have found the book useful in helping them to isolate important material to be used in examinations.

The primary aim of the book is to show the student *when* to use that material and *how* it should be done. Assessment procedures vary, from unseen papers to open book examinations and continuous assessment, so reference will be made to those different methods of testing the student's knowledge and ability to apply the law. I do not make the claim that in each chapter the material mentioned will necessarily be prescriptive for examinations, but I would claim that it is highly probable that such materials will have to be used and in the ways suggested in the text. The important element is, of course, *how* to apply the knowledge gained during the period of study. This is the very essence of the book – the thing that does not appear as significant in the other family law texts.

Glanville Williams has described his book, *Learning the Law*, 11th ed., as a 'guide, philosopher and friend'. It is hoped that students will be persuaded to believe that this book and indeed the series of which it forms a part, will guide them through their studies, and that they have 'a friend at court' – of which the *Concise Oxford Dictionary*, 7th ed. (Clarendon Press, 1982), gives the following apposite definition, 'one whose influence may be made use of' – so that on judgment day the student will be sufficiently skilled in order not only to pass but to pass with distinction.

It will undoubtedly be of help if the student appreciates why a particular format of examination has been chosen, information will be given on what the examiner is 'looking for' so that ultimately the examinee's thought processes will be activated as soon as he sees the style of the question set. In other words, matters of construction.

ONE

HOW TO STUDY AND WHY

If you have seen other books in this series you will be aware of the advice which has been tendered on a multitude of issues appertaining to the study of law. Authors have variously written on topics from the value of lectures, to the ability to answer examination questions. It may be confidently asserted that, irrespective of the branch of law under investigation the advice given is sound and therefore of immense value. However, the undergraduate reading family law is likely to do so in his second or third year and should, therefore, already be aware of the basic guidelines on study and examination techniques. It is not, therefore, my intention merely to repeat such general information but rather to address my comments directly to family law issues and where possible illustrate the point by reference to up-to-date case law or other authority.

More than a decade spent in higher education has led me to reach certain conclusions about how a student ought to approach the study of family law, thus leading to success in examinations in the subject. The first piece of advice I would offer is that students ought to believe in their own abilities. Most will have reached university or polytechnic on the strength of quite high-grade passes in A level subjects. At the time of writing a minimum combination for entry to university to read law would be BCC and admission to a polytechnic law degree would normally be on a range from CC to CCC. The institution is, at that stage, indicating that it believes that you have the potential to obtain a degree, the class of which will depend on your performance while on the course. (Take heart from this!) However, your task has not been to reach university or polytechnic, that is just a pre-condition to the ultimate goal of becoming a law graduate.

Once you have taken up your place on the course, seek to adopt a questioning approach to your studies. The law student ought to have an enquiring mind combined with a confident personality which will allow him to receive and express opinions on a whole range of legal disciplines ranging from the English legal system to the most complex matter of international law. Most degree courses are preceded by some kind of *induction course* which ought to introduce to students some of the skills which they will be expected to display during their time at the institution. Students who opt for family law will normally expect to face a programme of lectures and tutorials as with most other subjects on the degree and therefore it is legitimate to pass comment on these two features. The lecture format is generally accepted in higher education as a useful means of transmitting a body of knowledge appropriate to the abilities, needs and expectations of the student. The recipient is recognised as possessing certain skills in that he can receive and digest information, his needs are usually perceived to be to acquire a basic set of notes upon which to build and his expectation will be to use this material in a constructive way so as to achieve success in the examinations.

The student will undoubtedly expect that if he attends lectures and makes adequate notes of what is being said then he will have a context in which to work and prepare for examinations. He would not expect questions to be set upon topics which have not been covered in lectures. At the outset of the course the lecturer ought to make it clear to students whether or not there is an expectation that questions will be set upon topics discussed only in tutorials. Nevertheless one often finds that a student likes to 'play safe' and work only to material dealt with in lectures and backed up in tutorials.

The lecture in family law

It has already been mentioned in the introduction that the major student text in family law runs to nearly 800 pages. The lecture programme will last for approximately 24 weeks. It is therefore unreasonable and also unhealthy to assume that the lecturer will cover all the material listed in the textbook. It is permissible for students to enquire of their lecturer exactly what he hopes to cover during the year. This will help them to structure their work programme, in that certain parts of the syllabus will be likely to receive longer treatment, because, for example, the matter of law is currently under review or there has been a particularly controversial decision which has thrown the law into turmoil. This latter point may arise with some regularity in family law as judges struggle with policy issues or attempt to do justice between the particular parties, but where the existing law does not, they perceive, help them to achieve one objective let alone both.

The lecturer will endeavour to state the principles of family law and give references to case law and important legislation. Whilst family law can no longer be considered as a 'black letter' law subject it can still legitimately call in aid many thousands of decisions from which the general principles of the subject are meant to be gleaned. Therefore, listen carefully to any cases quoted. Make a note of the reference, if given, and pay attention as your lecturer seeks to explain the significance of the case. Note the level at which it was decided and whenever you are given a case of some significance, resolve to 'look it up' in the library later. As you do this you should have your lecture notes close at hand to provide guidance as you attempt to find the significant point of the case. A lecturer, aware that all too often students do not go to the law reports will sometimes give only the name and reference and advise students to 'read it'. It is likely that such a case will have significance and you ignore it at your peril. In addition, if you do read the case but have difficulty understanding the principles don't be afraid to challenge your lecturer or tutor when next you see him.

Family law is a subject which inevitably, year in, year out, produces topical and hopefully interesting material. A good lecturer will seek to incorporate this into his programme of work in the hope that the student will be stimulated by the fact that he is 'experiencing' a 'living' issue. A good example is when Parliament is seeking to introduce, consolidate or change legislation. Recently family law students have had the opportunity to listen to the arguments in favour of a radical alteration to existing child care law. The media attention which has focused on the issue of child sexual abuse in light of the *Cleveland* enquiry has given students a marvellous opportunity to understand the real dilemmas facing not just parents and children, but the agencies charged with the responsibility of investigating child sexual abuse. The inadequacies of the Children and Young Persons Act 1969 have been exposed and, hopefully, it is easier now for students to understand why change is necessary. In addition, a comprehensive review of child care law took place in 1985 which culminated in a government White Paper (Command 62) being published in January 1987, entitled *'The Law on Child Care and Family Services'*. The Government is committed to new legislation in 1989 and students therefore have all the basic information necessary from these sources, together with the Cleveland Inquiry Report, to underpin their study of changes in child care law. It also goes without saying that knowledge of important case law which has exposed deficiencies in the working of the 1969 Act is necessary to a full understanding. A good example of this is the House of Lords decision in *D (A Minor)* v *Berkshire County Council and others* [1987] 1 All ER 20.

The next point, of course, is that lectures on family law will often contain not only standard legal references but also touch upon the background issues such as those mentioned above. Family law teaching, it is argued, ought to reflect the social context of the subject-matter. One is, after all, dealing with people, feelings, moral, religious and ethical matters, policy, economics, politics, and more so perhaps than in any other aspect of law.

It is not expected that at the end of a lecture a student will, if cross-examined, be able to wax lyrical about all that he has just heard. More often than not he has had his work cut out just keeping up with the lecturer's comments. *Do not* attempt to take down every word. It is impossible. *Do* attempt to be selective and make a note of the major points raised. The notes, after all, are only the basic outlines from which to 'construct your case' to put to the court – in this case the examiner.

It is often alleged that students have few original thoughts. Let us be charitable and assume that you are an exception. Have you contemplated the possibility of noting down your own thoughts on issues raised by the lecturer? Does a question occur to you but the opportunity does not arise where it can be asked? If so, then make a note of it, possibly in the margin against the particular piece of information which has prompted you to assume the need for clarification. The writing of *effective* lecture notes ought to include not only important information but also your own thoughts and reactions to the matters mentioned. To think for yourself is no bad thing.

The induction course to which reference was made earlier will have introduced you to the techniques of how to analyse a law report. Those techniques will have been developed further in the course on the English legal system (or some other contemporary title). But they are also relevant beyond the bounds of such courses. Family law with its fair share of House of Lords and Court of Appeal decisions merits a 'judicial' approach to cases. The lecturer ought to endeavour to point out the *ratio* of a case or indicate that a comment was merely 'by the way'. It should never be thought that just because a statement is *'obiter dicta'* that it is irrelevant to the student. Eventually you will be collecting evidence upon which to make submissions and such information can be important to your case. Remember also that cases may be distinguished and thus an earlier authority appears to diminish in importance. Take care to note that in some areas of family law, especially in matters appertaining to custody and the matrimonial home, the courts prefer to talk of guidelines rather than precedents. It would be unusual, given the extent of the case law, to find lecturers spending a lot of time detailing facts of cases. The norm, it is suggested, would be for the lecturer to emphasise the crucial parts which have had some impact upon the decision. For example, if the case is concerned with what ought to be done with the matrimonial home upon divorce then the following points may be emphasised in the lecture:

(a)   Length of time the spouses have lived there.
(b)   Whether or not there are any children of the family and their ages.
(c)   The financial and in particular capital positions of the parties.
(d)   Their needs and obligations both now and in the future.

These sorts of matters would be extremely relevant to help a judge determine the correct course of action to take.

Given also that decision-making in family law is often intimately bound up with some social considerations then you should ensure that the full social significance of the case is mentioned in your notes. In 1976 Parliament passed the Domestic Violence and Matrimonial Proceedings Act, a response to the concern vociferously expressed by various pressure groups about wife battering or 'domestic hooliganism' as Sir George Baker P was later to call it. Civil remedies were created including the right to exclude a spouse or cohabitee from the matrimonial home. In *Spindlow* v *Spindlow* [1979] 1 All ER 169 Ormrod LJ had dealt with the matter of exclusion as 'essentially a housing matter, housing for the children', even though there was no evidence of violence or ill-will. The

New Law Journal referred to it as a case of 'domestic non-violence'. A lecturer therefore dealing with the case would mention the social background to the legislation and presumably endeavour to show how this influenced the judge's interpretation. However Lord Hailsham of St Marylebone LC in *Richards* v *Richards* [1983] 2 All ER 809 specifically disapproved of the *modus operandi* on the basis that relevant statute law had been ignored by the Court of Appeal. It was unlikely, said the Lord Chancellor, that s. 1 of the Domestic Violence and Matrimonial Proceedings Act 1976 'can be applicable unless there be shown violence, or the threat of it or reasonable apprehension that the presence of the man (or woman) in the house constitutes a danger to the physical or emotional health or well-being of the woman (or man) and the children'.

Therefore, if this was being discussed in lectures, the student would:

(a)   note the *legal* point made by Lord Hailsham — i.e., the Court of Appeal should not ignore statutory provisions, and

(b)   the social background which might have persuaded Ormrod LJ to adopt the course of action subsequently disapproved by the House.

Saving time

A great deal of time can be saved in lectures by the judicious use of abbreviation when taking notes. The use of H and W for husband and wife will be of great advantage and it is acceptable to shorten case names which involve husband and wife by using the figure 2 after the first name, e.g., *Brown* v *Brown* becomes *Brown 2*. Much consternation is caused to students by the standard practice of using letters when describing cases involving children. My advice is that a student really ought to try to remember the very important cases, gaining assistance both from the date *and* the subject matter, e.g., *Re B* [1981] (Wardship — mongol baby case) as distinct from *Re B* [1987] (Wardship — sterilisation case). We are not, as examiners, it must be stressed, out to test your ability to remember case names. So to use 'in an important Lords case' or 'the Court of Appeal ruled in a case in 1985' is quite satisfactory. Family law statutes often have lengthy titles and standard abbreviations abound, e.g., Matrimonial Causes Act 1973 (MCA), Domestic Violence and Matrimonial Proceedings Act 1976 (DVMPA), Guardianship of Minors Act 1971 (GMA), and so on. Some statutes have such lengthy titles that even the abbreviated form seems to create a new word, e.g., the Health and Social Services and Social Security Adjudications Act 1983 becomes HASSASSAA 1983.

Structure

Lecture notes ought to be structured so as to facilitate easy expansion, recall and act as a solid foundation for revision purposes. The task ought to be relatively straightforward as the lecturer ought himself to structure the delivery of the information. The student response would be to use headings emphasising by thick lines when one topic ends and another begins. It is advisable to use loose-leaf files for the collection of notes as this allows for easy insertion and expansion at a later stage. Write only on one side of the paper. It would be unusual for a new case not to be reported during the year and this can then be added at the relevant place.

Conclusion

Lecture notes are valuable providing they are accurate, comprehensible and structured. They ought to be expanded and reviewed regularly. Constant revision is the best. *Never* treat them as being sufficient for examination purposes. Lecturers are not flattered, and they do not expect, to see their notes quoted back at them in the examinations.

Tutorials in family law

It is normal to assume that students will need to acquire study skills. In lectures it is often assumed that the student is partaking in a passive activity although I have suggested above that this need not be necessarily the case.

However, when one comes to assess the relevance of tutorials or seminars in a family law programme it soon becomes obvious that many new study skills need to be acquired. The tutorial provides the student with the following opportunities:

(a)   To read and assess material set by the tutor in advance of the tutorial.

(b)   To advance ideas and opinions based upon (a) above.

(c)   To receive the same from other members of the tutorial group.

(d)   To argue, discuss, agree/disagree with others, thus aiding the student's ability to think spontaneously and as a result improve his self-confidence.

(e)   To take some notes for further study based upon comments made by the tutor or by colleagues which are endorsed by the group and/or the tutor.

They are not designed as an ideal climate or setting in which to cultivate academic wallflowers, yet we are all aware of students who do not make any voluntary contributions to such a gathering. In a subject like family law which takes a multi-perspective look at the subject-matter it should be possible for even the most timid of characters to make a meaningful contribution. Tutorial input is becoming increasingly important as many institutions move away from total reliance on traditional examinations in favour of assessed coursework, counting up to 30% of the final mark. Some departments now assess tutorial contribution and therefore thorough preparation and the confidence to contribute to the discussion are essential if you wish to gain a high rating.

Advance preparation

Many institutions will provide their students with 'tutorial sheets' listing relevant case law, statutes, articles, discussion points, past questions. Such material is usually too extensive to cover in one round of tutorials but the device is useful in that it provides information as to the extent to which the student ought to prepare the subject-matter. The tutorial itself may centre around discussion of a problem or assessing the validity of comments made in various leading cases and articles.

As the financial pressures in higher education mount the size of tutorial groups is likely to rise from a norm of around six or seven to a figure often in excess of ten. Some departments work on a minimum tutorial size of ten. It is thus becoming easier for the student who has done little or no preparation to escape without making a contribution to the discussion. Such students tend to exhibit the following giveaway signs:

(a)   Lecture notes spread out. Constant leafing through such notes every time a question is asked.

(b)   Eyes never raised from the folder until the question is answered by a colleague.

(c)   Often a student will attempt (a) and (b) above using a textbook and if challenged claim that he has forgotten his family law file! No file — no answer!

All this, of course, gives a clear indication that it is foreseeable that this student will have examination difficulties. I have stated that continuous work and revision is the best methodology to adopt but the student just described is not working and has therefore little or nothing from which to revise.

In colleges where tutorial contribution is not assessed an examinations board may have to consider student performance during the year in order to arrive at an appropriate degree classification in cases where a student's marks indicate that he is firmly fixed between classes. The board will consider not only marks gained for written work but also the general impression given to tutors throughout the session. Therefore your tutorial contribution may indeed have an important influence on your final classification.

One question you may care to consider is: Could my performance in tutorials be improved and if so how?

Tutorial preparation

A great proportion of your study time will be taken up in preparing for tutorials. If you are given tutorial sheets, make a careful note of the articles it is suggested that you read. It is most unlikely that you will have to read every one *in toto* in order to improve your chances of understanding the law and passing the examination. Indeed it may not be just articles but whole books which are cited. This is when your lecture notes may become invaluable. With these open at the relevant page you should be able to cross-reference your lecturer's comments with material listed on the sheets. For example, if you are studying custody of children your reading list may contain a reference to a book entitled *Child Custody and Divorce* by Susan Maidment (Croom Helm, 1984). Your first thought on seeing it is likely to be that a lot of law exists to deal with something as small as a child! The book then needs to be used as a reference text. Let us assume that your lecture notes dwell upon the feasibility of divorce courts awarding joint legal custody as the norm. The notes ought to have briefly rehearsed the arguments for and against such a presumption. Maidment deals with joint custody in Chapter II comprising twelve pages under six sub-headings. This makes it much easier for you to note relevant and important points. She also refers to key cases such as *Dipper* v *Dipper* [1980] 2 All ER 722 and *Jussa* v *Jussa* [1972] 1 WLR 881. One should then check to see whether or not such cases are mentioned in your notes. In addition do remember that it usually takes some three or four months from the manuscript being delivered to the book being available for purchase. Therefore are there any new cases which are not included in the text but which your lecturer has brought to your attention? If so consider whether or not they have any effect on the statements being made by the author. Do they confirm the line adopted in the previous cases or are they distinguished in any way? The availability of the Lexis computer facility in most law libraries now means that unreported cases are easily accessible to students and some of these may influence quite dramatically the issue under discussion. Look closely at the figures cited and ask yourself are they up to date. Mrs Maidment says that in 1981, 145,713 married couples divorced, 60% of whom had children under 16. Don't just quote that figure; check to see what the latest position is. You then may be able to draw a conclusion, e.g., that divorce has levelled out, or is in steep decline (unlikely) or continues to rise but slowly. Remember the things left unsaid in books and articles can be as or more important than some of the things taken up in the text. In addition to case law developments, one may also find that the particular area of law has attracted the attention of the Law Commission. This is a highly likely occurrence in family law as the Commission has a 'rolling' programme of revision in this field. Therefore, if the matter under consideration is joint custody of children, then you would be expected to be aware of two working papers published in 1986, dealing with the review of child law. Working papers Nos. 96 and 96(a) contain much valuable information on joint custody (see pp. 125-129 (No. 96) and pp. 41-62 (No. 96(a))), although it should be recognised that this only takes you up to August 1986 and must not be seen as representing the latest information on this subject.

When one refers to 'material' we are concerned not only with books but also case law. Cases listed on a tutorial sheet will, in the main, represent the leading cases on the matter under discussion. They are the ones that you are most likely to quote in examinations and as such must be read carefully. Family law possesses its own series of law reports dating back to 1980 and in addition cases are extensively discussed in the periodical *Family Law*, notwithstanding with the utmost regularity the appearance of such cases in the standard law reports. What, therefore, ought you to look for when reading a case in preparation for a tutorial? Students often ask whether or not they ought to go to the report of the case or is it permissible to use a casebook or a cases and materials text? My answer is that the student ought to attempt to read the case at first hand. Casebooks are invariably selective in that the lack of space means that whole cases cannot be cited. This can be confusing if a particular judgment is quoted without an adequate context being given for reference. Arguably to use a casebook stifles initiative – you are letting someone else determine what is important and significant. You are bound to feel pleased if you have picked out certain things which are later endorsed in the tutorial as being the *ratio* of the case.

With the case in front of you and your lecture notes close at hand, read the headnote to the case. This will give you the relevant facts, help to give the case a context and ascertain the issue before the court. Reference will be made to any statutory provisions and there will be a 'potted' version of the decision, usually citing supporting authorities.

Once you have read the headnote decide just how much of that information you need to note and when you do so try to put it into your own words. *Do not* simply copy out the headnote – a process which involves little skill and is of little use at that stage.

Consider whether or not you need to refer to the judgments in the case and, if so, to what degree. Is it vital to read *all* of them or can you select certain parts which are of use? For example, in *Burns* v *Burns* [1984] 1 All ER 244 the Court of Appeal delivered a most significant judgment, dealing with the proprietary interests of cohabitees. The approach adopted in *Burns* v *Burns* was more recently endorsed by the Court of Appeal in *Grant* v *Edwards* [1986] 2 All ER 426 in determining how and in what circumstances a trust would be created. The report of *Burns* v *Burns* extends to 20 pages and it would take an hour to read, let alone to digest, the information.

The headnote makes it clear that the matter uppermost in the court's mind was how the major authorities of *Pettit* v *Pettit* [1970] AC 777 and *Gissing* v *Gissing* [1971] AC 886 were to be used in deciding the issue. Thus when scouring the pages of the report you ought to look for references to these cases. In a tutorial that would be a major discussion point. Yet one vital component in the case appears in the last few lines of the judgments of Fox and May LJJ. Both judges refer to injustice suffered by (Mrs) Burns, who had lived in the property for nearly 20 years, and go on to say that such injustice as there was must be remedied by Parliament and *not* the courts. But do not be satisfied with finding this point. What needs to be considered therefore is what, if any, parliamentary reforms are necessary. This would certainly be a very important matter to discuss in tutorials. Thus a careful look at judgments will sometimes bring to the surface matters which do not affect the legal issue in the case but which undoubtedly would give great scope for examination questions. It will also indicate that you have adopted a thinking approach to the case. To find such points does not presuppose that you need read the whole of the judgment. To 'scan' carefully will in most cases give you adequate opportunity to spot such matters. Once isolated you will then have to get down to the serious task of thinking about them. I have tried to indicate that in preparation for tutorials you have to collect and assess material and to think about ideas and opinions based upon the subject-matter. Once in the tutorial you will be able to discover whether others have reached your own standard and in so doing hopefully impress your tutor with the produce of your labours.

Students often enquire as to the importance of dissenting judgments. The answer is that as the law rarely stands still today's dissenting judgment may be tomorrow's majority opinion. If there is sufficient dissent then others will start to take notice. There has to be a reason for dissent and if that can be proffered to an examiner when discussing the matter then credit will be given.

Information is likely to be gleaned from books, articles and case reports. However, the student of family law may care to browse through reports produced by the Law Commission. The reports are of great benefit to the student in that the Commission invariably details the existing law and its apparent defects before going on to make suggestions for reforms.

Armed with all this source material you should be in a position to make a large and satisfying contribution to tutorials. However, remember that both lectures and tutorials are preparation, in the short term, for the examination and you should always be seeking to jot down material from whatever source that you think may be appropriate for examination purposes. Remember that the relevant examination material may range from a long, complicated argument comparing cases and seeking to extract particular principles to discussion of one word in a statute which is or has caused difficulty in interpretation. Often the latter may lead to the former if enough judges are allowed to give their opinions. Many past family law students will be aware of the difficulty caused by the inclusion of the word 'and' in s. 1(2)(a) of the Matrimonial Causes Act 1973. The word appeared to link the adultery required to evidence irretrievable breakdown of marriage with the further fact that the petitioner found it intolerable to live with the respondent: 'that the respondent has committed adultery *and* the petitioner finds it intolerable to live with the respondent'.

Did the use of the conjunction mean that the intolerability had to stem from the act of adultery or was intolerability something that could be wholly unrelated to the adultery, e.g., the respondent only bathed once a month or smoked in bed etc? The little word generated four cases within the space of two years culminating in a Court of Appeal decision, *Cleary* v *Cleary* [1974] 1 All ER 498 which indicated that it was not necessary to show that the adultery was the cause of the intolerability. This in turn was followed by *Carr* v *Carr* [1974] 1 All ER 1193 where a differently constituted Court of Appeal felt bound to follow the *Cleary* line but at the same time indicated in no uncertain terms that it doubted the decision. As the matter was never discussed by the Lords the *Cleary* position holds good today. It is, however, a good illustration of how one small word can generate a large amount of case law.

A similar, but more recent example is the interpretation to be given to the word 'conduct' in s. 25 of the Matrimonial Causes Act 1973.

Section 25 indicated that in exercising its powers in proceedings ancillary to divorce, nullity or judicial separation, the court was to have regard to the parties' *conduct*. What type of conduct we are not told. Conduct in its ordinary, dictionary sense means behaviour. Yet, as most law students will be aware, the Court of Appeal in *Wachtel* v *Wachtel* [1973] Fam 72 put a gloss on the word by adding the qualifying words 'obvious and gross'. To understand why the Court of Appeal should do this one needs to be aware of the *context* of this particular piece of legislation, i.e., to make a clear distinction between the basis for the divorce, e.g., adultery, and other proceedings which were designed to be the basis for future planning. One ought not to be penalised in financial, property or custody matters for what might be termed the responsibility for or contribution to the breakdown of the marriage.

Now, of course, Parliament has considered the issue again in the Matrimonial and Family Proceedings Act 1984, which substitutes a new s. 25 into the Matrimonial Causes Act 1973. Section 25(2)(g) now says that the court must have regard to 'the conduct of each of the parties, if that conduct is such that it would in the opinion of the court be inequitable to disregard it'. Parliament hasn't put on to a statutory basis the words 'obvious and gross' but it is now understood that these words will still be relevant in helping a court to determine when and if it is *inequitable* not to look at the conduct of the parties. In *Kyte* v *Kyte* [1987] 3 All ER 1041, at p. 1047 Purchas LJ accepted that Parliament had chosen not to use the words 'gross and obvious' and accepted that the new wording 'may give a broader discretion to the court than that envisaged hitherto by the authorities'. However, the headnote points out that the wife's conduct was 'gross and obvious' which it would be inequitable to disregard.

Students preparing for tutorials will often be referred to legislation which will require them to give consideration to a particular word or phrase in an Act. In family law one needs to be fully aware of the proper *context* of the legislation posing questions such as: Why was it necessary? and: Ought certain words to be interpreted by reference to that context? Also remember that judges may place a restrictive meaning or conversely give a very wide and flexible meaning to a word or phrase. The major question though is *why* has the court chosen this particular option? The moral is, of course, that the undergraduate ought to begin thinking about his learning strategy from the very first day, even perhaps before he has addressed his mind to any substantive issues.

In a tutorial the tutor will be seeking, as will ultimately the examiner, to discover whether you *understand* the principles of law. To *understand* in this context does not mean simply to *remember*. He will require evidence that you comprehend the significance of a particular principle within the general framework of that aspect of the law. For example, it is generally accepted that the law relating to *nullity* of marriage seeks to provide remedies to those whose marriage was, *at its inception*, flawed, either fundamentally or less significantly. By contrast the law on *divorce* is centred on the provision of a remedy if a defect materialises which puts the marriage in jeopardy, e.g., adultery or desertion.

It is a relatively simple task to remember the relevant law in ss. 1, 11 and 12 of the Matrimonial Causes Act 1973. A student may believe at this stage that he 'knows the principles'. This would not be strictly correct. He must be able to comprehend why a marriage is *void* if the parties are for example not respectively male or female (s. 11(c)). He must realise that void means 'never having legally come into existence'. That no matter however hard the parties may desire their 'marriage' to be ratified this is impossible as the leading case of *Hyde* v *Hyde* (1866) LR 1 P & D 130 demands that in English law a marriage is a 'voluntary union for life between *one man* and *one woman* to the exclusion of all others'. Equally he must understand the difference in *philosophy* between *void* and *voidable* 'marriages' and why Parliament has given the option to couples whose marriages are affected by the criteria in s. 12 to ratify. The reason is that the impact of the 'defects' listed in s. 12 are not so fundamental and do not necessarily offend against the basic tenets of marriage. (It could be argued that s. 12(c) is the exception as *Hyde* v *Hyde* does require the union to be entered into voluntarily, although conversely, if a voluntary consensus is present at a postceremony stage, then there is no reason to force the parties to go through the relevant procedures.) As to divorce the student must point out that the marriage is valid at its inception and will remain so until dissolved by a court of competent jurisdiction.

At the end of the day probably the two most important words to a law student are *how* and *why*? Ask yourself: How do I use the information I am gathering together and why, i.e., to what end or purpose?

Conclusion

In this chapter I have endeavoured to draw your attention to the value of lectures and tutorials and how you ought to set about your preparation. The extent and success of that preparation will be amply rewarded in the examinations. In the next chapter I shall discuss the process of revision for examinations, how they are structured and for what the examiner in family law is likely to be searching.

TWO

ASSESSMENT

In this chapter I shall deal with different modes of assessment and the various types of question with which you may be confronted on your degree course. Despite evidence that academics are giving much greater thought to the process of assessment, the three-hour unseen examination paper is still the norm in most universities and polytechnics, although the mark may have to be combined with a continuous assessment percentage before the final result in a particular subject is known. Views vary on the merits and effectiveness of any particular form of assessment. It is argued that the three-hour unseen paper, if the only method of assessment for the course, is too arbitrary in that it places too much pressure on a student to perform well on one special day in the year. Students we are told do have 'off days'. As such is it fair to examine the student's understanding of a whole year's work by this method? Whatever one's views, the procedure is universally adopted and in my experience students are not unduly worried at the prospect of having to face this type of examination.

Continuous assessment is now incorporated into degree schemes as a legitimate means of testing ability, although normally it works in conjunction with an unseen final examination, rather than having superseded this mode of assessment. Advocates of such a system maintain that the pressure is taken off the student in that he can have access to legal materials when he is preparing his answer and that this more accurately reflects what would happen in practice. No solicitor, it is said, would tender spontaneous advice to a client. He would gather the relevant information, research the area and then produce his findings. He would not be expected to retain in his memory hundreds of cases or to learn statutory provisions verbatim. This would appear to be a compelling argument but its advocates have yet to persuade others to dispense with the traditional mode of examination. As with all methods of assessment it has its drawbacks. Students already used at school to three-hour examinations may not readily take to the new skills needed to produce assessment essays. What happens if a piece of work is not handed in by the deadline? Does the student then forfeit his total mark for the piece? It may also lead to continuous pressure on the student as he realises that he has to do well in each particular piece of work in order to stand a good chance of obtaining a high grade at the end of the year.

It is my task, therefore, to make suggestions on how best to cope with both of these procedures. However, before I deal in detail with the modes of assessment it will be instructive to make some general points relating to revision and examination technique.

Revision

This is the one aspect of study that students, in the main, prefer to leave as late as possible in the academic year. No student will actually confess that he looks forward to revision although sooner or later he is going to have to come to terms with it. One can always think of things that would take precedence over revision, if given a free choice. It has already been suggested that the best way to attain a good standard of knowledge is to employ a continuous revision approach, yet in practice very few students will adhere to this advice. Students who are not prepared to do this can still help themselves by ensuring that at very least their preparation of material throughout the year has been of a high standard. At least then when a decision has been taken to begin revision you are not faced with incomplete notes and the decision whether or not to spend effort making up for lost opportunities or risk a gap in your knowledge.

Students invariably seek advice as to when they ought to begin revision. This will usually mean that your conscience is beginning to assert itself and send messages out to the effect that if you wish to stand any chance in the forth-coming examinations then now is the time to begin revision. The tutor's response will probably be 'Now!' or perhaps even 'Last week!' You really must give yourself as long as you possibly can to prepare for examinations. Nevertheless whenever you start you should ensure that whatever you do constitutes constructive and effective revision. If you plan a revision programme it means that you can still continue a relatively normal and enjoyable lifestyle while still making sure that revision takes place. If you live in a hall of residence it may be agreed when examinations are imminent that no noise should occur in communal areas between the hours of 7 p.m. and 10 p.m. You ought therefore to utilise this period and ensure that you have no other commitments which may interfere with study. At 10 p.m. you may then decide to join others for the last half-hour in the union bar or your favourite local hostelry knowing that you have worked effectively for three hours. To plan your revision is most important and to this end you may care to jot down an outline of your daily routine including travelling time, meal breaks, study periods, shopping expeditions, social activities and plan your day so that the routine is not unduly affected by your desire to revise but also that the revision is not placed second to other events. Students are full of good intentions and meticulous planning will mean that the intentions are realised before it is too late.

Assessment

Constructive revision

Are you going to have the opportunity in the examination to mention the thousand or so cases mentioned in the family law course? And what about all the articles, reports and textbooks which you have read and made notes upon? Three hours is not a long time when set against perhaps 70 to 80 hours of lectures and tutorials let alone private work.

Topics

First of all make a list of the subjects or topics covered during the course of the year. These will broadly correspond with textbook coverage although there may be 'special' topics covered during the year. A family law topic list would probably look something like this:

(a) Introduction (Mi).
(b) Creation of marriage (Mi).
(c) Nullity of marriage (Ma).
(d) Magistrates' jurisdiction (Mi).
(e) Domestic violence (Ma).
(f) Divorce (Ma).
(g) Ancillary provisions (Ma).
(h) Cohabitation (Ma).
(i) Children, custody, adoption (Ma).
(j) Wardship (Mi).
(k) Special topic — e.g., The need for a family court (Ma).
(l) Special topic — e.g., Child Abuse: the remedies (Ma).

Against each category put a symbol indicating whether or not the treatment of the topic during the year warrants it being regarded as an important or subsidiary matter. I have used the letters Ma (major) and Mi (minor) to differentiate.

When allocating time to each topic do it on a basis which adequately reflects the amount of effort expended on the subject. Once you have done this take each heading in turn and underneath list the major features as indicated in lecture notes or from tutorial preparation and discussion. Let us take an example. Assume that you are dealing with topic (i) above, i.e., children. Your note might look something like this:

CHILDREN
   (a)   CUSTODY OF CHILDREN
      (i)   Relevant legislation:
Guardianship of Minors Act 1971, ss. 1 and 9 (as amended by the Family Law Reform Act 1987)
Children Act 1975, ss. 86 and 87.
Matrimonial Causes Act 1973, s. 42.
      (ii)   Cross reference: wardship: Supreme Court Act 1981, s. 41.
      (iii)   Major cases:
J v *C* [1970] AC 668.
Re W (1983) 4 FLR 492.
Jussa v *Jussa* [1972] 2 All ER 600.
G v *G* [1985] 2 All ER 225.
(and so on).
      (iv)   Law Commission Working Papers 96 and Supplement (1986).
      (v)   Points specifically discussed in lectures/tutorials:
         (1)   Joint custody.
         (2)   Actual and legal custody.
         (3)   Welfare principle.
         (4)   First *and* paramount not first consideration.
         (5)   Access.
         (6)   Kidnapping of children.
         (7)   Role of the appellate court in custody.
         (8)   Position of father in custody disputes.
         (9)   Wishes of the children — impact of the *Gillick* case.

Now take each of these sub-headings and under the particular subject-matter list those cases, statutes, articles, comments etc. that it would appear vital to mention if you were to answer a question on this topic in the examinations. For example:

      (vi)   (7)   Role of the appellate court in custody:
Competing case law see: *Clarke-Hunt* v *Newcombe* (1983) 4 FLR 482, cf. *Dicocco* v *Milne* (1983) 4 FLR 247. Recently resolved in *G* v *G* [1985] 2 All ER 225.
    Post *G* v *G* case law, e.g., *Re G* [1987] 1 FLR 164 and *May* v *May* [1986] 1 FLR 325.
    Key issues:
            Discretionary jurisdiction.
            Rehearing?
            Application of wrong law.
            Meaning of 'wrong'.
            'Balancing exercise'.
            Irrelevant considerations taken into account.
            Germane matter left out of account.

Blatant error.
Purpose of appeal in custody cases. No precedents?
Time factor.
Comment? Articles? Quotations?, e.g., Eekelaar, *'Custody Appeals'*,
(1985) 48 Modern Law Review 704.

The fact that cases have occurred since the House of Lords decision would indicate that examiners may still consider it an issue worthy of mention in the examination. You have therefore isolated certain factors which you consider to be of great importance. Other information, especially of a factual nature could then be ignored or given a low priority. You are engaging in a thinking and constructive approach to revision recognising the limitations of the three-hour examination.

(vii) Past questions. If you have been given past questions look to see how they have been structured. Would the information that you have picked out suffice to provide a satisfactory answer to a problem on custody? To come up with the correct answer you need to know how to apply your knowledge, but more about this later in the chapter dealing with the welfare of the child.

What is extremely important is for you to appreciate that revision is not just about how much you can memorise. If you are in the habit of taking a mechanistic approach to revision, i.e., trying to remember everything in your notes without giving thought to the purpose and applications of your knowledge then you are likely to be wasting time and heading for a traumatic examination period. Don't be taken in by this practice. You may convince yourself that three hours 'reading' of notes has been very valuable and you can now take a well-earned rest. In educational terms it would have been preferable not to have started at all.

Your family law examination will contain both problem and essay questions. The purpose of your revision is to enable you to answer both types of question with consummate ease. You must therefore continually pose the questions: What is the importance of this? and How would I apply it in an examination? One other general point needs to be made. Don't forget that the time available for revision must be allocated twice. First between the number of subjects in which you are to be examined and secondly on a subject-by-subject basis. Thus if you have five subjects in year three your programme of revision on a weekly basis may be

Sunday	Monday	Tuesday	Wednesday	Thursday	Friday	Saturday
PUBLIC	FAMILY	WELFARE	LABOUR	TAX	FREE	FAMILY

If you are only spending one or two revision sessions per week on a subject it becomes increasingly obvious that every second must be used as effectively as possible. It may be the case that you have a preference for particular subjects. If you expect to do well in family and welfare law then you might allocate a little more time to these subjects because you may be rewarded with a first or upper second. However, this should not be done at the risk of failure in the other subjects. Adopt this tactic only if you are convinced that you will succeed and that your overall classification will not be jeopardised. Final degree classes are usually decided on marks achieved over two academic sessions. Some students may require only one or two of their five subjects to be in the upper second or first category to ensure a high overall classification. Others may need all five subjects to count equally in order to compensate for a poor Part I performance.

So plan your revision timetable carefully and try so far as possible to adhere to it. Once you have considered material it is important to keep on recalling it throughout the whole programme. It may well be that you allocate half an hour at the beginning of each day's work to give thought to previous revision in that subject. You need to refresh your memory constantly and if the material can be recalled fairly easily then it will give you a great psychological boost in preparation for that day's revision.

Revision in any subject needs careful planning and family law is no exception. Treat the subject seriously and do not underestimate the standards required. There is no easy way to learn family law and because of the diverse range of issues it may be harder than most to structure. I have always found students complaining of too little time to answer family law papers to their own satisfaction. Maybe that says more about the student and his process of revision and application of knowledge than it does about the examination paper.

Planning for examinations

It may be useful at this point, as you look ahead to the examination, to say something about how examiners create papers in their subject. My feeling is that if students are aware of how questions are constructed then they will be in a better position to provide an effective answer to such questions. Indeed I devote one round of tutorials each year to asking students to prepare a mock examination question which is then photocopied and passed to others in the group. We then set about seeking to determine what points of law the student was hoping to pose in his question. By this simple device one can illustrate to students how effective they have been in this exercise of academic construction. They then appreciate how points are run together to form a complete question. They also come to appreciate how an examiner must check and double-check in order to ensure that the question set is free from ambiguity. Those tutorials are often the most amusing of the year as students realise that something they have written is capable of more than one interpretation. For example:

Fred has lived in England with his parents since birth. In 1963 Fred, whilst on holiday in Spain, meets and intends to marry Anabella.

Anabella has lived in Spain since birth. In January 1965 Anabella joins Fred in England, on a Spanish passport, already two months pregnant! Fred and Anabella marry that year and set up their matrimonial home in Kent.

Fred is employed as a travelling salesman, whilst Anabella is a housewife. Seven months later their son Horatio was born, living in England for ten years.

In 1975 Horatio is sent to Canada for educational purposes, residing with Aunt Gertrude. Every summer Horatio accompanied Anabella to Spain to visit her family. Fred and Anabella separate in 1976. Anabella remains in England and takes up employment as a teacher. On completing his education in Canada, Horatio takes up employment in Canada.

In 1981 Horatio marries an English-born girl, Bernadette, in Canada. She has lived and been educated in Canada. Early in 1982 Bernadette gives birth to Christine. Tragically, later that year Horatio dies in a car crash. Bernadette takes Christine to England in early 1983.

Assess Anabella's, Bernadette's and Christine's position.

Have you ever seen a two months pregnant Spanish passport?!! Equally, the students do not make it clear exactly what the examinee is expected to discuss. Assess the parties' position in relation to what?

The following question is taken from a three-hour unseen family law paper in June 1987. I will endeavour to show how the question was constructed so that you will be able to appreciate what the examiner was seeking and how best to respond with the relevant techniques.

Gillian and Clive lived together as husband and wife along with their child Max, now aged 4. They are joint tenants of a council house. Four months ago Clive met Andrea and invited her to live with him in the council property. After two months Gillian found the situation intolerable and moved out leaving Max with Clive and Andrea. She has been living with her mother for the past two months but wants to return 'home' to be with Max. She consults you on her chances of excluding Clive and Andrea from the property. It is conceded by all parties that Max is well cared for but occasionally he says he would like to be with his mother.

Advise Gillian.

The examiner had decided that he wished to incorporate into the paper a question which covered the interrelated issues of cohabitation, property rights, exclusion from property and custody of, in this case, an 'illegitimate' child. In other words, he was seeking to get the student to deal with issues that do in practice give rise to genuine problems for the cohabitee.

Having reached that decision he then had to decide what, if anything, of significance had materialised during the previous year or so. Both he and his students would, of course, have been aware of such events as one assumes that he would have drawn their attention to the particular matters during lectures and tutorials.

In the period under consideration, the Court of Appeal had taken the opportunity to consider the legal position of a cohabitee who was seeking an interlocutory injunction to exclude the respondent from the council house, of which they were joint tenants. So the question was set around the problems highlighted by the case of *Ainsbury* v *Millington* [1986] 1 All ER 73. This in turn would allow the examiner to expect reference to the leading case on exclusion from property, that being *Richards* v *Richards* [1984] AC 174. (Although this case related to a married couple, as distinct from a cohabitee.)

Therefore, before going on to deal with specific matters the examiner is giving the student the opportunity to pass comment on the relative positions of co-habitees and married couples, because undoubtedly if Gillian had been married to Clive then she would presumably have been seeking divorce based upon his adultery (and/or behaviour) and a property adjustment order, a facility which is not available to cohabitees. Whether it ought to be available is a matter which undoubtedly generates strong feelings, both for and against the idea.

The other general factor which this question brings into play is the number of pieces of legislation which affect this area of law. Lord Scarman had commented in *Richards* (at p. 206) that the statutory provision:

is a hotchpotch of enactments of limited scope passed into law to meet specific situations or to strengthen the powers of specified courts. The sooner the range, scope, and effects of these powers are rationalised into a coherent and comprehensive body of statute law, the better.

This statement has itself appeared on examination papers with the instruction 'Discuss'.

The major point to remember is that the examiner is quite prepared to give marks, indeed would expect to do so, for placing the question into a particular context, as in this case the disadvantaged position of a cohabitee and the avowed need for rationalisation of the law. To have the knowledge to cite from Lord Scarman's speech in *Richards* very early on in your answer would go a long way towards persuading the examiner that he could look forward to an informed answer.

A degree level problem can be expected to contain a number of points for the student to discuss. A brief analysis of each line of this question will indicate exactly what is of concern to the examiner.

The first line gives you the basic information required to put the question into context: Gillian and Clive are unmarried. They have a child and therefore the custodial position of cohabitees may be an issue. The child's age is given, and this will be one factor to be consider in deciding whether the mother or father should have actual custody.

We are then told that Gillian and Clive are joint tenants of a council property. In other words, neither has a pre-eminent right to occupy the property to the exclusion of the other.

The examiner then introduces a third party. The reason for this is that he is aware that the Domestic Violence and Matrimonial Proceedings Act 1976 does not give any remedy against a third party. Section 1 of the Act grants remedies to 'a party to marriage' against 'the other party to the marriage . . .'. The examiner is therefore posing the question: Where must the aggrieved party to the relationship look for a remedy?

Given that the parties are joint tenants, it must be assumed that either party is lawfully entitled to bring anyone he wishes into the property, even though that may prove intolerable to the other party. In this question the examiner is also giving you information on the time span, i.e., four months, and this is likely to be important when considering the future of Max.

The next piece of information is very important. Gillian has left and is living with her mother. She has also left Max with Clive. What has now become crucial is the question: On what criteria will a court exclude and under which legislation must she proceed? There is also the question of whether it can be said that her future is inextricably bound up with that of Max. Should she perhaps seek custody under the Guardianship of Minors Act and argue that it is in the child's best interests that his father and his new cohabitee should be excluded from the property? The examiner wishes for a full discussion of *Richards* v *Richards* to take place together, one suspects, with an analysis of *Re W (A Minor)* [1981] 3 All ER 401, a case which was in the event distinguished in *Ainsbury* v *Millington*.

The final area for discussion centres around the custody question. What is likely to be in the child's best interests? Would a court assume that his future is better served with the mother, especially as he is relatively young? Against that he is in his home and is well cared for; there is an element of stability but, of course, not necessarily continuity, as it is anyone's guess whether Clive's relationship with Andrea will survive. And what reliance, if any, will a court place on the comments of the child, that he would 'like to see his mother'. Should this be interpreted to mean access only? However the matter is eventually decided by you is relatively immaterial. There is no right or wrong answer. The examiner simply wishes you to state the relevant legislation and criteria to be applied based upon the dicta of the House of Lords in *J* v *C* [1970] AC 668.

The examiner asked the students to 'advise'. This is defined as 'offer counsel to, to recommend'. Thus, what would you recommend to Gillian? Can she exclude Clive and Andrea? Will she obtain custody of Max? Will she be allowed to re-enter the property more readily if she is the custodial parent? Which legislation are you going to use? The Matrimonial Homes Act 1983 is not available as the parties are not married. The Domestic Violence Act could be used providing the parties are 'living with each other in the same household as husband and wife', but this patently isn't the case here. Is there any possibility of using the Supreme Court Act 1981, s. 37 of which is applied to the County Court by s. 38 of the County Courts Act 1984? The drawback here is that before this section can be successfully used there must be evidence of a legal right which is capable of being supported. As neither party has the right to occupy to the exclusion of the other, this piece of legislation would seem to be less than helpful.

You can offer advice only when you are thoroughly conversant with the relevant legislation and case law. The examiner would expect you, for example, to know the case law which has developed in connection with the interpretation of s. 1(2) of the Domestic Violence and Matrimonial Proceedings Act.

By way of summary you could tabulate in the following way:

QUESTION AREA	EXAMINER EXPECTS
Cohabitation	*Introduction!*:
Exclusion from property	Context.
Custody	Major areas for discussion.
	Relevant legislation.
	Discussion:
	(a) Domestic Violence Act — meaning of living together.
	(b) Legislation to be applied and deficiencies in this case.
	(c) Principles to be applied when excluding — *Richards* v *Richards*.
	(d) Exclusion of third party.
	(e) Custody.
	(f) Wishes of child.
	Position of father.
	Different types of custody orders.
	Access.
	(g) Conclusion summarising advice to Gillian.

Useful advice to student

(a)   Remember that if dates are used in the question they are likely to have some significance.

(b)   If there are recent controversial issues then it is likely that the examiner will expect to see evidence of wider reading. Journals such as *Family Law* and the *New Law Journal* carry comment and articles on matters of topical interest.

(c)   Don't forget to refer to the essential legislation especially when dealing with the case law.

To understand exactly how the examiner pieces together particular aspects of law is important. Equally when preparing for examinations do not expect to find a compartmentalised paper. As with the above question aspects of occupation rights to property and custody were pulled together to make a question.

Form of answer required

It is fair to say that most examiners will want the student to pass his examination. After all too many failures may cast doubt on his competence as a teacher!

'if only I'd bought SWOT Family Law I wouldn't need to cheat'

So providing you have sufficient information at your fingertips and use it correctly then you can rely on the examiner to see you through. The extent of your success will depend on how you respond to the question set. The following are examples of 'last lines' that you may expect in family law papers and it is those which will provide the key on how to answer the question:

(a)   *'Discuss'*. Will usually appear after a quotation or pair of quotes. The expectation will be for you to grasp the significance of the quotation and to consider its implications. Often two quotes are given which are diametrically opposed yet dealing with the same point of law. As an example this question appeared on a 1988 Family Law degree paper:

'I conceive that marriage, as understood in Christendom, may be defined as the voluntary union for life of one man and one woman to the exclusion of all others.' (Lord Penzance in *Hyde* v *Hyde* [1866])

'This principle has a mythical status in English law; that is to say that it is widely cited, disregarding its inherent legal falsity.' (Anthony Bradney (1987) Vol 17 Fam Law)
Discuss.

At least you are aware that two points of view exist but unless you have extensive knowledge of these issues this type of question is best avoided. However, if you feel confident enough to attempt an answer then you should jot down a rough plan of campaign. Essay-type answers do need to be well structured and coherent. 'Discuss' is defined in the *Concise Oxford Dictionary* as 'examine by argument, debate'. Therefore you must not be purely descriptive of the problem but must attempt to compare and contrast. Work from the assumption that in this type of question there must be something to argue. There must be more than one point of view. Family law papers are often based upon answering four questions from the total set. You must therefore feel confident enough to write on one topic for something in the order of 45 minutes. Jot down briefly the factors you would raise and then consider whether this will sustain you for three-quarters of an hour.

(b) *'Advise'.* The standard notation for problem questions. Look carefully to whom you are deemed to be giving this important advice. Is it one or both parties to a marriage? Is it all parties to the problem which could involve advising four or five persons, perhaps grandparents or foster parents or a local authority. Does the question give a further clue about what you are expected to advise on? The question discussed earlier asked students to advise one party on issues of cohabitation, property rights, exclusion from property and custody of a child. Another recent example from a university examination paper was: 'Advise on the legal problems that parties will face if the local authority refuses to hand over the child'. Such a question allows great scope for an answer to raise the aspects of law that are problematical, which can range from statutory procedure under child legislation to the use of the prerogative jurisdiction.

(c) *'Critically analyse'.* Again you must do exactly as the question asks. You have, as the *Concise Oxford Dictionary* says, to 'examine minutely the constitution of', or 'ascertain the constituents of'. Once you have decided that you have the capacity to do so after receiving the facts of the problem, take each in turn and with a *critical* eye deal with the pertinent issues. To be critical will usually allow you to make extensive use of academic opinion and you ought not be tempted by such a question unless you can display evidence of wide reading.

(d) *And the others.* Scanning through past papers the following came to light:

(i) In the context of a quasi-practical question where you are asked to place yourself in the position of a solicitor giving advice to a client the student was asked to 'explain' to him various points concerning problems of custody, housing and maintenance. To 'explain' means to make known in detail or make intelligible. It is possible to distinguish an explanation from the giving of advice in that the latter relates to the offering of an opinion whereas the former suggests that something has happened and the reason has to be put over to the client.

(ii)   'Consider' is another word which appears frequently in questions. For example, 'Consider the adequacy, or otherwise, of the procedures and sanctions available to those who are victims of domestic violence'. To consider means to 'weigh the merits of' and as such suggests that more than one view must be tendered.

(iii)   The question which is relatively straightforward demanding only a descriptive response is often put in these terms: 'What appears to be . . .?' 'What are the practical difficulties . . .?' or 'Describe the present law on . . .'. All of these suggest a descriptive account of some particular matter but I would suggest that you ought to be critical wherever possible.

One other point to note is what one might refer to as the 'sting in the tail' question. It is usually indicated by further information being given after you have been asked to 'advise' or 'explain'. It is normally cast in these terms: 'Would your answer be different if . . .?' followed by a variation of the facts which formed the basic problem. In such cases you should indicate on the question paper that the answer requires two separate elements. Often in the heat of the moment the second, less obvious part of the question is missed and the student, as a result denied perhaps five or six marks. The simple expedient of writing 'Do not forget' in red ink at the relevant point on the question paper should ensure that you do not miss it out in your answer.

The day of the examination

In addition to planning for the questions which are likely to appear on the paper, you must plan for the examination itself. Double-check that you have the correct details of all of your examinations which should include:

(a)   Date.

(b)   Whether or not it is a.m. or p.m.

(c)   Precise starting time and whether or not you are advised to be present a certain number of minutes before the examination commences.

(d)   Venue. It may not be a bad idea if beforehand you can check out the room.

Will you have an examination number and therefore have to sit at a particular desk or will you have a free choice? Remember that the examinations invariably coincide with a heatwave and therefore to have to sit near a window presents two hazards. The first is susceptibility to distraction and outside noise while the second is the 'greenhouse' problem. This latter problem becomes all the more difficult to alleviate especially as to let in more air means increasing the noise level and chances of distraction. Therefore if you are allowed to sit anywhere arrive early at the examination room and as soon as you are admitted aim for the desk which you have previously considered the most appropriate.

(e)   Check your travel arrangements. Is your car very reliable? Does it start when you want it to or when it wants to? It is certainly not a good idea to rely on others to get you to the examination on time. Is there a suitable mode of public transport? Does the particular train always arrive?

If you are travelling by car make sure that there are no road-works or diversions which may delay your journey. I am aware of one student who arrived 15 minutes late for an examination after being caught up in a long traffic jam. He was breathless and had to take another five minutes or so to settle down. Certainly not the best way to start an examination.

(f)   Ensure that you arrive at the examination hall in good time. I would suggest 20 minutes before the scheduled start. This will give you the chance for a few words with your fellow students and ought to enable you to relax a little. It is vital to ensure that you have with you all those things which you are permitted to take into the room. An adequate supply of pens and markers, rulers, ink plus any academic material. For a family law examination it is usual for the student to be permitted to take a copy of *Sweet and Maxwell's Family Law Statutes* into the examination. Make certain that you do not have anything which could be construed by an invigilator as giving you an unfair advantage over other students. I am aware that it is jokingly suggested that the only sure way to pass an examination is to cheat. However the penalties for 'unfair practice' are harsh, usually the failure of the complete diet of examinations. It is wise to read the regulations which are posted outside the examination room because 'unfair practice' offences are normally written on a strict liability basis, so that even though it was through sheer negligence that certain papers found their way into your pocket it could still be sufficient to establish the offence and mean that a whole year's study has been wasted. Carry out a body search for anything that may be construed as giving you an unfair advantage. If in doubt about any material seek the advice of an invigilator before the commencement of the examinations. Sometimes invigilators will warn everyone of the consequences of cheating and invite you to declare anything of a suspicious nature.

You ought to have a watch or travel clock to help you when allocating time for each answer and many students come armed with packets of Polo and fruit gums which they claim helps them to concentrate when the examination is under way.

The examination begins

Check the rubric. Ascertain the number of questions you are expected to answer and look carefully to see whether or not there are any compulsory questions or if the paper is sectionalised. If there is a compulsory element then it is wise to determine that it will be attempted early in the examination. Two years ago one of my students left a compulsory question on the family law paper which was worth 40% until the end. He only attempted one of its three parts and denied himself nearly 30 marks. He had done sufficiently well on the other three questions to acquire 41% overall but a bare pass was hardly good compensation for a full year's work. From his point of view it was as well that he had attempted the question. Failure to do so would have invalidated his whole paper. Sometimes a paper will contain an 'either/or' question. This should be clearly marked so as not to confuse it with an '(a) and (b)' type question which demands that both parts must be attempted. More than one student has in the past fallen into the trap of doing both and thus diminishing the maximum mark available to 80%.

Read the examination paper carefully. If on your first reading you think there are a couple of questions that you would not wish to answer, determine to re-read them most carefully before you make your final decision.

Once you have established which four or five you are going to attempt to answer then you must decide in which order you are going to proceed. It is usual to attempt your 'best' question either first or second. However, you should seek to ensure that you do not devote too much time to these answers to the detriment of later answers. Extra marks may be gained and then lost as you fail to do yourself justice in the later answers.

Just as you planned your revision so must you plan within the examination room. Check and recheck in order that you are convinced that what you are writing continues to answer the question set. It is very easy to move off at a tangent. Most common is the student who introduces a particular matter and then proceeds to discuss it at length, the problem being that it ought not to have been mentioned in the first place.

If you are attempting to answer a problem question then application of knowledge is crucial. Do not regurgitate masses of material even though it may well relate in some way to the area of law under discussion. The most obvious way in which this is done is through using too many cases which are purely illustrative and add little to the argument which is being developed.

Wherever possible think of yourself as being not in an examination room, but in a court of law. The primary purpose of doing this is constantly to remind yourself that the best evidence needs to be presented in order to ensure success. While it may not be a marvellous idea to put forward your own theories, it is advisable to make submissions based upon relevant academic or legal opinion.

Towards the end of the examination, say when there are 15 minutes left, it is suggested that you attempt to finish your final question leaving perhaps ten minutes or so for a reading of your answers. Examiners all too often find that a candidate has failed because of a combination of lack of detailed knowledge combined with minor mistakes which have appeared in the paper. It is the latter which can be spotted if you can give yourself sufficient time to read your answer.

Remember that one word can change the whole gist of a sentence or quoting a wrong case can mean lost marks. This tidying-up exercise could save perhaps five marks which in the final analysis may be crucial.

A last point in this section is to advise you not to leave the examination hall early unless, of course, you are totally and utterly unprepared for the examination. Many students leave when there are still 20 minutes or so left. To leave means that there is no chance to improve your position, to stay might just result in something coming back to you which means an extra mark or two.

The examiner's hope is that he will be presented with a legible script which is well-structured and argued. Some scripts give us a torrid time but in the main we decipher almost everything the student throws at us and hopefully achieve justice.

Other forms of assessment

I have spent a lot of time discussing the general approach to examinations and mentioning specifically the three-hour unseen paper. However, many courses now include continuous assessment as part of the examination process and some degree courses also have provision for a project to be written in lieu of a taught course in the final year. It is therefore legitimate and necessary to say something about this mode of assessment. Students ought to be aware of the requisite techniques in order to ensure a good mark for the written work. When one considers that 20% of the final total for family law may be based upon an extended essay or project then one realises its importance for inclusion in a book of this type.

Continuous assessment

A programme of continuous assessment may result in the student having to produce two or perhaps three pieces of written work. Often the student's mark for the assessment is based upon the best two of the three pieces of work submitted.

It is far more likely for the assessment to be based upon the submission of an answer to an 'essay'-type question than to a problem. If, however, it is the latter then the process and points to note mentioned above will still be valid, although the problem may well be more expansive than one which generates a 35 to 40-minute answer. Turning our attention to concentrate on the assessment essay we may attempt a similar analysis to the one above. As the examiner will expect an essay of a particular length, say 5,000 or 6,000 words, he will have to alight upon a topic that has been or is currently being studied which will provide the student with the necessary array of materials to produce an 'extended' essay. The lead may be given by a new report or particularly controversial case. A good example at the time of writing, is the continuing problem of how best to deal with child abuse, and in particular child sexual abuse. The whole debate has recently been heightened by the publicity surrounding the so-called Cleveland sex abuse scandal, which culminated in a statutory inquiry chaired by Lord Justice Butler Sloss, the report of which was published in July 1988 (Cm 412).

From the viewpoint of both examiners and students this would be a good area upon which to set an assessment essay because, as with many family law matters, it touches upon moral, medical, ethical and practical issues. An examiner would be convinced if he chose this topic that the student would have sufficient material upon which to produce a work of high standard. Once the examiner has determined the topic, then he must frame the question to pose. The analytical and critical skills so vital to budding lawyers will again have to take a high priority. He will wish to indicate to the examinee that discussion of 'broader' issues is not only permissible but essential. At the same time he must indicate that the student should take a legal perspective, which will involve commenting on existing legislation and case law. He might wish to consider whether the legislation is in need of reform, whether or not it is sufficiently extensive to give adequate protection to a child who it is alleged has suffered non-accidental injury. He would certainly wish to consider the role played by the wardship jurisdiction to supplement the statutory powers when it is thought that a child should be in local authority care but insufficient evidence is thought to exist to support a care order being made under the Children and Young Persons Act 1969.

In addition to a critical study of the existing law, he will need to ask whether new laws are needed and, if so, why and to what purpose. Overall he will have to discuss how best to balance the interests of the child with those of parents, especially, as in Cleveland, when mere suspicion was in some cases deemed sufficient to take children away from the parents. If the parents have not abused their children in any way, as was established in some cases in Cleveland, then it is wrong that families should be brought to breaking point. The criminal law after all demands that a person is presumed innocent until proved otherwise. Should the civil law not work to such a presumption? The student could also assess the role of the criminal law in these cases.

The examiner's first draft could be along the following lines:

Critically analyse the legal problems that stem from the proposals of the Buttler-Sloss Committee.

He may reject this on the grounds that it emphasises *legal* problems and also doesn't seek to discriminate between the various proposals.

His second attempt could read:

Consider the problems which may arise in seeking to reduce child abuse.

This form of words still means the question is very wide. To use the word 'problem' without qualification may be deemed unfair.

Finally he may decide on the following structure:

'We were told of the inadequacy of the present child care legislation and its failure to balance the interests of the child and the rights of parents.' (para. 13.31 of the *Cleveland Report* 1988)

Consider the changes needed and the additions required to the existing law in order to ensure that a correct balance is maintained between the rights of parents and their children when abuse of whatever kind is suspected.

This structure has certain advantages. The examiner can, by using a quotation, direct the student's attention to what he considers to be the point or points of major concern: in this case the inadequate child care legislation and the interests of families. The student is therefore aware that he must give some thought to the quotation.

The second part of the question sets some parameters to the answer. It emphasises the *changes* and *additions* to the existing law and what they would seek to *achieve*.

Finally, because the quotation comes from a report, then by implication it must be important and thus warrant some attention being paid to it.

However, ultimately the student will have to be selective with his source material and decide what sort of priority should be given to the material. The student should provide an answer profile which may look something like this:

(a) *Background:* Evidence of continuing child abuse. Various reports into child death, e.g., the Beckford, Tyra Henry, and Kimberly Carlisle Reports. Non-accidental injury as opposed to sexual abuse which may cause only psychological harm.

(b) *Professional involvement:* Medical Practitioners, GPs, Consultants, Local Authority, Social Services, The Police, Legal Departments of local authority.

(c) *Present law/procedures:*
   Children and Young Persons Act 1969.
   Child Care Act 1980.
   Children and Young Persons (Amendment) Act 1986.
   Care Orders.
   Place of Safety Orders   *How effective?*
   Wardship proceedings.
   Control of local authority.
   Welfare of the child.

(d) *Case law:* e.g.,
   D v Berkshire CC [1987] 1 All ER 20;

A v *Liverpool City Council* [1982] AC 363;

W v *Hertfordshire CC* [1985] AC 791.

(e)   *Reports:*

Child Care Law Review [1985];

Law on Child Care and Family Services [Cm 62] [1987];

Butler-Sloss Report, July 1988 [Cm 412].

(f)   *Points to consider:*   e.g.

(i)   How does one challenge the 'professionals' before any court proceedings?

(ii)   Is the place of safety order and its 28 day duration working against the best interests of the family?

(iii)   How does the law deal with possible future harm as distinct from present harm?

(iv)   Should the 'welfare principle' be specifically written into the Children and Young Persons Act or its successor?

(v)   What appeal rights do parents have at the moment? Is the position suitable for change?

(vi)   Could a Family Court be the answer to some, if not all, the legal problems?

Remember the above is just a brief outline of how you might prepare to answer the question. It is obviously not a question which asks you to write everything you know about child care.

In your introduction to the answer state what you think the question is asking and then you will have a ready-made structure for your discussion, and keep referring back to the question just to check that you continue to be relevant.

Summary

In this chapter I have tried to illustrate how problem questions and essay questions are constructed in the belief that if the student realises how this is achieved then he will be able more clearly to set about answering the question set.

You should, therefore, note the differences in expectation between unseen papers and those forms of assessment where material is at the disposal of the student. In the latter case the examiner will expect bibliographies to be submitted and will throughout be looking for evidence of plagiarism which would count quite dramatically against a good mark being achieved. You should seek to show *understanding* of the question set. A brief comment in the introduction pointing out what you believe to be the thrust of the question is often found helpful by the examiner. It may be a perfectly legitimate interpretation yet one that the examiner has not considered.

You must then show the ability to deal with the material available. To collate, assess and reject information requires patience and quite often causes frustration.

The most difficult decision is often what to exclude, not what to retain. You should be constantly seeking to introduce opposing views and collecting evidence to support the arguments. You should be following a work plan similar to that listed on p. 19 but it should always be capable of being amended if new information should come to light.

You should attempt a draft answer and re-read it thoroughly once the first draft is finished. Amend accordingly and check that references are correctly cited as this will add to the overall impression, and extra marks may be available for style and presentation. Most of all ensure that any potential material is used correctly *and* if a viva voce examination is included as part of the assessment that you are fully familiar with the material you have used. In other words try not to quote references from secondary sources. You must end with a conclusion that in our example points out the existing problems and what you consider ought to be the way forward. If you follow these guidelines then you should have few problems in achieving a creditable mark.

In assessing answers to an unseen paper the examiner will expect a logical approach. There should be a statement of what the examinee believes the question to entail. Legislation wherever necessary should be quoted but not necessarily verbatim. Never lead with cases. Remember that you must be clear about the impact of a case. You do not have sufficient time to give lots of facts which in most cases will be irrelevant to your answer.

Make sub-conclusions before you go on to deal with the next point. Finally sum up and ensure that you have answered the question set. If it says 'Advise Bill' give that advice. If it says 'Discuss' then arguments both for and against should have been included.

In the rest of the book I will be looking at selected areas of family law and I will seek to isolate important cases, articles and legislation that ought to be vital in answering *any* question on that particular area.

THREE

VOID AND VOIDABLE MARRIAGES

Many family law courses proceed on the basis of creation of marriage, marriage breakdown, ancillary matters and aspects of the law relating to children. In this chapter we shall be concentrating on the defects which sometimes exist which may cast doubt upon the validity of the marriage. In the textbooks the law on this area is summarised under the heading 'Nullity' or sometimes 'Void and voidable marriages'. When one compares the number of nullity decrees granted by the court with those in divorce it would appear that nullity is far less important than divorce. In 1986, the latest year for which figures are available at the time of writing, only 554 nullity decrees were made by comparison to 179,844 petitions for dissolution of marriage.

Nevertheless the issues raised in the law of nullity go to the root of the marriage and as such are rarely ignored by family law examiners. Nullity, at present, provides a foundation both for problem and essay questions, the latter often concentrating on the criteria listed in s. 11 of the Matrimonial Causes Act 1973 which, if established, will result in the marriage being declared *void ab initio*.

Background information

Before we proceed to look at the details of the law it is advisable that students come to grips with the relevant terminology and statutory provisions. The key sections are ss. 11 to 16 of the Matrimonial Causes Act 1973 although most of the questioning will centre around ss. 11, 12 and 13. Remember that I have suggested that a verbatim statement of sections is rarely going to produce a lot of marks so you could concentrate on remembering that s. 11 lists those *grounds* upon which a marriage will be declared *void*. A cursory look will tell you that they are fairly fundamental concepts supporting the established idea of marriage in English law and defined in the important case of *Hyde* v *Hyde* (1866) LR 1 P & D 130 as being 'the voluntary union for life of one man and one woman to the exclusion of all others'. Although as to whether this remains an accurate appraisal of what constitutes a valid marriage in English law see Bradney, 'Transsexuals and the Law' (1987) 17 Fam Law 350.

When dealing with so-called void marriages it is advisable to include this definition in your answer as it will help to put any critique of the law into a relevant context. Marriage as defined above will not occur, if, for example, the parties are of the same sex or one party is already lawfully married.

Note also that there are various *grounds* upon which a nullity decree may be obtained, unlike divorce where there is only one *ground*, irretrievable breakdown of marriage, and five facts, any one of which is deemed sufficient from which to draw the conclusion that the marriage has totally and irretrievably broken down. The use, by Parliament, of the word *grounds*, may indicate that each in itself is regarded as making some significant impact on the idea of marriage and the status, rights, duties and obligations which marriage bestows upon those who commit themselves legally to each other.

Section 12 lists those grounds upon which a marriage can be declared *voidable*. It becomes immediately apparent that you ought to be aware and be prepared to make an examiner aware of the distinction between the two notions of void and voidable marriages. Thus any standard textbook will inform you that void marriages do not legally need a decree of nullity as a marriage has not come into existence, whereas a voidable marriage is one which is valid unless steps are taken to have it annulled. This distinction is itself based upon varying philosophies. It is evident that public policy considerations form the rationale for s. 11 because marriage as we know it could not be recognised if such fundamental defects were present. However, the problems mentioned in s. 12 relate in the main to individual imperfections which do not have a devastating effect on the idea of marriage but which relate to the parties themselves. It is therefore accepted that only the parties to the marriage can take action to have it annulled whereas the public interest requires that *anyone* can, if they desire, challenge the validity of a marriage on the grounds listed in s. 11. It may be worth just making the comment that it is virtually unknown for strangers to challenge the validity of a marriage and to query whether it is worth retaining the legal right to do so. For some support for this view see Law Commission Working Paper No. 48.

Once you have drawn the examiner's attention to the distinction you ought to quote authority to support your assertion. One of the most widely accepted judicial statements continues to be that of Lord Greene MR in *De Reneville* v *De Reneville* [1948] P 100 where he said:

[A] void marriage is one that will be regarded by every court in any case in which the existence of the marriage is in issue, as never having taken place and can be so treated by both parties to it without the necessity of any decree annulling it: a voidable marriage is one that will be regarded by every court as a valid subsisting marriage until a decree annulling it has been pronounced by a court of competent jurisdiction.

Other introductory points remain to be mentioned. First look closely at the dates in any problem that you are faced with. The statutory provisions apply only to marriages celebrated after 31 July 1971. Section 12 contains reference to time-limits within which proceedings may be brought and s. 12(c), (d), (e) and (f) are subject to a time-limit of three years from the date of the marriage. Note, however, that as a result of s. 2 of the Matrimonial and Family Proceedings Act 1984 leave may now be granted out of time to bring proceedings for nullity on grounds (c) to (f), provided the judge is satisfied that the *petitioner* has at some time during that period suffered from mental disorder within the meaning of the Mental Health Act 1983 *and* that in all the circumstances of the case it would be just to grant leave for the institution of proceedings.

This provision implements the proposal made by the Law Commission in its Report on Time Restrictions on Presentation of Divorce and Nullity Petitions (Law Commission No. 116, 1982). It is therefore unlikely that nullity problems will be set relating to marriages celebrated before 1971 especially as s. 13 would allow a court to consider that prolonged lapse of time is evidence from which it could be concluded that the marriage, despite the defect, had been 'approbated'.

Secondly it is often worth mentioning that the full range of ancillary provisions relating to maintenance and property adjustment are available whether or not a nullity decree is obtained on void or voidable grounds. Thus, even though it is not strictly necessary to obtain a decree under s. 11, later financial relief will depend on such an order being obtained.

To sum up the introductory points worthy of mentioning in an answer on nullity.

(a)   Definitions of void and voidable.
(b)   Reference to dates in statute.
(c)   Reference to modification by recent legislation.
(d)   The relevance of a decree for void marriages.
(e)   The rationale and context of ss. 11 and 12.

Nullity and the examinations

I will now endeavour to list the types of issues that could be raised by the examiner who has decided to include a question on nullity on his examination paper. Some aspects of the law lend themselves more readily to a discursive question while others are usually set in a problem. The distinction is usually between factors mentioned in s. 11 of the Matrimonial Causes Act 1973 and which tend to support the former assertion while those in ss. 12 and 13 are likely to appear in problem questions. I would warn though that this is only a rule of thumb and ultimately everything will depend on the personal preferences of your tutors. I will take each section in turn and comment on the various criteria while at the same time giving you an understanding of what an examiner may be looking for and how you may work at and revise the topic.

Section 11: Void marriages

This section is concerned with fundamental problems which affect the validity of a marriage. It is made clear in s. 11(a) that a marriage will not come into existence if the parties are within the prohibited degrees of relationship, if either of them is under the age of 16 or if they have married in disregard of certain requirements laid down by the statute as to the formation of marriage.

Taking the latter point first it is a truism that this issue often crops up in a problem question although many examiners would take the view that procedural points such as these are not the stuff upon which undergraduates should cut their academic teeth. It is argued that a practitioner would simply check the facts against a standard reference work in order to ascertain whether or not the parties have complied with the formalities. If you check the standard textbook it will be obvious that case law is virtually non-existent leading one to the conclusion that there is little worth discussing in this area of law, other than perhaps, in an essay context, the justification for the requirements and whether or not reform is necessary.

However, if your examiner chooses to include this material one or more of the following points may be covered:

(a)   Parental consent.
(b)   Publication of banns.
(c)   Prohibited degrees of relationship.
(d)   Age.
(e)   Bigamy.
(f)   Male and female.
(g)   Domicile and polygamous marriages.

Requirements of the Marriage Acts

Parental consent

Where either party to the ceremony is under the age of 18 a consent is required which may be from parents if the infant is 'legitimate' or guardian and parent if one parent is dead or guardian(s) where both parents are dead. Admittedly parents don't always live together and in cases of divorce then the law looks to the custodial parent, but where custody is jointly awarded both will need to consent.

The Family Law Reform Act 1987 has amended the Marriage Act of 1949 with regard to the consents required when the child is born out of wedlock. Essentially the mother will be the person to give consent, unless the father has been given by court order actual custody of the child *or* the right to consent to the marriage of the child. For other circumstances, e.g., when mother or father is dead, see the 1987 Act. In cases where an infant is a ward of court, then the court's consent is required.

Where this issue is raised in a question look carefully to see whether or not the ceremony was civil or by common licence, because the Marriage Act 1949 requires that where the marriage is to take place after banns have been published then any objection to the ceremony should be 'openly and publicly' declared 'in the church or chapel' (s. 3(3)). The publication of the banns then becomes void. By way of example I reproduce a small part of a university examination question which touched on the point:

> Nancy and Donald married in a Manchester registry office in 1984. At the time, she was 17 and he was 29; she married without her parents' consent by using a forged letter of consent allegedly signed by them.

One would thus raise the registry office point, indicate the necessity for parental consent but at the same time conclude that s. 48 of the Marriage Act 1949 makes it clear that the essential validity of the marriage is not jeopardised from failure to have the necessary consent. It will, of course, be usual for the marriage to be valid otherwise the rest of the question would be undermined. It is interesting to note that Cretney, in *Principles of Family Law,* 4th ed. (p. 16), concludes that 'These provisions are now outdated and unsatisfactory', and the material therefore could be useful evidence to adduce if faced with a question enquiring about possible reforms of s. 11. The matter of parental consent has not recently been reviewed although it was given a welcome airing by the Latey Committee on the Age of Majority in 1967 (Cmnd 3342) and the Kilbrandon Report inquiring into the marriage laws in Scotland in 1969 (Cmnd 4011).

Publication of banns

Another point which may be raised is that dealing with the publication of banns, a procedure used for the overwhelming majority of Anglican weddings. One major purpose of this procedure is to give the intended marriage sufficient publicity to allow any objections to be raised by members of the public. Thus a question may inform you that one party had the banns published using a false name or had omitted to use one of his names by which he would have been instantly recognisable. Some case law, albeit dated, does exist and you ought to be aware of *Dancer* v *Dancer* [1949] P 147 and *Chipchase* v *Chipchase* [1939] P 391 by way of example. These cases would seem to hold that the concealment of one's true identity must be deliberate before the court will conclude that due publication has not taken place.

Disabilities

A third and final point on this particular aspect of formalities relates to the Marriage (Registrar General's Licence) Act 1970, and the more recent Marriage

Act 1983. In some cases it is not possible for parties to attend at a building designated for the purposes of marriage. Age, infirmity, disability, accident are but some of the reasons why individuals who wish to marry may not be able to attend at an authorised building. Therefore, if your question makes reference to so-called 'deathbed' marriages, or the fact that the parties were geriatric, then it is inviting you to outline the purpose of this legislation and to mention the circumstances in which it will apply. Under the 1970 Act the Registrar General is empowered to issue a licence once he is satisfied that the terms of the Act have been complied with. Under s. 1(2) he has to be satisfied that one person to be married is seriously ill and not expected to recover *and* cannot be moved to a place at which the marriage could be solemnised.

The 1983 Act is wider in scope in that a superintendent registrar's certificate can authorise the marriage of persons who are house-bound, detained in hospital or prison to take place at the place where they are 'for the time being'.

Revision note   Formalities such as mentioned above are likely to appear in nullity questions but rarely nowadays form a major part of the question. You ought to note any aspect to which your tutor draws your attention. Look then at the particular piece of legislation, isolate the key words and check to see whether or not any case law exists on the point.

If you expect an essay question you should seek out any readings noting points for and against the retention of such provisions in the relevant legislation.

Prohibited degrees of relationship

The report of the Archbishop of Canterbury's review group, entitled *No Just Cause* (1984), was the basis for amendments to the existing law on prohibited degrees. Despite wide ranging discussions of the restrictions, the new legislation could hardly be construed as radical. The Marriage (Prohibited Degrees of Relationship) Act 1986 amended the Marriage Act 1949 so as to relax the law which bans marriage between those related only by marriage, such as in-laws and step-relations. Parts II and III of the Schedule 1 Marriage Act restrictions have been retained for specific reasons, although there will be those who find them unacceptable. Basically the legislation permits affines to marry but restricts marriage to stepchildren or step-grandchildren unless certain conditions are fulfilled. Thus both parties must be over 21 and the stepchild must never have been in a *loco parentis* situation before the age of 18. If the stepchild has been brought up by someone else then there is no restriction. The rationale of the law is to prevent adults seeing their stepchildren as potential marriage partners and minimise the risk of 'exploitation'. Secondly, marriage to a daughter or son-in-law is prohibited unless both are over 21 and, for a man, both his son and the son's mother are dead. As may be expected very few people will fulfil these criteria.

When one turns to Part I of the Marriage Act Schedule one finds restrictions based not upon affinity but consanguinity. It goes without saying that most people would support, probably on eugenic grounds if nothing else, prohibitions preventing a man from marrying his mother, sister, grandmother, daughter, or aunt. However, the weakness of all these restrictions is that they prevent only marriage. The parties are free to cohabit, produce children and live ostensibly as a married couple.

Questions on this area are becoming more frequent as the policy behind the restrictions is called into doubt. It is unlikely that such matters will arise in problems and, therefore, when revising such a topic it will usually be in your best interests to note material which is of a critical nature. A good basic source of information is the family law 'reader', *The Family, Law and Society: Cases and Materials* by Brenda Hoggett and David Pearl (2nd ed., Butterworths, 1987). On this point see pp. 21-25. Positive benefit can also be gained from reading the article by Robert Chester and Martin Parry (1983) 13 Fam Law 237, entitled 'Reform of the Prohibitions on Marriage of Related Persons'. Reference is made to the practice in Australia, Sweden, the USA, Federal Republic of Germany, France, Spain and New Zealand, and while all countries have some restrictions there is no unanimity on where the line is drawn. Any critique of the United Kingdom position will be enhanced by reference to the position in other Western industrialised nations. See also the Law Commission Report No. 33 (1970), upon which the Nullity of Marriage Act 1971 was based and which lists arguments for and against change in the law.

Orfe positive benefit of the 1986 Act is that it reduces the need to promote a private Act of Parliament in order to avoid the restrictions. As the restrictions are imposed by Parliament, then equally they may be taken away by Parliament. For example, the John Francis Dare and Gillian Loder Dare (Marriage Enabling) Act 1982 permitted a man aged 66 to marry his stepdaughter aged 49. This would now be unnecessary providing he had never been *in loco parentis* to her.

Questions may therefore be expected. Work on a 'for' and 'against' basis and, of course, refer to the experience of other jurisdictions. You may also note a possible overlap with the criminal law, and in particular the law on incest. Intercourse between a man and his niece is not incestuous nor any criminal offence providing she is consenting and over sixteen, although as things stand they are not allowed to marry. Thus you may pose the question: What is so special about marriage? The couple do not attract criminal sanctions if they produce a child, yet they cannot marry and socially the child remains 'illegitimate'.

Age

Little need be said on this point. The law requires both parties to be 16 before the marriage is valid. This point may appear in a problem question where the marriage has taken place overseas. The attitude of the law may differ depending on the status of the parties. Thus in *Pugh* v *Pugh* [1951] P 482 a man domiciled in England and Wales had married a 15-year-old girl in Austria. Although the marriage was valid under Austrian law it was void by English law as he could not have the capacity to marry someone under 16. However, in the unique case of *Mohammed* v *Knott* [1969] 1 QB 1 a Nigerian domiciled there had married a 13-year-old girl according to Muslim law. They came to England and proceedings were started on the basis that the girl needed care and protection. The Divisional Court decided that the marriage was valid and thus the girl was in law his wife.

It is far more likely that you will have to give thought to the policy considerations. In your revision, note the following points:

(a)   The law has not been altered on this point since 1929.

(b)   The Latey and Kilbrandon Commissions, and the Law Commission Report No. 33 (1970) give consideration to the matter.

(c)   The criminal law, which makes 16 the age of consent to intercourse.

(d)   Medical evidence on the age of maturity but consider not just physical but emotional maturity.

(e)   The law makes 18 the age for drinking in public houses, entry to a cinema to see an X film, to vote and 17 to drive a car. It is arguable that the consequences of an ill-advised marriage at 16 are equally if not more harmful to society than allowing the age for the above activities to be reduced.

(f)   Should the age remain as it is, rise or fall?

For statistical evidence see Hoggett and Pearl, *The Family, Law and Society,* (2nd ed.), pp. 25-7 and for a review of the arguments, Cretney, *Principles of Family Law*, 4th ed., pp. 55-61.

Revision note   Generally unless your tutor has emphasised this area you need only consider the legal impact of one party being underage in the context of a problem question and even then it is certainly not an area to spend many hours on.

Other reasons for a marriage being void

The preceding section dealt with requirements demanded by the Marriage Acts. The following areas still lead to the conclusion that a marriage is void but are based upon s. 11 itself and not upon other legislation.

Bigamy

The accepted definition of marriage, stated in *Hyde* v *Hyde* (1866) LR 1 P & D 130 precludes one party who is already married from taking a second wife. If by chance a question should refer to the issue of bigamy, the major point for you to mention is whether or not immediately before the ceremony either party was already lawfully married. Bigamy, of course, is a criminal offence so you ought to bear that factor in mind. It is far more likely that questions on bigamy will appear on criminal law papers rather than family law.

Male and female

The common law definition of marriage refers to it being a voluntary union between one man and one woman. The advance in medical science has resulted in the performance of sex-change operations designed to create physical attributes possessed by the opposite sex to which the individual feels a strong psychological affinity. Is, therefore, a person who has undergone such an operation, who may look and act like a person of the opposite sex, to be given in law a new legal status? An examiner may frame a question which allows you to raise and discuss the following points:

(a)   Section 11(c) of the Matrimonial Causes Act 1973 says that a marriage is void if the parties are not respectively male and female. The leading case at the moment is *Corbett* v *Corbett* [1971] P 83 where Ormrod J concluded that biological criteria must be used to determine a person's sex. In this case the respondent, a male at birth, having male chromosomes, gonads and genitalia, was a male for the purposes of marriage notwithstanding his psychological identity. You would have to state the implications of this case and at the same time point out that the decision was based upon the common law terms 'man and woman'. Parliament has, however, chosen the words 'male and female' in s. 11(c) and this raises the question whether or not they would be given the same meaning as 'man and woman'.

The matter has recently been given an airing before the European Court of Human Rights. In *Rees* v *United Kingdom* [1987] 2 FLR 111, the applicant claimed that as a transsexual he was the victim of national legislation and practices, contrary to his right to respect for his private life as enshrined in Article 8 of the European Convention on Human Rights. He also sought to maintain that as English law prevented him from entering into a valid contract of marriage with a woman, then Article 12 of the Convention had been violated. This Article guarantees the right of people to marry freely. He lost his case on both points. On the former point the Registrar General had refused his request to amend his birth certificate, although other national documents indicated his new status. The Court held that Articles sought to protect individuals against 'arbitrary interference' by public authorities, but that the 'mere refusal' to alter the register could not be considered as interference. As to Article 12 it was decided that it related only to the 'traditional right' to marry, which in turn meant to members of the opposite biological sex. National laws which limited marriage to this traditional concept of marriage could not be said to breach Article 12.

Therefore any questioning on this matter will demand reference to the European Court decision. This case should be read together with the decision of the European Commission in *Van Oosterwijck* v *Belgium* (1980) 3 EHRR 557 and see also the Australian decision in *Re C and D* (1979) 28 ALR 524 (briefly mentioned at p. 16 in Hoggett and Pearl).

(b) That the matter again cannot be confined purely to family law. As the case of *R* v *Tan* [1983] 2 All ER 12 indicates, the word 'man' in s. 30 of the Sexual Offences Act 1956 has to be interpreted by using the same criteria used by Ormrod J. In fact *Corbett* was applied in this case in which a 'man' who had undergone a sex-change operation and was to all intents and purposes a woman was found to have been rightly convicted of living on the earnings of a prostitute, namely Tan. 'His' claim that he was not a 'man' was rejected by the Court of Appeal. (For a commentary on the case and the wider issues of sexual identity see P. J. Pace, 'Sexual identity and the criminal law' [1983] Crim LR 317.)

(c) You ought to be aware that other jurisdictions have faced this problem. For example the American case of *M.T.* v *J.T.* (1976) 355 A2d 204, 2 Fam L Rep (BNA) 2447 asserts that in cases of genuine transsexualism if the anatomical features conform to the psychological identity, then for marital purposes identity by sex must be governed by those standards, which would have left both Corbett and Greaves (the 'man in *Tan*) as women.

West Germany passed legislation in 1980 that post-operative transsexuals belong, for legal purposes, to their chosen sex and as such acquire the rights and duties of their new sex. Other countries have passed similar legislation and thus appear to take a more enlightened approach to a very sensitive matter.

(d) The area of law raises the major question of what in the mid 1980s we ought to understand by the word 'marriage'. Ought we to recognise homosexual or transsexual 'marriage'. The problem is that those with sexual identity problems cannot be left in a legal vacuum. They ought to know what their position is with regard to 'marriage' which according to Ormrod J is 'essentially heterosexual'.

Revision note As you can imagine this is a fairly controversial topic. You ought therefore to distinguish between the present legal position based upon case law and the wider issues raised by transsexualism and the definition of marriage in English law.

Domicile and polygamous marriages

Major problems arise from the uncertainty which surrounds the concept of domicile and therefore the *capacity* of someone domiciled in England and Wales to contract a polygamous or potentially polygamous marriage outside the jurisdiction. From an examination viewpoint a student must mention the complications that may arise as a result of the decision of the Court of Appeal in

Hussain v *Hussain* [1982] 3 All ER 369 as well as the recommendations contained in the Law Commission Report No. 146 (Cmnd 9595) entitled Polygamous Marriages: Capacity to Contract a Polygamous Marriage and Related Issues. In its report the Commission advocate that men and women domiciled in England and Wales should not lack capacity to contract a marriage which is *de facto* monogamous merely because it has been celebrated in polygamous form; what is referred to as 'potentially polygamous' as opposed to 'actually polygamous marriages'. Clause 6 of its draft Polygamous Marriages Bill makes it clear that the wording of s. 11(d) of the Matrimonial Causes Act 1973 will of necessity have to be repealed. The result of *Hussain* meant that a woman who was domiciled here and went through a polygamous marriage ceremony would not have the capacity to contract such a marriage even though a man domiciled here could, so long as the marriage was not actually polygamous. Thus s. 11(d) cannot stand with the new clause 1(1) of the draft Bill, which states, 'A marriage between parties neither of whom is already lawfully married shall not be void on the ground that it was entered into under a law which permits polygamy', and will thus have to be repealed if the draft Bill becomes law. It should be emphasised that s. 11(b) of the Matrimonial Causes Act 1973 is to remain in force and renders void an actually polygamous marriage entered into by a man or woman whose capacity to enter into such a marriage is governed by English law.

As usual the Law Commission has produced a report full of information for the student wishing to understand the present legal position and any defects inherent in the law. It is made clear at para. 2.17 that no commentator upon the Working Paper No. 83 (1982) actually opposed the proposal that persons domiciled in the UK should have capacity to enter a marriage celebrated outside the UK which was polygamous in form. The Commission give extensive coverage to the impact of the *Hussain* decision and students should read the appropriate paragraphs in Part II of the Report in order to understand fully the implications of that decision. In addition you ought to be aware of the relative merits of the dual domicile, the intended matrimonial home, and most recently the 'real and substantial connection' tests, the latter having been discussed in *Lawrence* v *Lawrence* [1985] 2 All ER 733. Students who wish to pursue the issue of capacity to marry and the whole debate on polygamous marriages are referred to Cheshire and North's *Private International Law*, 11th ed. (1987), published by Butterworths. A further source of information using a critical perspective is the Law Commission Report No. 168 on private international law (1987), with particular reference to the law of domicile.

Sub-conclusion

Marriages ought to be declared void if they suffer from a substantial and funda-mental defect. It is worth bearing in mind this point because I am now going to examine the circumstances in which a marriage is likely to be deemed voidable, i.e., valid until one of the parties takes action to have it annulled. This presupposes that Parliament is not prepared to see the defects listed in s. 12 of the Matrimonial Causes Act 1973 as being, from a public policy viewpoint, on a par with those in s. 11.

As some of the issues covered by s. 11 are relatively controversial it is always going to be worthwhile checking on family law periodicals to see whether or not anything new has been written. Look also at publications such as the *Journal of Social Welfare Law* and the *Journal of Medical Ethics* as occasionally articles appear on topics dealing with s. 11. The footnotes contained in the standard texts, especially Cretney, *Principles of Family Law*, cover a wide range of material and should be checked carefully.

Voidable marriages

A good starting-point for an answer on s. 12 of the Matrimonial Causes Act 1973 is the definition quoted on p. 37 from the case of *De Reneville* v *De Reneville* [1948] P 100. In addition you should emphasise the purpose of the nullity laws which with one exception refer to defects which exist at the time of the marriage and apparently prevent it from coming into existence. However, s. 12 makes it clear that the marriage is now to be deemed valid until one party takes action to have it annulled.

Incapacity

Section 12(a) of the Matrimonial Causes Act 1973 indicates that a marriage is voidable if the marriage has not been consummated owing to the incapacity of either party to consummate it. This section is full of key words and you ought to extract the following for examination and revision purposes:

(a) consummated,
(b) incapacity,
(c) either party.

Consummation is the first post-marital act of intercourse between the spouses. Intercourse must be 'ordinary and complete, not partial and imperfect' per Dr Lushington in *D* v *A* (1845) 1 Rob Eccl 279. As with many areas of law once a key word is defined then that very definition will need of itself to be further refined in light of particular circumstances. Thus in *Baxter* v *Baxter* [1948] AC 274 the husband was not allowed by his wife to have sexual intercourse with her unless he used a contraceptive sheath because she did not want children. Eventually he sought a decree of nullity arguing that his wife had wilfully refused to consummate the marriage. Being the only House of Lords case to have dealt with the matter it is, from an examination viewpoint, vital that you list the points raised by the Lord Chancellor, Viscount Jowitt. In summary these were:

(a)   That procreation of children is not a 'principal end' of marriage. Sterility will not prevent consummation.

(b)   The House left open the point whether coitus interruptus could amount to consummation although it is now accepted that it does (see *White* v *White* [1948] P 330 and *Cackett* v *Cackett* [1950] P 253).

(c)   That Parliament when using the word 'consummated' in the Matrimonial Causes Act 1937 (now s. 12 of the 1973 Act) did not intend that the courts should be involved in enquiries of a most intimate nature. The word consummate has to be understood in 'common parlance and in the light of social conditions known to exist'.

It therefore follows that if the parties in an examination question have had intercourse before their marriage, this cannot be consummation. That after the ceremony there must be an act capable of amounting to intercourse in line with the *D* v *A* statement. Thus it has been held that there has to be penetration which is more than transient, although one could not imagine the judges turning to their stop-watches in order to give a precise definition of 'transient' (see *W* v *W* [1967] 1 WLR 1554). Credit would be given if you contrast this requirement for consummation with the degree of penetration required by the criminal law for rape or any offence involving sexual intercourse. Recently the Privy Council had to consider whether under New Zealand legislation sexual intercourse was a continuing act. The relevant legislation, the New Zealand Crimes Act 1961 provides that sexual intercourse is complete upon penetration. The Board concluded that if the woman withdrew her consent to intercourse, yet nevertheless the man continued and failed to withdraw then he could be guilty of rape even though the entry was consensual (*Kaitamaki* v *R* [1984] 2 All ER 435).

Note also that a woman may give birth to her husband's child yet this is not conclusive evidence that the marriage has been consummated. The conception may have occurred as a result of *fecundatio ab extra.*

Incapacity refers to the inability of the spouses to perform the act of intercourse. Failure may be due to physical or psychological factors, the latter being a fertile area for inclusion in examination questions. For example, in *D* v *D* (1982) 12 Fam Law 101, the petitioner, a party to an arranged marriage, proved to the satisfaction of the court that at the time of the ceremony and ever since she was incapable of consummating the marriage due to her invincible repugnance to the act of intercourse with her husband. You should inform the examiner that the incapacity must exist at the date of the hearing and the issue is whether or not there is any practical possibility of intercourse taking place. This would include circumstances where the defect could be cured only as a result of a dangerous operation or where one spouse refused to undergo an operation in which case the petition is likely to be brought on wilful refusal to consummate (Matrimonial Causes Act 1973, s. 12(b)).

Either party means in practice that a spouse may petition on his or her own incapacity. The old case of *Harthan* v *Harthan* [1949] P 115 acknowledges this possibility but only if the petitioner was unaware of the defect at the time of the marriage and that in all the circumstances it would not be unjust to grant the decree. 'Unjust' may mean with respect to the respondent or on public policy grounds. More will be said later about this aspect as it would now appear to fall within the ambit of s. 13 of the Act.

Revision note   An area of law well liked by examiners. If you consider the three areas above and arrange your notes around these headings you will have covered the majority of points likely to be raised. Sadly there is very little recent case law and you may therefore wish to ponder on whether the statements in the older cases would automatically apply today. Give thought also to how much of the old common law has survived the Matrimonial Causes Act 1973. For example, the Act does not say that any defect must exist at the time of the marriage, although that could be countered by stating that the assumption has always been implicit in the law of nullity, and certainly the Law Commission in 1970 did not wish to change the common law position.

Wilful refusal

There has been continuing controversy as to whether or not this matter should be part of the law of divorce or nullity. The proponents of the former feel that this is a problem which manifests itself after the ceremony and is more akin to adultery or 'unreasonable' behaviour. Those in favour of the latter maintain that the reticent spouse is merely exhibiting feelings held, possibly subconsciously, at the time of the ceremony. Whatever line you prefer, the fact remains that it is and has been since 1937 part of the nullity laws. What has already been said about the word 'consummation' will hold true for this subsection. The key words here, of course, are 'wilful refusal'. These have been judicially defined and therefore the case of *Horton* v *Horton* [1947] 2 All ER 871, HL, *must* be noted for examination purposes. You should become familiar with the following definition of Viscount Jowitt LC:

The words connote, I think, a settled and definite decision come to without just excuse, and, in determining whether there has been such a refusal, the judge should have regard to the whole history of the marriage.

When one refines this definition further it becomes apparent that you need to consider what will amount to a 'settled and definite decision' and secondly the meaning of the words 'without just excuse'. The Lord Chancellor pointed out that the whole history of the marriage ought to be considered. An interesting example involving discussion of the former is *Potter* v *Potter* (1975) 5 Fam Law

161, where the wife's petition on the grounds of wilful refusal by her husband was met with the rejoinder that his refusal was not deliberate in that he had lost his sexual ardour for his wife. The Court of Appeal accepted that what was a natural occurrence was not a deliberate decision to refuse intercourse.

Of equal importance to a petitioner is the ability to prove that the respondent's refusal is without just excuse. The courts have held that 'just excuse' can be implied from the circumstances, as, for example, in *Kaur* v *Singh* [1972] 1 All ER 292 where the respondent husband had refused to make arrangements for a religious ceremony to follow their civil marriage, and thus comply with Sikh custom, of which he was aware.

This latter issue is often incorporated into examination papers through the device of so-called 'companionship marriages'. The facts usually relate to a couple who prior to the marriage agree that it shall not be consummated. If subsequently one spouse changes their mind can the other plead the agreement and thus have 'just excuse' for refusing intercourse? A case decided during the First World War years is authority for the proposition that public policy cannot allow parties unilaterally to vary the obligation imposed by law to consummate. However, in later cases the courts have recognised that this would not be a strong argument especially if the couple are elderly. Your authorities on this point would be *Morgan* v *Morgan* [1959] P 92 and *Scott* v *Scott* [1959] P 103. In *Morgan*, Mr Commissioner Latey said: 'In the ordinary case of a younger couple, the agreement itself would be void *as against public policy*.'

In the case the judge recognised the agreement as valid and refused in the circumstances to allow the petitioner to succeed on the grounds of his own impotence which, given the agreement and age of the parties, could hardly be seen as a factor undermining the marriage. The petitioner was 72 and the respondent 59.

Revision note   Another popular area for references. Given that both s. 12(a) and s. 12(b) of the Matrimonial Causes Act 1973 concern matters affecting consummation of marriage you really ought to consider them in the alternative when revising. In (b) it is the refusal to have intercourse, in (a) the inability to have or permit intercourse. Cases such as *Baxter* v *Baxter* [1948] AC 274 have implications for both heads. As a final point your lecturer may have raised at some stage the possibility of wilful refusal being a 'fact' from which irretrievable breakdown of marriage may be inferred. Therefore cross-reference this with divorce matters. As to the reasons you can do no better than read the Law Commission Report No. 33 (1970) and the summary of the arguments in Cretney, *Principles of Family Law*, pp. 69-72.

Lack of a valid consent

Hyde v *Hyde* (1866) LR 1 P & D 130 makes it clear that marriage is a voluntary union, hence the requirement for a freely given consent stemming from a full appreciation of all the relevant facts. This area is again popular with examiners and it is worth expending some effort to appraise yourself of the law. Section 12(c) of the Matrimonial Causes Act 1973 states that there will be no valid consent if there has been evidence of duress, mistake, unsoundness of mind or *otherwise*. It is possible that questions dealing with duress are more likely than ones raising the other points because of recent developments in the law, which it can be argued became necessary because of the changing nature of the United Kingdom population; as it becomes more cosmopolitan the law has to respond to new practices and decide what place if any they have in English law.

The test for duress was formerly based upon the decision in *Szechter* v *Szechter* [1971] P 286 where Simon P said:

> it must ... be proved that the will of one of the parties ... has been overborne by genuine and reasonably held fear caused by threat of immediate danger (for which the party is not himself responsible) to life, limb or liberty, so that the constraint destroys the reality of consent to ordinary wedlock.

Since that statement cases have come before the court in which lack of consent has been pleaded because one spouse was a party to an arranged marriage. The suggestion is that a young female faced with such a request from her parents cannot exercise a free choice. Tradition means that she is bound to acquiesce. But, however real the problem to the female it will only be in very rare circumstances where she is in immediate danger to life, limb or liberty. Therefore the Court of Appeal in *Hirani* v *Hirani* (1982) 4 FLR 232 held that the previous test was now superfluous and replaced it with the question, 'Is the threat or pressure such as to overbear the will of the individual petitioner so as to destroy the reality of consent?'

From a student viewpoint when working on the topic or revising you need to consider the following:

(a)   The issue of precedent. Was the court in *Hirani* bound to follow *Szechter* and the Court of Appeal decision which endorsed it, *Singh* v *Singh* [1971] P 226? Bear in mind also that *Szechter* was followed by Ormrod LJ in *Singh* v *Kaur* (1981) 11 Fam Law 152 only months before the *Hirani* decision.

(b)   Consider whether the *Hirani* test is more acceptable than *Szechter*. It would appear to give a court far more flexibility to respond to individual circumstances and thus to achieve justice in the particular case.

(c)   Quite a lot has been written on the issue of duress. For a recent discussion see Ingman and Grant, 'Duress in the law of nullity' [1984] Fam Law 92, where the authors argue that duress covers two sets of circumstances. First, what they term 'the lack of conscious volition' and secondly 'where the petitioner claims his will was "deflected" by improper pressure'.

See also Christine Davies, 'Duress and nullity of marriage' (1972) 88 LQR 549; S. Poulter, 'The definition of marriage in English law' (1979) 42 MLR 409; A. Bradney, 'Arranged marriages and duress' [1984] JSWL 278.

(d)   Other issues include:

(i)   Whether or not the test for duress should be objective or subjective. *Hirani* would suggest a subjective assessment but compare with Scarman J in *Buckland* v *Buckland* [1968] P 296.

(ii)   Whether the fear must stem from the other party. In *Szechter* the threat came from the Polish authorities. The respondent had married the petitioner in order to effect her release from prison and once this had been achieved they emigrated to this country. She then petitioned, successfully, to have the marriage avoided although patently the threats did not emanate from her 'husband'.

(iii)   The theory of duress. You could when seeking an appropriate basis for the theory refer to both criminal law and contract as both disciplines have recognised the concept of duress. In the criminal law see *DPP for Northern Ireland* v *Lynch* [1975] AC 653; *Abbot* v *R* [1976] 3 All ER 140 and *R* v *Howe* [1987] 1 All ER 771; and in contract *Pao On* v *Lin Yiu Long* [1979] 3 All ER 65, HL.

(iv)   Spend some time thinking about the overlap with so-called sham marriages, a good example of which is *Vervaeke* v *Smith* [1983] 1 AC 145. English law takes the view that mental reservations about the purpose of marriage, e.g., to acquire status rather than a husband, will not affect what is an otherwise good marriage which the parties intended to contract. However, if there is fear or duress then the marriage may become voidable.

'shall we have a joint service . . . the outcome is just the same'

Mistake Mistake to be accepted in this context must vitiate consent. Thus mistake as to the identity of the other party or mistake as to the nature and purpose of the ceremony will be acceptable. Case law is in limited supply but nevertheless mistake has been known to appear in nullity questions. See in particular *Kassim* v *Kassim* [1962] P 224 and *Mehta* v *Mehta* [1945] 2 All ER 690 by way of example.

Unsound mind The only question to pose here is whether or not the person was capable of understanding the nature of the contract into which he was entering. It has to be shown that he is capable of appreciating that marriage involves certain responsibilities. You need concern yourself with only two cases, namely, *Park* v *Park* [1954] P 89 and *Roberts* v *Roberts* [1978] 3 All ER 225. In the latter case the deceased suffered from senile dementia at the time of marriage and the court was of the opinion that the marriage was voidable. The marriage, though, remained valid as it could no longer be avoided due to the death of one party. Before his marriage he had made a will and it was held that his marriage being valid had the effect of revoking the will by virtue of s. 18 of the Wills Act 1837.

Otherwise It is suggested without supporting authority that this could cover cases of drunkenness, amnesia, hypnotism and drug taking. You may add your own suggestion as to what else may invalidate consent.

Revision note A fair amount of case law, some of recent ilk and controversial at that, makes this area a good one to revise for examination questions. But remember any question will normally demand an *application* of knowledge rather than a descriptive account of the law.

Section 12(d), (e) and (f)

Minor provisions which are unlikely to trouble the examinee. By way of revision note that s. 12(d) is now amended by the Mental Health Act 1983 to include reference to the Act which defines mental disorder as mental illness, arrested or incomplete development of mind, psychopathic disorder, and any other disorder or disability of mind. The 1984 Act also allows for petitions to be brought after the expiration of the three-year limitation for commencement of actions on these grounds and s. 12(c) (see s. 2(3) of the 1984 Act).

As to the last two grounds both the venereal disease and pregnancy *per alium* must exist at the time of marriage.

Sub-conclusion

Despite the low number of nullity decrees granted each year this area of law is popular with examiners. You should therefore devote a reasonable amount of time to working on ss. 11 and 12 of the Matrimonial Causes Act 1973, both on the legal implications of the sections and the rationale behind them. A 1985 examination paper contained this question:

'It is sometimes suggested that, although the concept of the void marriage must clearly be preserved, that of the voidable marriage might be abolished' (Cretney, *Principles of Family Law*, 4th ed.).
     Discuss.

After working on the sections ask yourself the question: Do I have sufficient information to answer this question? If so how would I structure my answer? Your model could look something like this:

(a)   Must void marriage *clearly* be preserved?

(i)   Rationale for void marriage. Never came into existence. Fundamental defects.

(ii)   Meaning of marriage. Section 11 would be undermined if wider definition of marriage acceptable.

(iii)   What is achieved by preventing parties, say within prohibited degrees, from marrying?

(iv)   Is marriage in decline anyway? Could it be bolstered by this device?

(b)   Voidable *might* be abolished.

(i)   What is a voidable marriage? Valid until action taken by parties.

(ii)   Possesses similar effects to law on divorce.

(iii)   Similar ancillary provisions available.

(iv)   Valid consent ground could be returned to s. 11. Wilful refusal to law on divorce.

(v)   Mental disorder more likely to lead to divorce petition on grounds of behaviour. Pregnancy and VD could be covered by extension of law on behaviour.

(vi)   What therefore are the overriding reasons for present position? See Law Commission (1970).

To jot down points similar to the above will concentrate the mind on the issues and ensure that you do not meet them for the first time in the examination room.

     The remaining part of this chapter will refer to the bars to a nullity decree and advice on how to analyse a nullity problem.

Bars to a decree

Under this heading we shall investigate the elements of s. 13 of the Matrimonial Causes Act 1973. It is generally assumed that there are no bars to granting a decree where the marriage is void, although estoppel may have a role to play where a party may be estopped from denying the validity of a bigamous marriage.

Section 13 is likely to appear at some point in a nullity question and as such you must become familiar with the essential elements of the section which are:

(a)   That it applies to voidable marriages only.

(b)   That if the provisions are fulfilled the court is under a mandatory duty not to grant a decree of nullity.

(c)   The respondent must satisfy the court as to the following:

(i)   that the petitioner knew he could have the marriage avoided – thus knowledge of his remedy is important;

(ii)   and still conducted himself in such a way as to lead the respondent *reasonably* to believe that he wouldn't seek to avoid the marriage and

(iii)   that it would be unjust to the respondent to grant the decree.

From a revision viewpoint you should be aware of the significance of *D* v *D* [1979] Fam 70, which confirms that both (a) *and* (b) of s. 13(1) must be satisfied before a decree can be refused. In this case the husband by his conduct had satisfied s. 13(1)(a) but not (b) because the parties had lived apart for a number of years.

Examples of what in the old law amounted to 'approbation' and may now be considered as conduct by the petitioner *vis-à-vis* the respondent are contained in the cases of *Slater* v *Slater* [1953] P 235 and *W* v *W* [1952] 1 All ER 858. For comparison purposes see *Tindall* v *Tindall* [1953] P 63.

Sample question

Prior to his marriage to Jill in 1982, Jack, to save himself embarrassment, did not tell the vicar that his middle name was Ebenezer. As a result the banns were published without this information. Soon after the ceremony Jack discovered that Jill suffered from a minor physical defect which prevented intercourse. Being frightened of operations Jill refused to undergo treatment despite assurances from a medical friend that the operation was a simple one. In 1984 Jack was told by his brother that because of the defect the marriage could be 'dissolved'. Nevertheless in 1985 the parties adopted a child. Throughout this three-year period, Jack has tried to persuade Jill to change her mind and have the operation, but she stubbornly refused his requests. In 1986 Jill, after learning that Jack was associating with another woman, Anne, decided to have treatment. Unfortunately the hospital could not give her a date for the operation but promised that it would be 'before the end of 1988'.

Jack now says that it is too late as he has 'lost his ardour' for Jill. She is determined to proceed with the operation but insists that she would only permit intercourse if Jack's relationship with Anne ceases.

Both Jack and Jill seek your advice as to possible grounds to have the marriage terminated.

Analysis

Examining each line in turn the following points are to be noted:

(a)   The first sentence raises the issue of undue publication of banns. One therefore assumes an Anglican ceremony. You are told that he did not reveal his middle name because of likely embarrassment and from this you are meant to conclude that he does not possess the intent to deceive or deny publication of the marriage plans. Thus the marriage is likely to be declared valid.

(b)   The second point relates to Jill's *minor* physical defect and thus her *inability* to permit intercourse. Will this give Jack a basis for petitioning for nullity under s. 12(a)? The next sentence informs us that she refuses to undergo an operation which is likely to cure the problem. We have already noted that as the operation is not attended with danger her refusal may give Jack the evidence he needs to bring a petition based upon wilful refusal to consummate. We are not actually told that consummation has not taken place but it is a safe conclusion on the facts. In these instances you would need to tell the examiner the meaning of consummation, wilful refusal and incapacity.

(c)   The next sentences raise the s. 13 defence and whether or not because the parties adopted a child this would prevent Jack from successfully petitioning. Remember that 'knowledge that it was open to him to have the marriage *avoided*' is a strict requirement. Will therefore the information given by his brother suffice? It informs him of a remedy but not one based in nullity. The legislation does use the word 'avoided' not 'dissolved'.

(d)   Jack has used tact and persuasion but Jill has refused to have the operation. However, in light of further information she changes her mind. For Jack to be successful he must show inability at the date of the hearing and as Jill cannot have the operaiton until later in the year he may well succeed on this basis.

(e)   Jill may be able to petition for divorce against Jack on the assumption he is committing adultery with Anne.

(f)   Jack has 'lost his ardour'. A reference to *Potter* v *Potter* (1975) 5 Fam Law 161 where the Court of Appeal required a deliberate decision. If Jack can substantiate his claim then Jill will be unable to succeed on the basis of Jack's wilful refusal to consummate.

(g)   The fact that Jill, if the operation is successful, will only permit intercourse if Jack's relationship with Anne ends means that you will have to consider the meaning of 'just excuse' in the definition of wilful refusal noted in *Horton* v *Horton* [1947] 2 All ER 871.

(h)   Terminated refers to remedies in divorce and nullity.

Conclusion

The law on nullity is relatively straightforward. Look for key words in the question such as impotence, defect, psychological, threat, mental illness, banns, terminal illness etc. and these will lead you directly to the relevant sections on nullity.

FOUR

MAGISTRATES' DOMESTIC JURISDICTION

Undoubtedly the jurisdiction of magistrates' courts is very wide. This in itself has raised questions as to whether or not the court has any particular rationale or any rational structure and there is a school of thought which says that the 'domestic jurisdiction' can be dispensed with. The magistrates' court has often been referred to as a 'first-aid post' to those who are experiencing matrimonial difficulties. The Law Commission in its report No. 77, upon which the Domestic Proceedings and Magistrates' Courts Act 1978 was based, saw it as a 'casualty clearing station'. It can therefore be seen as a local court to which spouses can turn in their hour of need. Whether or not it is effective in the role it assumes is another matter. You may initially begin to think about including information concerning the magistrates' jurisdiction if faced with a question on restructuring of the family court hierarchy or in attempting to answer a question asking you to discuss the merits or otherwise of a family court along the lines advocated in the Finer Report on One Parent Families (1974) the recommendations of which were promptly shelved by the government in Spring 1975 on the all too familiar grounds that the cost of implementation would be prohibitive.

The following question, which appeared on a university examination paper in 1984, may be taken as a model:

'For nearly a decade family courts have received support from lawyers, social workers and politicians: for example the Labour Party Manifesto of 1974 and reports from "Justice" in 1975, from the Conservative Party Lawyers Group in 1978 and from the Law Society in 1979' (Morris, Giller, Szwed and Geech 1980).

Discuss the present structure and arrangements of jurisdiction, showing what you perceive as its particular strengths and weaknesses, and where you see a need for reform.

This type of question allows you to introduce material from a wide range of sources but it is important that you have given preliminary thought to the structure of your answer. It refers you to jurisdictions of which the magistrates' is just one. You then are asked to assess the strengths and weaknesses of those jurisdictions and finally to consider the need for reform, drastic or otherwise including the setting up of a family court. Therefore information about the role of the magistrates' court, the substantive law and its effectiveness in particular will allow you to go some way towards providing an answer to a question similar to the one quoted.

One important point is that in many areas of family law the magistrates' court and higher courts have similar or overlapping powers. For example, powers to exclude a violent spouse are possessed, albeit not equally, by the High, county and magistrates' courts. Similarly in adoption and custody proceedings. This will mean that an examiner before asking for comments on the substantive law may ask for your advice on which court provides the most effective forum to resolve the problem and why.

I therefore propose to range briefly over the material which may be raised in an examination question, making, hopefully helpful, suggestions as I proceed. I will in conclusion introduce a sample question of the type that has appeared on examination papers. You may also wish to consider this area as the subject of an extended essay or project which counts towards your final assessment. Quite a lot of literature has appeared commenting on the wider issues and you will also have the benefit of the Law Commission Report in assessing whether its expectations in 1976 have been fulfilled in the last decade.

Scope of the jurisdiction

The areas of domestic jurisdiction most likely to arise in examination questions are:

(a) Domestic violence and exclusion from property.
(b) Maintenance and related orders.
(c) Affiliation proceedings.
(d) Custody and custodianship and care proceedings.
(e) Adoption.

I shall take each of these areas in turn.

Domestic violence and exclusion from property

Always a likely source for an examination question, which may take the form of a problem or a more general question on how the courts can respond to what Sir George Baker in *Davis* v *Johnson* [1978] 1 All ER 841, CA, called 'domestic hooliganism'. I shall say more later about the powers of the county court and High Court but here I am concentrating on the magistrates' court. Remember therefore, when revising, to list the differences between the magistrates' court exercising powers given by the Domestic Proceedings and Magistrates' Courts

Act 1978 and those exercised by the county court under the Domestic Violence and Matrimonial Proceedings Act 1976.

Magistrates' Courts (1978 Act)	*County Court (1976 Act)*
Restricted to spouses.	Spouses and those living together *as man and wife.*
Has to be violence or the threat of violence.	The test is based upon the word 'molestation'.
Orders can only be made in respect of children of the family.	Any child 'living with the applicant'.

The 1978 Act, sections 16-18   First note that an application under s. 16 may be made, depending on the circumstances, for a personal protection order and/or an exclusion order. You must then become familiar with the criteria, proof of which will result in the order being made. A personal protection order can only be made if the court is satisfied that the respondent has used, or threatened to use, violence against the person or the applicant or child of the family *and* it must be shown that such an order is *necessary* for the protection of the applicant or child of the family.

A key word in the application of this section is *'violence'*. While judicial interpretation of this Act is not extensive the Court of Appeal has in the case of *Horner* v *Horner* [1982] 2 All ER 495 had the opportunity to pass comment on the word 'violence'. The wife had obtained an order under s. 16 stating that the husband should not use or threaten violence. He then began harassing her but in such a way as not to use or threaten to use violence. The wife's solicitors commenced proceedings in the county court being of the opinion that the magistrates' court order was inadequate to restrain this type of conduct. The Court of Appeal agreed. Ormrod LJ commented: 'I have no doubt that the word "molesting" in s. 1(1)(a) of the 1976 Act does not imply necessarily either violence or threats of violence. It applies to *any* conduct which can properly be regarded as such a degree of harassment as to call for intervention of the court'. The conclusion is that while the word 'molest' is wide enough to include violence the word 'violence' is limited to the application of force or in s. 16 the threat of. Thus *Horner* is an important case, and your choice of forum may depend on the impact of this case.

Next you will have to consider s. 16(3), that is, whether or not an exclusion order is needed. It is obviously a drastic step to exclude a spouse or prevent him or her from entering the matrimonial home. (It would appear necessary for there to be a property which the parties consider to be the matrimonial home.) Do emphasise to the examiner that rigorous conditions have to be established in order to obtain the remedy, namely that:

(a) there is danger of physical injury to the applicant or a child of the family *and*

(b) the respondent has used violence against the applicant or child of the family *or* has threatened to use violence against them and there is evidence that he has used violence against some other person *or*

(c) he is contravening a personal protection order and has threatened to use violence against them.

For judicial authority examine *McCartney* v *McCartney* [1981] 1 All ER 597 where Arnold P said (at p. 600):

If there is to be demonstrated a danger, such as is mentioned in the last part of s. 16(3), it must in my judgment be an objectively observable danger, one which the magistrates think to exist and not one which the complainant thinks to exist.

The case should also be used as authority for the proposition that the danger need not necessarily be immediate to justify an exclusion from the matrimonial home. Other points which may find their way into examination questions are the 'immediacy' issue and it is possible for a court to grant an expedited order but only in cases of imminent physical danger and only then for personal protection orders. An expedited order is for a limited period. The other point, and this again may raise comparisons with the county court's powers under the 1976 Act, is the matter of attaching a power of arrest under s. 18(1). This order is designed to give added protection to the applicant in that if a breach of the protection order occurs then the respondent can be arrested without warrant. There are really only two cases to which you need to pay particular attention, *viz: Widdowson* v *Widdowson* (1982) 4 FLR 121 and *Head* v *Head* [1982] 3 All ER 14, which deal with when a power of arrest should be attached and what the consequences will be for failure to comply with the order.

Revision note A good chance that this topic will appear on the question paper. List the points of interest in the sections noting carefully the words which have received judicial consideration. Note the overlap of jurisdictions and list the relative merits of both county and magistrates' courts. It is argued that the county court and solicitors are now geared up to respond quickly to domestic violence cases, yet some evidence exists to show that *provided the more limited criteria* can be established the magistrates do provide a speedy remedy. Look also at the Court of Appeal decision in *O'Brien* v *O'Brien* [1985] FLR 801, which considers the interrelationship between the county court and magistrates' jurisdictions in cases of violence.

Maintenance and related orders

The 1978 Act repealed the Matrimonial Proceedings (Magistrates' Courts) Act 1960 within which was enshrined the concept of the matrimonial offence, abolished in divorce proceedings in 1969 and now dispensed with in the magistrates' court. One of the major purposes of the 1978 Act was to bring the magistrates' court more into line with the divorce court.

If anything this aspect is the true 'first-aid' function referred to earlier. Look carefully at ss. 1 and 2, the former listing the *grounds* of application for *financial provision*, and the latter indicating the orders which the court can make. The *application* is therefore for an order under s. 2 not s. 1. Note the similarity between s. 2 of the 1978 Act and s. 23 of the Matrimonial Causes Act 1973. The magistrates' court can now make in appropriate circumstances a lump-sum order which has recently been increased from £500 to £1,000. This is one example of the powers of the magistrates being brought more into line with those of the divorce court.

The grounds are not as extensive as the 'facts' for divorce, being based upon the failure to provide reasonable maintenance, 'unreasonable behaviour' and desertion. There is little that is controversial in these provisions and as long as you are familiar with the corresponding divorce cases on behaviour and desertion then you will be adequately equipped to deal with any problem the examiner cares to throw at you. One case you might mention is *Bergin* v *Bergin* [1983] 1 All ER 905 as it is authority for the proposition that when magistrates are considering s. 1(c) of the 1978 Act they should apply the same test as used by the High Court under s. 1(2)(b) of the 1973 Act. That test was said by Heilbron J (at p. 908) to be the one stated by Dunn J in *Livingstone-Stallard* v *Livingstone-Stallard* [1974] 2 All ER 766:

> I ask myself the question: would any right-thinking person come to the conclusion that this husband has behaved in such a way that this wife cannot reasonably be expected to live with him, taking into account the whole of the circumstances and the characters and personalities of the parties.

This test has most recently been confirmed in the case of *Buffrey* v *Buffrey* (1988) 138 NLJ 107 when the Court of Appeal held that the correct test was not whether the behaviour had been 'grave and weighty' (the old constructive desertion test) but the one laid down by Dunn J.

Another point that could be raised is the role of adultery in such proceedings. Unlike the divorce legislation adultery does not rate a mention in the Domestic Proceedings and Magistrates' Courts Act 1978. The assumption therefore is that adultery must be categorised as 'behaviour' but *quaere* adultery on its own? In light of the above test for behaviour all the circumstances will have to be considered together with the reaction of the other spouse. As yet there appears to be no direct authority on the point.

As to desertion note that in the magistrates' court there is no minimum period of desertion. In divorce it is desertion for a *continuous* period of two years.

Section 2 of the 1978 Act should be read together with s. 3 which lists those matters to which a court must have regard in dealing with an application for reasonable maintenance. The following points are important:

(a)   A new s. 3 has been substituted by s. 9 of the Matrimonial and Family Proceedings Act 1984. The court is under a *duty* to examine certain matters but in the context of giving *first consideration to the welfare of any child of the family under the age of 18*. For full background information on this innovation see the Law Commission Report No. 112, Financial Consequences of Divorce. The new s. 25 inserted by the 1984 Act into the 1973 Act contains the same statement of priority as when the divorce court is asked to consider financial provision.

There are probably two cases which will of necessity have to be cited if discussing the approach of the magistrates' court to s. 3. The Court of Appeal in *Vasey* v *Vasey* [1985] FLR 596 said that the correct approach was for the magistrates to deal with each issue on a point-by-point basis, making whatever finding they felt appropriate. It was then up to them to balance those factors against one another so as to arrive at an order which was both just and reasonable. The weight to be attached to any particular item is for the magistrates to decide, but they *must take account of all of them*. However, the most important function is to balance needs and responsibilities against financial resources.

The latest reported case would appear to be *Day* v *Day* [1988] 1 FLR 278 where Wood J held that there was no basis for interfering with the magistrates' conclusion that a husband who had deserted his wife should pay £15 per week to her and £5 each to the two children. The justices had taken the whole history of the relationship into account, had directed themselves in accordance with s. 3 and accordingly the appeal was dismissed.

The meaning of 'first consideration' has now been determined by the Court of Appeal in *Suter* v *Suter and Jones* [1987] 2 All ER 336. It was stressed that in deciding whether to make a periodical payments order, the welfare of the children was *not* the paramount consideration. The court had to consider all the circumstances, keeping in mind the welfare of the children, and then attempt to attain a financial result which was just between *husband* and *wife*.

(b)   Most of the matters listed in the new s. 3 are repeated from the old section. But there are some major differences which could form part of a question, e.g., to discuss the differences as a part (a) and then follow it up with a problem in part (b).

The following differences between the paragraphs of the old s. 3(1) and the equivalent paragraphs of the new s. 3(2) may be noted:

(i)   Paragraph (a) has been expanded by putting the court under a duty to consider future earning capacity of the parties. This would apparently allow the court to consider whether one or both parties, but usually the wife, can become more financially independent especially if she has a particular skill or professional qualification which may be exploited. This factor though is more important when considering the aftermath of divorce as the Law Commission was particularly anxious that one spouse should not see the other as providing a 'meal ticket' for life.

(ii)   Paragraph (f) has been added to by instructing the court to take into account likely contribution in the foreseeable future to the welfare of the family. This addition reflects the new responsibility to make the children's welfare the first consideration.

(iii)   As to paragraph (g), it was always a matter of some debate whether or not conduct by the parties should be taken into account when apportioning out the family assets. 'Taken into account' in practice will mean penalise. One of the most famous cases of the decade, *Wachtel* v *Wachtel* [1973] Fam 72, concerned the phrase 'having regard to their conduct' in s. 25(1) of the Matrimonial Causes Act 1973 as originally enacted, and it decided that conduct ought to be a factor only when it was 'obvious and gross misconduct' (per Lord Denning MR). Parliament has now inserted a new test in s. 25(1) that conduct shall be taken into account, *if that conduct is such that it would in the opinion of the court be inequitable to disregard it.* One can at this stage only speculate on how this differs, if at all, from the previous test. The last important case under the old s. 3 of the Domestic Proceedings and Magistrates' Courts Act 1978 was *Robinson* v *Robinson* [1983] 1 All ER 391 when the Court of Appeal confirmed that past conduct was only to be taken into account in exceptional cases where it would offend a reasonable person's sense of justice to disregard such conduct. The court felt on the facts that the husband was completely blameless and that the marriage had broken down *solely* on account of the wife's decision to end cohabitation and thus fell into the 'exceptional' category. Now this test does not appear to be substantially different from the one contained in the new s. 3: 'if that conduct is such that it would in the opinion of the court be inequitable to disregard it'. As *Robinson* purported to follow the obvious and gross misconduct test enunciated by *Wachtel* one could conclude that the new section will not lead to a radical reappraisal of the approach previously adopted and applied by the Court of Appeal. This has been confirmed by the latest reported case, *Kyte* v *Kyte* [1987] 3 All ER 1041.

(c)   The Act gives no guidance on how much magistrates ought to order by way of financial provision. It is desirable that a court should have the utmost flexibility in reaching a decision given the income of the parties. During the 1970s and especially after *Wachtel* it became common to speak of one-third of joint incomes as being the starting-point although the so-called one-third 'rule' has been much criticised (see below). The one-third rule often appears on papers with the thrust of the question being a discussion of the usefulness of the 'rule' in practice. You ought therefore to be familiar with the following group of cases – a quote from one will set the tenor for the others. In *Furniss* v *Furniss* (1982) 3 FLR 46 at 51 Ormrod LJ said:

> Many times this court has said that in these days the one-third approach is not helpful. It may help sometimes, it may give a rough idea of the position, but generally it misleads.

Gengler v *Gengler* [1976] 2 All ER 81 applied the one-third principle to the magistrates' court. For the general background to the approach see the following cases:

Cann v *Cann* [1977] 3 All ER 957;
Slater v *Slater* (1982) 3 FLR 364;
Stockford v *Stockford* (1982) 2 FLR 58;
Potter v *Potter* [1982] 3 All ER 321.

For recent judicial comment on the working of the one-third principle in ancillary proceedings see: *Bullock* v *Bullock* [1986] 1 FLR 372, which clearly stated there was substantial authority for the one-third approach which had not been followed of late but had never been disapproved; and *Dew* v *Dew* [1986] 2 FLR 341 in which Lincoln J said that the true position was that it was a 'helpful guide in some but not all cases'.

Revision note An area of substantial overlap with divorce court legislation as was bound to be the case given the rationale of the 1978 Act. Even for refusal to provide reasonable maintenance there is a corresponding section, 27, in the Matrimonial Causes Act 1973 (as partially substituted by s. 4 of the 1984 Act). The revision tip is to list the various points on this topic raised by your tutor and then search out the similar provision in the 1973 Act. A body of case law will often have built up under the 1973 Act and this will be of great assistance in making submissions on the *likely* interpretation of the 1978 Act.

Affiliation proceedings

One of the major changes to affect the magistrates' court since the first edition of this book has been the abolition, by s. 17 of the Family Law Reform Act 1987, of affiliation proceedings. Proceedings have until the coming into force of the section been based in their entirety in the magistrates' court, but the new Act allows for an action to be brought under the new s. 11B of the Guardianship of Minors Act 1971, the text of which is to be found in the first schedule to the

1987 Act. For the first time either parent may apply for a periodical payments order in their favour for the benefit of the child, which order may in turn be secured if application is made to the High Court or county court, but not the magistrates' court.

It is also possible to seek a lump sum order for the benefit of the child. Much more controversially, if application is made to the High Court or county court, a property transfer can be made.

Although significant changes have been effected, the issue of paternity is still likely to present problems to the court. Section 23 of the Family Law Reform Act 1987 amends s. 20 of the Family Law Reform Act 1969 and allows the court on its own motion to give a direction for the use of scientific tests to ascertain paternity or even maternity, as the case may be. Of particular significance will be the new DNA fingerprinting procedure which can establish paternity as a virtual certainty.

Recent cases which clearly indicate the current position on establishing paternity are: *Turner* v *Blunden* [1986] Fam 120; *Re I (A Minor)* (1987) The Times May 22; *McV* v *B* (1988) 138 NLJ 106. In the last case the putative father had failed to comply with a blood test direction. Wood J held that this was 'other evidence' capable of corroborating the mother's evidence as required by s. 4(1) of the Affiliation Proceedings Act 1957.

It should be noted that at the time of writing s. 17 of the 1987 Act has not been brought into force, although many other sections including s. 23 came into force on 4 April 1988.

From a student viewpoint an examiner may decide to ask you to compare the new position for maintenance of a child — whether born in wedlock or not — with the pre-FLRA position. Remember that the principal reason for abolishing affiliation proceedings is to help to eradicate the proceedings which existed purely because the child was illegitimate. By integrating such claims for maintenance within the Guardianship of Minors Act any distinction becomes superfluous.

Custody, custodianship and care proceedings

As the subheading indicates, the magistrates have a wide jurisdiction to deal with many problems involving children. The most obvious is that of allocating legal custody when spouses separate. Section 8 of the 1978 Act applies when an application has been made for financial provision. It may be useful at this stage to introduce you to two terms which have great significance in family law, namely, 'legal custody' and 'child of the family'. The magistrates can only make a custody order if the child in question is a child of the family. It will be helpful if you list the occasions when you may have to consider its meaning. The following spring to mind:

Legislation	Sections	Purpose
Matrimonial Causes Act 1973	21, 23, 24, 25	Financial provision on divorce.
	27	Failure to provide reasonable maintenance.
	52	Definition.
Domestic Proceedings and Magistrates' Courts Act 1978	1	Application for financial provision.
	2, 3, 7	Orders for financial provision and factors to take into account.
	8	Orders for custody of children.
	16-18	Protection.
	88	Interpretation.
Matrimonial and Family Proceedings Act 1984	3, 4	Substituting new sections for s. 25 of the Matrimonial Causes Act 1973 and amending s. 27 of that Act.
	27	Interpretation.
	Part III	Financial relief after overseas divorce.
	9, 10, 11	Provisions relating to powers of magistrates to order financial relief.

The above list is meant only to be indicative of the approach to be adopted and not to list every piece of legislation which refers to 'child of the family'. The words are quite popular with examiners because of the existence of case law and the difficulty in applying the statutory definition to any given set of facts. A child of the family is one who is a child of both parties to a marriage or any child, except one boarded out with the couple by, for example, a local authority, who has been *treated* by both as a child of their family. The key words are thus 'treated' and 'family'.

Treated   In dealing with this word in an examination it is worth mentioning that the test prior to 1973 was whether or not a child had been 'accepted' as a child of the family (see the Matrimonial Proceedings (Magistrates' Courts) Act 1960 – now, of course, repealed). This was held to mean that a party to a marriage must consent to receive the child as one of the family and in order to give that consent he must be in possession of the material facts (see *R* v *R*

[1969] P 414). The material fact in *R* v *R* was paternity. The husband believed he was the father of the little girl, but on finding out the truth some five years later he rejected her. The court held that his conduct in the previous five years was not carried out in knowledge of the material facts and therefore as he rejected the child at the first opportunity after learning of the truth he had not accepted her.

It is always useful to compare and contrast. As the test has changed ponder whether the latter is preferable to the former. To treat was held in *A* v *A* [1974] 1 All ER 755 to mean to 'act or behave towards' but not to include knowledge of material facts. In this case it was decided that a man could not act or behave towards a child in the womb, and therefore not assume responsibility to maintain it after its birth. It goes without saying that the child was not the respondent's. In the later case of *D* v *D* (1981) 2 FLR 93 the stepfather was held not to have treated his wife's daughter as a child of the family because she lived for the most part with her grandparents and was essentially a visitor to the mother's house. The fact that the stepfather had acted kindly towards her did not justify a conclusion that she had been treated as a child of the family. In *M* v *M* (1981) 2 FLR 39 the court decided that to 'treat' was a matter of fact to be culled from the available evidence. Thus, where the husband had behaved for certain limited purposes as though the child was his own, it was insufficient to show that he had treated the child as a child of the family.

The Court of Appeal in *Teeling* v *Teeling* [1984] FLR 808 held that the test was an *objective* one. The wife had left the husband, and after an affair became pregnant. Encountering difficulties she prevailed upon the husband to allow her and the child back into the martimonial home. Ormrod LJ considered that the fact that the child had lived 'as part of the family' for six months was conclusive (at p. 809):

> The husband did various things for the child and was obviously willing and prepared, if the wife had been prepared, to accept the child as his own child and live together as a family and they did so for six months.

Similarly in *Carron* v *Carron* [1984] FLR 805 the children had been living with the parties for four years. 'It could not be said that they had not been treated as children of the family.'

However, this in itself does not mean that husbands will automatically have to assume large financial responsibilities towards the children. The final amount will depend upon an assessment of s. 25(3) of the Matrimonial Causes Act 1973.

It is therefore important when considering liability to maintain a child that you fully appreciate the law on this point. However, it ought to be pointed out that from the male viewpoint justice may not be achieved as a result of applying the treated test. The husband in *R* v *R* (above) would in all probability be found liable to maintain the child under the new test although he was completely ignorant of the truth at the time of the conduct upon which his liability is based. Under the 'accepted' test a man could be forced to admit responsibility for a child in the womb, e.g., with knowledge of the pregnancy and knowing it was not his child, marrying the mother. Of, course under the *A* v *A* test he could not now behave towards a child in the womb.

Family   In *M* v *M* (1981) 2 FLR 39 the Court of Appeal accepted the submission that a prerequisite to applying the treated test was a determination of whether or not the child had ever been part of a family unit. In the case the husband and wife separated and one year later the wife gave birth to a child of which the husband was not the father. Although he didn't repudiate the wife's implied suggestion to her family that he was the father the court concluded that there had never been a family once the separation had taken place in 1971.

This case is worth noting because the court was of the opinion that the word 'family' is a 'popular loose and flexible description and not a technical term and that its exact scope must depend on its context' (per Ormrod LJ at p. 44). To hold that a family subsists as long as the marriage is legally in existence would lead to the most extraordinary conclusion, e.g., 'that when one of the spouses had deserted . . . so that for five, six or ten years one was in America and the other in China, the family would be said to continue to exist.

M v *M* was applied in *W* v *W* *(child of the family)* [1984] FLR 796. The husband married the wife knowing that she was pregnant by another man. However, his only contact with the child was at the birth and subsequently for two weeks at his wife's parents home when he was on leave from his army unit. He then effectively ended the marriage. The basis of the husband's argument was that there had never been a family within which the child could be treated as a child of the family. The Court of Appeal, having regard to the parties' initial intention to live together combined with the two weeks they actually spent together, thought there was sufficient evidence from which to conclude that 'a family, even though an exiguous one, came into existence at the date of the marriage'.

For a full discussion of this issue see Jacqueline Priest, 'Child of the family', [1984] Fam Law 134. The author gives many examples from Court of Appeal transcripts in order to supplement the evidence to be gleaned from reported cases.

Legal custody   This is defined by s. 86 of the Children Act 1975 and means 'so much of the parental rights and duties as relate to the person of the child (including the place and manner in which his time is spent)'. The magistrates can also order access to any child of the family. See s. 14, which gives power to the court to order access for grandparents.

The principles upon which custody decisions are based will be discussed in chapter 10. The application for custody is ancillary to other proceedings in the magistrates' court, namely, an application under ss. 2, 6 or 7 of the 1978 Act.

Revision note   A problem question may raise the following points:

(a)   The problems connected with breakdown of the marriage, most usually maintainence and the custody of any children of the family. You would need to point out that the spouse can seek an order in the magistrates' court or may proceed straight to divorce and make applications for the above as issues incidental to the divorce proceedings.

(b)   The discussion of maintenance will normally involve consideration of the factors in s. 3 of the 1978 Act. Note that this is a substituted section as a result of s. 9 of the Matrimonial and Family Proceedings Act 1984.

(c)   Maintenance for children will depend on whether or not they are children of the family. In most cases they will be children of both parties and thus liability to maintain will not be in doubt. But look carefully at any problem to see whether or not the facts reveal that the husband married the wife knowing that she had a child from a previous marriage or relationship. If so note the points raised above.

Care proceedings   The latest statistics available show that 86,600 children were in the care of local authorities in England and Wales. 38,658 ended up in that position because of care orders granted by the juvenile court, a court composed of magistrates but to which special rules apply. I will say more in chapter 10 about the substantive law, which has been subject in the last decade to almost continuous judicial scrutiny and is, as a result, popular with examiners. Here it is sufficient to note the role played by the magistrates acting as the juvenile court. The responsibility placed upon their shoulders by Parliament is an onerous one as they are dealing with the difficult question of parental rights yet at the same time making decisions about the future welfare of the child. Presumably we would only wish to see a family split up if sufficient evidence existed to show that the child's welfare was better served if he was away from his parents.

The juvenile court exercises powers contained in the Children and Young Persons Act 1969 and the Child Care Act 1980. The major distinction between these two pieces of legislation is that the former relates to children who have to be *taken* into care while the latter puts local authorities under a duty to *receive* children into care on a voluntary basis. Thus in the former case the legal basis for retention by the local authority is the care order, granted by the juvenile court. In the latter case only if the local authority wishes to retain the child in care will it have to take action under the 1980 Act which may eventually lead to the juvenile court if the parent wishes to challenge a parental rights resolution made by the local authority. Most family law question papers will contain some reference to local authority powers in respect of children. Without at this stage going into the substantive law you may care to give thought to the potential for overlap between jurisdictions. A major controversy had arisen (now resolved, see for example, *W v Hertfordshire County Council* [1985] 2 All ER 301, HL) about the role of the wardship jurisdiction as a means of challenging the decisions made by juvenile courts and local authorities. What the courts had to decide was how far the exercise of statutory powers could be challenged by the use of the prerogative jurisdiction. The House of Lords in the *Hertfordshire County Council* case, together with its decision in *A* v *Liverpool City Council* [1982] AC 363 made it quite clear the wardship jurisdiction had an extremely limited role to play (see chapter 11 for greater detail and discussion of the law).

Custodianship   The provisions contained in ss. 33-46 of the Children Act 1975 were brought into force in December 1985. Aimed primarily at those who have a long established relationship with a child, e.g., foster parents, the law is based upon the recommendations of the Houghton Committee on Adoption of Children (Cmnd 5107, 1972). The purpose is to give those who are not entitled to apply for custody in the usual way an opportunity to gain what is in effect legal custody so as to enable them to resist the claims of natural parents wishing to resume care of their children, particularly those who had been fostered for a long period.

As legal custody includes regulating the place and manner in which the child's time is spent, then the applicant will possess the ability to care for and control the child.

Suffice it to say at this stage that the magistrates' court, along with the High Court and county court, may make a custodianship order. There are, however, some limitations on the magistrates -- for example, the child may not be made a party to the proceedings as he can if they are instituted in the High Court. More will be said about the recent case law developments, together with a more detailed discussion of the new law, in chapter 9.

Adoption

As with matters relating to custodianship, I do not at this stage propose to look at the substantive law on adoption. The present position is that the High Court, county court and magistrates' court all possess jurisdiction to make adoption orders. The latest figures show that nearly 90% of all adoptions are processed by the county court with the magistrates dealing with the majority of the remainder. However, it should be noted that in *Re PB* (a minor) (application to free for adoption) [1985] FLR 394 Sheldon J was of the opinion that the magistrates' court was an unsuitable venue for long contested adoption cases. A similar comment was made by Neill LJ regarding the length of interim care proceedings in the juvenile court. He said:

I was very concerned to hear in the course of this appeal that there have been cases of contested care proceedings . . . where, before the magistrates felt able to make even an interim order, the hearings had extended over a period of three days. . . . hearings of this length cannot have been intended by those who framed this legislation, nor can they be in the interests of justice.

(*R* v *Birmingham City Juvenile Court*, ex p. *Birmingham City Council* [1988] 1 All ER 683, at p. 689j)

It is reasonably safe to assume that detailed questioning on adoption in the context of the magistrates' court is unlikely to occur. What is far more feasible is reference to adoption in the context of discussing what ought to be the proper role of the magistrates' court, one aspect of which ought to be the eradication of duplication of business between the various courts dealing with family matters. (For a discussion of this together with comments about a family court see Cretney, *Principles of Family Law*, 4th ed., pp. 971-82 and Bromley and Lowe, *Family Law*, 7th ed., pp. 15-16.)

Sample question

'The Domestic Proceedings and Magistrates' Courts Act 1978 contains a number of significant, if cautious, reforms intended to improve procedures. . . . However, it is unlikely that these reforms will satisfy that substantial body of opinion, which believes that the matrimonial jurisdiction of the magistrates should be abolished.' (Cretney, *Principles of Family Law,* 4th ed., p. 879.)
Discuss.

Suggested model for answering the question

Remember that you must analyse the words of an essay question equally as closely as those of a problem. Therefore:

(a)   The first line introduces the 1978 Act and makes a comment about it – i.e., that it introduced *significant,* but *cautious* reforms. It also mentions the intended *purpose* of such reforms – to improve procedure.

(b)   Take each of the above italicised words and pass comment. What is meant by the word 'significant' – *significant* in what sense? You are aware, for example, that new grounds for an order were introduced scrapping the long list contained in the 1960 Act. I have also said that the magistrates were given greater powers with which to deal with applications for financial provisions, e.g., to award a lump-sum payment. Also new powers were allocated to combat violence between spouses and this would be classed as a significant development.

If we now take the word 'cautious' we can say that Parliament was not prepared to be radical and seek to finance a family court. It could be argued that the 1978 Act was really an updating measure rather than a radical attempt to provide a new structure to help those whose marriages are breaking down.

Finally the quote says that the reforms were intended to improve procedure. Was that all? One purpose was to bring the law administered by the magistrates more in line with that administered in the divorce courts. That aspect was certainly not procedural. It can also be said that there can be little improvement while the magistrates' powers are so restricted. You may pose the question: What is the point in being able to make financial provision and allocate custody when their powers regarding the matrimonial home are so limited? Apart from exclusion powers where violence exists they cannot take the home into account with the result that a complete 'package' cannot be dispensed upon initial breakdown of marriage. Conversely you could maintain that the magistrates' court has a different philosophical basis from that of the divorce court and anything that resembles a permanent solution could inhibit the possibility of reconciliation.

At some stage in the discussion of the first part of the quote you ought to mention the Law Commission Report No. 77 upon which the Act is based. In addition the Finer Report on one-parent families certainly did not see the magistrates' court as a 'casualty clearing station', and was very alive to the possibility of it serving only one section of the community, i.e., the poorer. The *purpose* of the reforms can therefore be readily gleaned from the Law Commission Report. This will also highlight some of the deficiencies of the 1960 Act and help you to get a clearer picture of why Parliament thought legislation was needed.

(c)   The latter part of the quote tells you of a 'substantial body of opinion' which believes that the matrimonial jurisdiction should be abolished. Note that the quote implies the continued existence of the court for criminal law purposes and indeed one of the complaints has been that, given the 'police court' origin of magistrates' courts, to possess a matrimonial jurisdiction in such an environment is wrong. To satisfy the examiner you would have to make an attempt to isolate this 'substantial body of opinion'.

Patricia Garlick in her article 'Judicial separation: a research study' (1983) 46 MLR 719 points to the reluctance of solicitors in her survey to seek orders in the magistrates' court. They speak of the 'barbaric atmosphere', the 'rough and ready' justice, that all solicitors interviewed saw the court as 'the courts of the poor'. You could quote Garlick at p. 736: 'It was found that the antipathy to magistrates' courts' domestic jurisdiction, which is still widespread amongst solicitors results in the use of county courts whenever possible in preference to the magistrates' courts'.

Conversely Colin Gibson in an article entitled 'Maintenance in the magistrates' courts in the 1980s' (1982) 12 Fam Law 138 concludes: 'Those who believe that the magistrates' court criminal work and atmosphere is an unsuitable environment for the hearing of family matters will be disturbed by the possibility that an *increasing* amount of matrimonial work is being handled by these courts' (emphasis added).

The further implication is that despite the changes that have been made the major problem has not been faced. Thus, it is submitted the question is whether or not there is a need for a magistrates' court matrimonial jurisdiction at all and whether it can be replaced and its powers transferred. Could, for example, the High Court and county court inherit its powers especially as they are in essence already duplicated or even wider, e.g., to exclude from the matrimonial home on the basis of molestation *not* violence. And behind all this are implications of cost, new procedures, legal aid which would mean perhaps the most positive commitment this century to change the court structure administering family law. Finally reference should be made to proposals to set up a family court first mooted by Finer. For a fairly comprehensive review of the arguments see Hoggett and Pearl, 2nd ed., pp. 625-636 and [1987] Fam Law, at pp. 64 and 96. However, it has been widely reported that proposals for a Family Court have been shelved indefinitely, and the Lord Chancellor has made it clear that the financial implications for such a move are a major obstacle to reform. (See the New Law Journal 1987, at p. 580.)

Conclusion

Overall, given adequate planning and revision, you should be able to deal quite successfully with such a question. Analysis of the wording used is vital. Even though it is not a problem question you are still applying your knowledge of the law. Note also that case law is virtually irrelevant to answering this question.

FIVE

DIVORCE

As a result of the divorce laws having been reformed in 1969 every one of the facts which provide evidence of irretrievable breakdown of marriage were subject to judicial scrutiny, and in some cases judicial interpretation resulted in greater uncertainty being caused for divorce practitioners. For example, the meaning of the word 'and' in s. 1(2)(a) led in one case to Lloyd-Jones J holding that adultery and intolerability were entirely separate requirements (*Goodrich* v *Goodrich* [1971] 2 All ER 1340). However Faulks J in *Roper* v *Roper* [1972] 3 All ER 668 came to the opposite conclusion. It was then two years before the conflict of opinion was resolved by the Court of Appeal decision in *Cleary* v *Cleary* [1974] 1 All ER 498 which followed the *Goodrich* line.

Now those heady days are behind us and it is virtually impossible to discover a reported case which seeks to interpret one of the five facts. The decline began in 1977 when legal aid was abandoned for undefended divorces. Concurrent with this development was the extension of a special divorce procedure to all undefended divorces which has had the effect of reducing the opportunity for further judicial consideration of the 'facts' and limiting it to defended divorces which are still listed for the High Court. In *R* v *Nottingham County Court ex parte Byers* [1985] 1 All ER 735 Latey J described the objectives of the special procedure to be to 'achieve simplicity, speed and economy'.

The family law student is therefore unlikely to spend much time in lectures and tutorials dealing with s. 1(2) of the Matrimonial Causes Act 1973 although there are still some points which examiners are prone to insert into their examination papers. It is these, together with related matters in s. 3 and s. 5, which I shall discuss first of all.

When can divorce proceedings commence?

Until October 1984 a petition for divorce could not be presented to the court before the expiration of a period of three years commencing from the date of the marriage. However, the restriction was not absolute and s. 3(2) of the Matrimonial Causes Act 1973 allowed for the petition to be presented within this three-year period if it could be established that the petitioner was suffering 'exceptional hardship' or there was 'exceptional depravity' on the part of the respondent. As can be imagined these phrases attracted the judiciary's attention and thus divorce questions were frequently found to contain reference to the interpretation of s. 3. In practice it transpired that virtually all applications for leave were granted and this factor was taken into account by the Law Commission when it examined the matter in 1982. (See Law Commission Report No. 116 entitled Time Restrictions on Presentation of Divorce and Nullity Petitions.) The result was a recommendation that the three-year *discretionary* bar be replaced by a one-year *absolute* bar and this now appears as s. 1 of the Matrimonial and Family Proceedings Act 1984 substituting a new s. 3 into the Matrimonial Causes Act 1973.

It is therefore suggested that for examination purposes the new s. 3 (effective from 12 October 1984) is likely to appear in one of two ways. First in a problem question which may want you to rule out divorce as a possible option for the parties, wanting you instead to look at judicial separation or possibly nullity remedies. Secondly, and more likely at the moment, a question which asks you to attempt to justify any prohibition on when divorce proceedings can commence. The following represent some of the issues you may choose to raise:

(a)   The merits or problems of an *absolute* prohibition.

(b)   The problems associated with discretionary bars especially in seeking to achieve equality of application throughout the country. The difficulties associated with definition of words such as 'exceptional depravity'. This will allow you to introduce some of the old case law by way of showing the problems associated with any discretionary bar based upon some objective criteria. In particular see *Fay* v *Fay* [1982] AC 835; *C* v *C* [1979] 1 All ER 556; and *Nota* v *Nota* [1984] FLR 573.

(c)   The difficulty of legislating on this, and whether or not the new law is a compromise. On the one hand Parliament ought to be seen to uphold the sanctity of marriage by not allowing people to divorce soon after vows have been taken committing each to spend their lives together. Equally Parliament showed in 1969 in passing the Divorce Reform Act that the underlying purpose of the legislation was to get rid of the 'empty shell of marriage' with the minimum of bitterness.

(d)   A restriction does not exist in Scotland and it is argued that Scottish couples do not rush headlong into divorce simply because they are entitled to do so once the marriage ceremony is complete.

(e)   It can be argued also that Parliament is not by this restriction preventing a party from seeking other matrimonial remedies. Thus if the wife is being assaulted by her husband she may still seek an order excluding him from the home, even though she cannot divorce him. Equally this conduct can be used to establish that she cannot reasonably be expected to live with him and making it almost inevitable that the court will hold the marriage to have irretrievably broken down once the one year is complete.

Revision note   If such a question appears on your examination paper you will be in a strong position to answer it if you have studied the Law Commission Report No. 116 because most of the arguments, if not the answers, are to be found between its covers. However, if this issue were to be raised it would probably be a 'half' question as it is not something which is *at the moment* attracting critical attention.

The 'facts' for divorce

A primary consideration is to clearly understand that proof of any one of the 'facts' required by s. 1(2) of the Matrimonial Causes Act 1973 does not automatically result in a decree nisi being granted. Section 1(4) states very clearly that even though a 'fact' may be proved the court may still find that the marriage has not broken down irretrievably and it is this factor *alone* which determines the outcome of the petition.   Recently the Court of Appeal has taken a disjunctive approach to the construction of s. 1(1) and (2) by holding that there does not need to be a causal connection between the 'fact' alleged and the sole ground for establishing 'irretrievable breakdown'. In *Buffrey* v *Buffrey* [1988] Vol 138 NLJ 107 the court seemed to follow the independent construction strategy seen in *Cleary* v *Cleary*. However, they found that as neither party was to blame for the breakdown the recorder had been right to dismiss the petition.

I would certainly expect this issue to be raised in a problem question on divorce, if only because examiners so very rarely have a new case to deal with in this particular area.

In practice it is virtually impossible for a court to conclude that a marriage has not irretrievably broken down once one of the 'facts' is established, e.g., after five years' separation. This contention would be supported by the lack of case law and even the one case which may be cited has rather unusual facts. In *Biggs* v *Biggs and Wheatley* [1977] 1 All ER 20, Payne J refused to say that the marriage had irretrievably broken down because the husband on his release from prison had recommenced cohabitation with his wife. This was after she had been granted a decree nisi based upon his adultery. This decree was, in the circumstances which existed, rescinded. It is more likely, but not at all common given the special procedure for divorce, that a court will conclude that the marriage had irretrievably broken down yet one of the five facts is not established. (See, *Buffrey* [1988] and *Stevens* v *Stevens* [1979] 1 WLR 885 where Sheldon J concluded that it was the petitioner's conduct and not that of the respondent which had caused the irretrievable breakdown and therefore went on to dismiss the petition.) I will now take the five 'facts' and try to indicate the issues which may present themselves on your examination papers. I shall deal with them under the following headings:

(a)   Adultery and intolerability (s. 1(2)(a)).
(b)   Behaviour (s. 1(2)(b)).
(c)   Desertion (s. 1(2)(c)).
(d)   Living apart (s. 1(2)(d) and (e)).

While these are the 'facts' for divorce at the time of writing, it is unlikely that they will continue to be by the end of this decade. The Law Commission has produced a paper entitled *'Facing the Future – A Discussion Paper on the Grounds for Divorce'* (HMSO £5.90, May 1988). The Commission suggest that divorce should be based upon a fixed separation period or what it refers to as a 'process over time' approach which requires a statement to be made to the court indicating that the marriage had broken down. This would be followed by a period of reflection and give time for discussion of financial and custodial issues.

If either of these recommendations is implemented it will mean the end of 'fault' as part of our divorce laws. The Commission was of the opinion that neither of these two suggestions, if accepted, would push the incidence of divorce to new heights. The Commission is in fact recognising the reality of divorce, which is that the major problems centre around children and cash. It would seem there is little in these proposals which will exacerbate the potential for conflict over ancillary matters.

From the student viewpoint it looks as though a subject which has been languishing in an academic backwater because of the lack of case law and a positive movement to reform may start to reappear on examination papers, concurrent with any new legislative proposals which stem from the Law Commission's work.

Adultery and intolerability

As with the matter of 'consummation' in nullity you ought to give some thought to the meaning of 'adultery' in English law. Essentially it is voluntary sexual . tercourse between a married person and someone of the opposite sex. Questions therefore may be set on the following:

(a)   Whether a woman who is raped may be said to have committed adultery. As a result of the Privy Council decision in *Kaitamaki* v *R* [1984] 2 All ER 435 what commences as a voluntary action may become rape if the woman withdraws her consent during intercourse. Adultery does not take place if a woman is raped according to *Redpath* v *Redpath* [1950] 1 All ER 600 but in the above case adultery would have taken place as a result of the consensual act even though it later led to a conviction of the man for rape.

(b)   There has to be sexual intercourse. The authorities indicate that there must be penetration of the woman by the man although it does not have to be 'ordinary and complete' which is necessary for a marriage to be consummated (see *Dennis* v *Dennis* [1955] P 153).

(c)   The requirement of sexual intercourse with someone of the opposite sex raises the spectre of facts of the type found in *Corbett* v *Corbett* [1971] P 83 being pleaded by way of a defence to an assertion of adultery by the petitioner.

(d)   Given the present advances in medical science an examiner may respond by asking for your comments on whether a wife inseminated artificially commits adultery. The point has never been decided in English law although the Scottish courts have concluded that she would not commit adultery. These advances beg the question of whether adultery should be confined to acts of normal intercourse. Further support for this view can be implied from s. 27 of the Family Law Reform Act 1987 which came into force in April 1988. It makes it clear that a child born to a married woman as a result of artificial insemination by donor, with the consent of her husband shall be treated as the child of the parties to the marriage. It would be ironic in the extreme if this consensual (between husband and wife) act should be evidence to support a divorce petition based on adultery. However, if the husband did not consent, then in divorce terms that could be different and certainly the child would not be treated as a child of the marriage under this section. Also, given that Parliament did not see fit to list adultery as a separate head in the Domestic Proceedings and Magistrates' Court Act 1978, should it cease to be an independent 'fact' and be included as part of s. 1(2)(b) dealing with behaviour by the respondent which means that the petitioner cannot reasonably expect to live with him?

(e)   The intercourse must be voluntary. Again parallels can be drawn with nullity and s. 12(c) of the Matrimonial Causes Act 1973 although in practice the law is more closely related to criminal law principles. Thus drunkenness by the woman may negative consent but if she voluntarily consumes alcohol then she may be considered reckless and her lack of understanding will not be a defence. (For a parallel with the criminal law approach see *R* v *Hardie* [1984] 3 All ER 848 where the consumption of a 'sedative or soporific' drug was not to be automatically considered reckless behaviour so as to deny an individual a defence to a basic intent crime, i.e., criminal damage.)

Intolerability   The exact relationship between adultery and intolerability in s. 1(2)(a) taxed the judiciary in the early 1970s. The prevailing view is that the section must *not* be read as though it says that intolerability must result from the act of adultery (see *Cleary* v *Cleary* [1974] 1 All ER 498). Unfortunately a differently constituted Court of Appeal in *Carr* v *Carr* [1974] 1 All ER 1193 was most reluctant to follow *Cleary* and suggested: 'it might be desirable that the matter should come in some form before the House of Lords so that the profession may have clear guidance about it'. Since then, of course, the special procedure has taken over and all that is now required is a positive declaration that living with the respondent is intolerable. This is all the more surprising because Scarman LJ said in *Cleary* (at p. 503) that the Act:

does put on the court the duty of satisfying itself on a balance of probabilities that the petitioner is in fact telling the truth.

And Lord Denning MR said (at p. 501):

> judges . . . should not accept the man's bare assertion that he finds it intolerable.

An examiner may therefore ask you to imagine that you are a Law Lord and that this issue has finally reached the Lords. He may ask for your opinion on each line of authority supported by reasons. Those are cogently set out by Cretney, *Principles of Family Law*, 4th ed., pp. 120-4 and Bromley, 7th ed., pp. 179-80. It is submitted by Cretney that the *Cleary* view is correct and that the two concepts need not be linked, although he accepts that 'apparently bizarre results' may ensue.

Carr v *Carr* relied upon the wording of s. 3(3) of the Divorce Reform Act 1969 for support (see now s. 2(1) of the Matrimonial Causes Act 1973).

It is suggested that when revising you become familiar with the adultery and intolerability dichotomy because in any question where a spouse has apparently committed adultery you *must* refer to the necessity of showing that there is some evidence upon which the petitioner can say that he finds it intolerable to live with the respondent. Remember also that the examiner may imply adultery rather than state that it did take place as in this passage from a recent examination paper:

> She nagged Fred mercilessly about their financial situation and he finally turned for comfort to the local barmaid, Peg. One afternoon . . . Mavis followed them to the cinema and caused an uproar, screaming that Peg was a 'man-eating' whore.

The question proceeds to give further details of disharmony between the spouses and you are asked to advise both parties as to temporary and permanent matrimonial remedies which include whether one spouse should be excluded from the property, the custody of the children of the marriage and divorce on the basis of adultery combined with intolerability or 'unreasonable' behaviour.

Revision note   In addition to the points raised above, please note the following points as they may appear in examination problems:

(a)   The Matrimonial Causes Act 1973 imposes a time-limit for divorce petitions based upon adultery. If the parties have lived together for six months or more after the discovery of the adultery then it will be presumed that the adultery has not had a damaging effect on the marriage and the ability to petition is lost. Look closely at any dates mentioned and equally any evidence of attempted reconciliation. The Act does through the six-months time-limit seek to encourage reconciliation and will assume it has been achieved after six months together.

(b)   It is possible, but unlikely, that you could be questioned about the standard of proof required. This is because of the conflict created as a result of the decisions in the House in *Preston-Jones* v *Preston-Jones* [1951] AC 391 and *Blyth* v *Blyth* [1966] AC 643. It is suggested the standard is based upon the civil test of balance of probabilities for reasons which will be found in any good textbook on the law of evidence. However, look at the report of *Serio* v *Serio* [1983] 4 FLR 756 where Sir David Cairns suggested that the normal civil standard of proof might be 'too low'. He went on to suggest the novel test of 'a standard commensurate with the seriousness of the issue involved'!

(c)   Note the overlap between the act of adultery and the birth of an 'illegitimate' child. Therefore you may be advised at this stage to cross-reference adultery with the law relating to paternity and the use of scientific tests allowed by s. 20(1) of the Family Law Reform Act 1969, as substituted by s. 23(1) of the Family Law Reform Act 1987. Interestingly because a child may be conceived *fecundatio ab extra* proof of 'illegitimacy' will not necessarily be conclusive evidence of adultery, remembering that adultery requires sexual intercourse to have taken place. In *Hodgkiss* v *Hodgkiss* [1984] FLR 563 the wife admitted adultery in uncontested divorce proceedings. There were two children who had always been treated as children of the family. On an application by the husband a registrar ordered blood tests to be carried out to ascertain paternity. The wife appealed. The Court of Appeal in allowing the appeal confirmed that before blood tests would be ordered paternity had to be an issue in the proceedings. As the children were accepted as children of the family it was unnecessary to determine paternity.

(d)   There is a tendency to assume that to constitute adultery there must have been sexual intercourse by a spouse *after* the marriage ceremony. But if you read s. 1(2)(a) closely no reference is made to the intercourse happening subsequent to the ceremony. Thus the section could be used where before the marriage one party has had intercourse with a married person, has then married and subsequently the partner discovers the truth about his spouse's infidelity. Providing he takes action within six months then he could presumably obtain a decree. It is thought unlikely that in practice many such cases will occur, but as an academic exercise in statutory interpretation the issue could well face the examinee at some stage.

Behaviour

An area of divorce law mulled over quite extensively by the judiciary in the early to mid 1970s. The factual circumstances which may be covered by this section are legion and the Civil Judicial Statistics indicate that this is the most popular 'fact' used to support the allegation of irretrievable breakdown. Students are initially reminded that although the common shorthand is 'unreasonable behaviour' s. 1(2)(b) of the Matrimonial Causes Act 1973 does not mention either 'reasonable' or 'unreasonable' *behaviour*. The question is whether the petitioner can *reasonably* be *expected* to live with the respondent in light of his behaviour. No definition is given in the Act of the word 'behaviour' or as to the degree of behaviour required. As a student you should merely note the bare facts of these behaviour cases and instead concentrate on anything which illustrates the legal approach to the section. The most widely quoted test is that found in *Livingstone-Stallard* v *Livingstone-Stallard* [1974] 2 All ER 766. This has become known as the 'judge and jury' test because of the analogy drawn by Dunn J (at p. 770) with a criminal trial:

> one approach . . . is to assume the case was being tried by a judge and jury and first to consider what the proper direction to the jury would be, and then to put oneself in the position of a properly directed jury in deciding the question of fact.

The point for the student to indicate is that the test mixes both objective and subjective factors in seeking to reach the correct decision. Having noted the test it would be worthwhile to chart briefly different elements of 'behaviour' which have been accepted by the court as being sufficient to warrant the granting of a decree, e.g.:

Case	Behaviour	Comment
Buffrey v *Buffrey* [1988] 138 NLJ 107	H didn't take W out on social occasions plus financial problems.	Rejection by CA of test based upon the old notion of constructive desertion.
O'Neill v *O'Neill* [1975] 3 All ER 289.	DIY renovations extreme embarrassment caused to wife and daughter.	Rejection by CA of the notion that a spouse is taken 'for better or for worse'.
Bannister v *Bannister* (1980) 10 Fam Law 240.	Taking very little interest in his wife.	Rejection by CA of idea that behaviour had to be unreasonable.
Livingstone-Stallard v *Livingstone-Stallard* [1974] 2 All ER 766.	Extreme criticism of wife which was totally unjustified.	Key case, see above.
Ash v *Ash* [1972] 1 All ER 582.	Alcoholic husband. Violence both actual and threatened.	If each equally bad, each can reasonably be expected to live with the other.

There are many other examples of behaviour quoted in the standard textbooks. The above is an attempt to illustrate the type of format that you might adopt when revising this area of law.

Revision note   The following points may also appear on examination papers:

(a)   Ask yourself the question: Does it matter what is the cause of the behaviour? It would appear that a spouse who deliberately engages in a course of conduct designed to affect the other ought not to command our sympathy. However, what of the person whose behaviour is irrational and unexpected, perhaps resulting from physical or mental illness?

The response is that *Wachtel* v *Wachtel* [1973] Fam 72 emphasises that modern divorce law is not about attributing blame or fault. It is to decide whether the marriage has broken down. Thus *Thurlow* v *Thurlow* [1975] 2 All ER 979 decided that 'behaviour' included negative conduct, e.g., prolonged silences or total inactivity as well as positive conduct. It also included conduct which was involuntary and stemmed from mental or physical illness or injury, in the particular case caused by epilepsy and a severe neurological disorder. This resulted in the wife becoming incontinent, displaying bad temper, throwing objects and causing damage by burning various household items. The impact of all this on the husband led to great stresses being imposed upon him and to a breakdown in his own health. Rees J granted a decree nisi to the husband but warned that:

In a case where a spouse is reduced to a human vegetable as a result of an accident and is removed at once to hospital to remain there for life, the other spouse may face very considerable difficulties in establishing that there has been any, or any sufficient, behaviour towards him . . . or ai ...natively t at such behaviour as there has been justifies the conclusion that the other spouse cannot reasonably be expected to live with him.

It would appear that this is still an open question and thus examiners may include it on their papers. (See also *Smith* v *Smith, The Times,* 15 December 1973 and the facts of *White* v *White* [1983] 2 All ER 51.)

(b)   The word 'behaviour' should not be automatically linked with 'intolerable' in s. 1(2)(a). Try to avoid writing a sentence such as 'W found it intolerable to live with H because of his behaviour'. There may be reasons why a spouse finds it 'intolerable' to live with her husband, including the fact that he has committed adultery but which would be insufficient on an objective/subjective assessment to amount to 'behaviour'.

(c)   I mentioned when discussing the adultery provision that it could be maintained that an act of adultery before the marriage could be relied upon in a subsequent petition. Similarly with 'behaviour', for example, if the wife in

Thurlow had concealed her epilepsy and its effects from her husband then after the marriage the husband could bring a petition based upon the medical condition and presumably the deceit on the wife's part. It is interesting to speculate on whether he would be successful if the condition had at the time of the petition failed to manifest itself although it was predicted that it would at some future stage.

(d)   The case of *Stringfellow* v *Stringfellow* [1976] 2 All ER 539 held that conduct which amounted only to desertion or behaviour leading to desertion could not ground a petition under s. 1(2)(b), the appropriate remedy being under s. 1(2)(c). The reason why this had to be spelled out was to prevent attempts to avoid the two-year waiting period under the latter subsection.

(e)   Note that unlike s. 1(2)(a) there is no six-month bar to proceedings. If the parties have cohabited for less than six months after the final incident relied upon then the court must disregard it. However cohabitation for over six months, if satisfactorily explained will not prevent the divorce being granted (see *Bradley* v *Bradley* [1973] 3 All ER 750).

Resumed cohabitation may also be a factor after the granting of the decree nisi as in *Savage* v *Savage* [1982] 3 All ER 49. In this case the parties were reconciled for 4¼ years before their relationship deteriorated again. On an application by the wife under r. 65(2) of the Matrimonial Causes Rules 1977 for leave to make absolute the decree nisi notwithstanding the lapse of time Wood J refused to grant the decree absolute. Having regard to the long period together, there was a public policy element involved and one could not treat the 1977 decree nisi as reflecting the current position.

Desertion

The law recognises two types of desertion, simple and constructive. The former covers one spouse leaving the other for no good reason and the latter where one spouse has been forced to leave because of the other's 'grave and weighty' conduct. In this latter case it is the spouse remaining in the home who is deemed in desertion, the other having good reason to leave.

Although a large body of law has built up over the years, judicial authority from the 1980s is difficult to find. The following represent the key elements of the section:

(a)   Desertion.

(b)   *Continuous* period of two years immediately preceding the presentation of the petition.

Desertion   It is generally asserted that four things go to establish desertion. Firstly there needs to be separation. The standard examination question is whether or not a couple living under the same roof can be said to be 'separated', so that one spouse may allege that the other has deserted. It was said in *Pulford* v *Pulford* [1932] P 18 that 'desertion is not the withdrawal from a place, but from a state of things'. Thus the courts have looked to see whether the incidents of consortium have been extinguished. The major case for you to mention is *Hopes* v *Hopes* [1948] 2 All ER 920. The spouses although living in the matrimonial home slept in separate bedrooms, did not have sexual relations and the wife refused to do domestic work for the husband. However, the whole family did eat their meals together. The Court of Appeal found insufficient separation. Note Denning LJ who said:

In cases where they are living under the same roof, [the point where the parties are living separately and apart] is reached when they cease to be one household and become two households, or, in other words, when they are no longer residing with one another or cohabiting with one another.

Hence was born the 'two households' test subsequently adopted in the Matrimonial Causes Act 1973 relating to two and five years' living apart (s. 1(2)(d) and (e)). The Domestic Violence and Matrimonial Proceedings Act 1976 also incorporated the idea in s. 1(2) which makes clear that s. 1(1) shall apply to 'a man and woman who are living with each other in the same household as husband and wife' (see *Adeoso* v *Adeoso* [1981] 1 All ER 107 for discussion in the context of the 1976 Act).

Note also that if the spouses are forced to live apart, as when the husband is jailed upon conviction of a criminal offence, for the purposes of the law they are living separately. But be careful not to confuse proof of separation as being synonymous with desertion.

Secondly, the law also demands that there is an intention on the part of the deserting spouse that married life should be brought to an end. In an examination question you should look closely to see if the 'deserting' spouse has the mental capacity to form the necessary intention.

Thirdly, ask whether there is any evidence of an agreed separation, either express or implied, because if so then neither party can be in desertion. One harsh rule has now been abrogated. It was the rule that if mental incapacity prevented the *continuance* of the animus then desertion could not be asserted. However, s. 2(4) allows the court to infer from such evidence as is available that desertion would have continued.

Fourthly, if the person leaving has good cause then he is not in desertion. However, if the circumstances change for the better but he refuses to return then he may find himself in desertion from the moment of refusal. It was also held in *Glenister* v *Glenister* [1945] P 30 that a reasonable belief in grounds, which, if true, would entitle the spouse to cease cohabitation, was a defence to a charge of desertion. Questions are frequently posed on this latter point and my advice would be to look closely at the textbooks. Note circumstances which would entitle someone to withdraw from cohabitation in the same way as was suggested above for 'behaviour'. Similarly list occasions when the spouse would be under an obligation to return or risk a finding of desertion against him. So if the husband's behaviour had forced the wife to leave and he subsequently by his conduct and assurances convinced her that there would be no repetition then she would be expected to return. (Although it is now ten years old, Lionel Rosen's *Matrimonial Offences*, 3rd ed., deals extensively with the case law which in the main is still authoritative today.)

Two years   Students should ensure that they are familiar with the meaning of 'continuous'. Reference should be made to s. 2(5) which may be referred to as a 'reconciliation' provision. No account is to be taken of a period or periods not exceeding six months during which the parties resumed living together but it is still necessary to show a total of two years when the state of desertion existed. Again look very carefully at any dates especially when the spouse left home and when the petition was presented. In *Warr* v *Warr* [1975] 1 All ER 85 it was held that the day on which the separation had taken place was to be excluded when computing the periods of time specified in s. 1(2)(c), (d) and (e). The wife had presented her petition two years to the day after separating from her husband in 1972. Her petition under s. 1(2)(d) was dismissed.

Revision note   You could spend a month doing nothing else other than read old cases on simple and constructive desertion. To avoid this you must work very closely in conjunction with your tutor and any hand-out material. I would be surprised if your course includes a great deal of material on desertion but the elements which are mentioned are strong contenders for the available space on examination papers.

Living apart

I can adequately cover both s. 1(2)(d) and s. 1(2)(e) under one heading. By way of introduction I would ask you to remember the following points:

(a)   While the Act refers to 'two' and 'five' years' separation the crux of both sections is proof of *living apart* for a continuous period of two or five years. According to s. 2(6), 'a husband and wife shall be treated as living apart unless they are living with each other in the *same household*' (see p. 85).

(b)   That s. 1(2)(d) requires the *consent* of the respondent to the decree being granted.

(c)   Section 1(2)(e) is perhaps the most controversial of the five facts evidencing irretrievable breakdown. Referred to as a 'Casanova's charter' when it was introduced into the Divorce Reform Act 1969, it does allow divorce to take place without any blame being attached to the respondent. So concerned was

Parliament that a limited defence to such a petition is contained in s. 5. Ironically one could not seek better evidence of irretrievable breakdown than separation for a lengthy period.

(d)   The decision of the Court of Appeal in *Santos* v *Santos* [1972] Fam 247 has focused attention on the *intention* of the separated spouses. This investigation of the belief or purpose underpinning separation would appear to complicate what ought to be a relatively straightforward interpretation of the subsections. The impact of the decision in *Santos* should be examined closely as it is a favourite examination point.

Separate households   It is generally assumed that what was stated above about separation in establishing desertion is equally valid here. The two major authorities you would need to cite in an examination are *Mouncer* v *Mouncer* [1972] 1 All ER 289 where living in the same household even though it was purely to give support to the children proved fatal to the husband's petition and *Fuller* v *Fuller* [1973] 2 All ER 650. In the latter case the husband was 'taken in' by the wife and her cohabitee because the medical prognosis after he suffered a serious heart attack was poor. However, he proved the doctors wrong and survived to resist his wife's petition under s. 1(2)(e). Even so, he failed to convince the court that he and his wife still constituted one household. As the court said he was 'to all intents and purposes a lodger in the house'. The Act presupposed the parties to be living together as husband and wife.

Intention   Sachs LJ in *Santos* v *Santos* [1972] Fam 247 said:

> The cogent volume of authority to which we have been referred makes it abundantly clear that the phrase 'living apart' when used in a statute concerned with matrimonial affairs normally imparts something more than mere physical separation.

You have to show to an examiner that the Court of Appeal envisaged evidence that one of the parties clearly recognised the marriage to be at an end, even though he is under no obligation to communicate that fact to the other spouse. The report is littered with reasons why this should be so ranging from overseas decisions illustrating a similar approach to the assertion by Sachs LJ that it was vital 'for the judge to examine closely exactly how the separation originally came about'. (What price this statement in light of the special procedure?)

You must therefore study the case closely noting the reasons supporting the decision and then turn to academic comment, most of which it must be said is unfavourable to the court. (See for example, A. Bissett-Johnson in Seago and Bissett-Johnson, *Cases and Materials on Family Law*, p. 189. It would be useful if you could look at some of the examples of potential hardship quoted by Cretney, *Principles of Family Law*, 4th ed., p. 154, and the questions posed by Hoggett and Pearl, *The Family Law and Society*, 2nd ed., pp. 192-3.

Consent   The respondent has to consent to the decree being granted under
s. 1(2)(d) and he has therefore the right to withdraw that consent at any time
up to pronouncement of the decree. In *Beales* v *Beales* [1972] 2 All ER 667
Baker P said that consent *must* continue up to the decree nisi otherwise Parliament
would have used the words 'has consented'. The consent has to be freely given
and he must have the requisite mental capacity which should be the same as for
formation of marriage. Finally there has to be evidence of positive consent and it
should not be assumed from the circumstances, for example in *McGill* v *Robson*
[1972] 1 WLR 237 where the husband returned from England to Rhodesia and
told his wife just to go ahead with the divorce. The proceedings were adjourned
to enable consent to be given.

Grave financial or other hardship   As a result of concern expressed at the
predicament of the 'innocent' spouse being divorced after five years' separation,
Parliament gave the court the power to refuse to grant a decree in circumstances
where the divorce would result in grave financial or other hardship *and* where in
all the circumstances it would be wrong to dissolve the marriage. This provision
has spawned a lot of litigation and your family law course will in all probability
contain more than a passing reference to the interpretation of s. 5. You will find
on further investigation that the court is often faced with a major dilemma. On
the one hand the spouses have been apart for at least five years and it is an
undeniable fact that the marriage has irretrievably broken down. The object of
the legislation is to end the empty shell of marriage with the minimum of fuss
and bitterness and thus encourage the parties to look to the future. In many
cases the petitioner will already be living with a new partner and there may even
be children of that relationship. There will in such circumstances be no possibility
of a reconciliation. Yet the court is faced with the respondent opposing the
granting of the decree on the grounds that she (invariably) will suffer grave
financial or other hardship. It does not matter that the respondent may have
suffered tremendous hardship since the petitioner left because the section
demands that the court concentrate on hardship which will result from the
decree being granted. In practice respondents have argued that the loss of
marital status will affect their pension entitlement or succession rights. As such
it must be seen as being of limited benefit to the respondent and the courts
have undoubtedly placed a restrictive interpretation on the section. They have
striven to ensure that the husband is given the opportunity to put forward
proposals to mitigate the hardship claimed by his wife to result from the divorce.
See for example *Parker* v *Parker* [1972] Fam 116 where the petitioner could
afford to compensate the respondent for her loss of pension rights by the
purchase of a deferred annuity or policy producing a specific sum on maturity.
In consequence the decree was granted. By way of revision technique may I
suggest you jot down the relevant cases with accompanying comment, e.g.:

Cases	Hardship	Comment
Reiterbund v *Reiterbund* [1975] Fam 99.	Widow's pension.	On death of H supplementary benefit available. H not casting his duty to maintain on to State.
Le Marchant v *Le Marchant* [1977] 3 All ER 610.	Loss of pension rights.	Petitioner to be given opportunity to present reasonable proposals to mitigate hardship.
Johnson v *Johnson* (1982) 12 Fam Law 116.	Index-linked pension.	H unable to mitigate hardship. Decree refused. Unfair to H in circumstances?

Other cases which may be listed are: *Mathias* v *Mathias* [1972] Fam 287; *Dorrell* v *Dorrell* [1972] 3 All ER 343; *Purse* v *Purse* [1981] 2 All ER 465.

Also give consideration to whether such a section is necessary in light of the court's practice to allow the husband to mitigate the loss. Could this not be adequately dealt with under the new s. 25(2)(h) which imposes a duty on the court when deciding how to exercise its powers under ss. 23 and 24 to consider the value to each of the parties to the marriage of 'any benefit (for example, a pension) which, by reason of the dissolution, . . . that party will lose the chance of acquiring'. If one examines *Johnson* v *Johnson* it is difficult to feel anything but sympathy for the husband who when he left his wife tried to make life easier for her by spending £2,000 reducing the mortgage, transferring his interest in the home to her and paying more maintenance to her than a justices' order had required. He was living with a woman whom he wished to marry, apparently according to Reeve J for 'sentimental reasons' (judges have never been strong on romance!). As a result of using most of his money to help his wife while they were apart he had no cash to mitigate her loss of pension entitlement and thus the decree was refused. This in spite of the wife living in a house with an equity of £24,000!!

'Other' hardship   While judges have tended, in the main, to help petitioners to succeed even when grave financial hardship is pleaded, they have it seems *never* allowed a plea of 'other' hardship to prevent a decree being granted. One must therefore question the need for s. 5. When 'other' hardship has been raised it has been in the context of religious or social objections to divorce. Again I would suggest a checklist of cases:

Case	Hardship	Comment
Rukat v *Rukat* [1975] Fam 63	Hostility in her Sicilian homeland	The word 'grave' qualified 'other' hardship. Important case on measuring of hardship.
Banik v *Banik* [1973] 3 All ER 45	Social outcast in Indian community	CA said it was a possible defence but on further investigation W failed to establish case.
Parghi v *Parghi* (1973) 117 SJ 582	W and children at grave disadvantage in Indian society if divorced	As wife highly educated and living in city would not expect same hostility as if in rural area.

See also and list:

   (a)   *Balraj* v *Balraj* (1981) 11 Fam Law 110, where Brandon LJ pointed out that 'other' hardship had not yet succeeded either because although there is hardship it is not grave enough or the hardship though grave is caused by the separation not divorce.

   (b)   *Grenfell* v *Grenfell* [1978] 1 All ER 561, in which it was held that W could not succeed with grave other hardship when she had herself previously petitioned for divorce on the basis of her husband's behaviour.

Wrong in all the circumstances   If the court does find hardship proved it will still have to consider whether in all the circumstances it should prevent dissolution of the marriage. The court's attention is specifically directed to certain criteria with which you ought to become familiar (see s. 5(2)(b)). You must therefore remember that proof of hardship alone is insufficient to prevent the decree being granted. Of the few cases which have been reported on this point you might read: *Julian* v *Julian* (1972) 116 SJ 763; *Brickell* v *Brickell* [1974] Fam 31.

Revision note   In terms of protection for respondents divorced under the separation facts you should look closely at the provisions of s. 10 of the Matrimonial Causes Act 1973 which apply once the decree nisi has been granted but before the decree absolute can be pronounced. In seeking to ensure 'reasonable and fair' provision for the respondent one must wonder if the section has an important role, given the vast discretionary powers held by the court to award financial provision. Indeed Balcombe J said in *Robertson* v *Robertson* (1983) 4 FLR 387 at p. 393: 'It does not seem to me that the wife's application under s. 10 in this case has added anything to her application for financial relief'.

(Cross-reference Ormrod LJ in *Cumbers* v *Cumbers* [1974] 1 WLR 1331 at p. 1334.)

Generally this area of law is popular with examiners and you may be asked to comment on the working of s. 5 as well as applying the case law to a set of facts. An example of the former is given here being the second part of a two-part question:

(b) 'As a safeguard of religious and social susceptibilities the defence ["grave other hardship", in s. 5(2) of the Matrimonial Causes Act 1973] has proved, as was predicted seven years ago, ineffective' (M. D. A. Freeman, 'Divorce reform − seven years later' 9 Fam Law 3 at p. 7)

Discuss.

Sample questions

As may be expected with such a diverse range of issues subsumed under the heading 'divorce' you are unlikely to see one question attempting to cover the whole area. I will therefore give a selection from examination papers and then pass general comments on them in an endeavour to aid your revision.

1 (a) 'The word "hardship" is not a word of art. It follows that it must be construed by the courts in a common-sense way, and the meaning . . . should be such as would meet with the approval of ordinary sensible people' (per Lawton LJ in *Rukat* v *Rukat* [1975] 1 All ER 347 at p. 351).

Discuss by reference to the words 'grave financial and other hardship' in s. 5 of the Matrimonial Causes Act 1973.

(b) Jill petitioned for divorce from her husband, Colin, on the basis of five years' separation. Colin had been sentenced to 12 years' imprisonment and even with remission still has to serve another three years. He does not want a divorce.

Advise Jill and Colin with regard to the relevant law of divorce.

2 Paul and his wife Vera agreed that in order to improve their financial standing he should take a well-paid job in Saudi Arabia, the contract for which was of two years' duration. Paul left in January 1986. He returned home periodically to visit his wife but unknown to him in June 1986 she committed adultery with Alan and has continued to see him. Alan has intimated that he would like to marry Vera if she can obtain a divorce from Paul. Vera determined in July 1986 that she did not wish to live with Paul but did not tell him as she wanted him to continue maintaining her. Alan has been separated from his wife Maud since 1982 but she has persistently refused to consider divorce because of her religious beliefs. In addition her job as a

teacher at a Roman Catholic School is dependent upon her remaining married as the school will not employ divorced persons. She is 40 years of age.

Advise all parties with regard to the law of divorce. There are no children of the marriages.

3 Jack and Jill married in February 1985. Jack had shown signs of depression before the marriage but Jill was not unduly worried. The marriage was relatively successful until August 1986 when Jack became extremely disinterested in everything that Jill did and contented himself by watching television and going for long walks alone. On two occasions when very depressed he hit Jill, on the second occasion causing severe bruising to her left eye. In July 1987 Jack told Jill that he had committed adultery with Marcia in 1986 and in the ensuing row he threw Jill out of the house, not letting her in again until next morning. Since then Jack and Jill have lived separate lives although they have lived in the same house. In October 1987 he was diagnosed as a manic depressive, an illness which required continuous treatment.

Consider any action that Jill may take to terminate her marriage.

Suggested approach to the questions

Question 1(a)

(a)   If the examiner has taken a quote from a case then there will be an expectation that you are familiar with the issues raised by it.

(b)   The emphasis is on the word 'hardship' and how it is to be assessed in the context of s. 5. It may be useful therefore to begin by saying something about the *purpose* of s. 5 so that your discussion on 'hardship' will have a context. In particular mention that the hardship must result from the granting of the decree and that it invariably results from the loss of marital status.

(c)   By reference to case law you can show what the courts have and have not accepted as amounting to 'financial' and 'other' hardship.

(d)   But the crux of the question is *how* is hardship to be determined. Ought the courts to take an objective, subjective or other approach? Certainly subjectivity must be involved – the section says 'will result in grave financial or other hardship *to him*'. Yet Lawton LJ refers to the 'approval of ordinary sensible people'. So in the end both subjective and objective criteria are taken into account. In the case Lawton LJ accepted that Mrs Rukat 'undoubtedly feels that she has suffered a hardship'. But then his Lordship questioned 'whether sensible people, *knowing all the facts,* would think it was a hardship'. You may quote the judge's 'homely example':

The rich gourmet who because of financial stringency has to drink *vin ordinaire* with his grouse may well think that he is suffering hardship; but sensible people would say he was not.

(e) In conclusion you may assert that the courts are more ready to find hardship when financial considerations are involved. There is more tangible evidence of likely hardship. In most of the 'other' hardship cases the respondent is maintaining that she will suffer hardship although this may be subjective fear rather than an objective assessment of the circumstances.

Question 1(b)

As only half a question is involved the examiner will not expect you to write for more than 15-20 minutes. You may expect in this type of question only a limited range of issues to be included. Reading the question carefully you are told that the petition is based upon five years' separation. Thus this is normally good evidence of irretrievable breakdown. From your investigation into the legal issues concerned with 'separation' you should mention:

(a) Separation really means 'living apart'.

(b) To 'live apart' requires a mental endorsement. Refer to *Santos* v *Santos* [1972] Fam 247.

(c) Does it matter how the separation came about? One could hardly maintain that it was voluntary! See *Beeken* v *Beeken* [1948] P 302 which indicates that it is irrelevant how the separation came about.

(d) Thus in this problem the crucial matter will be whether Jill has harboured, albeit secretly, the necessary animus to recognise the marriage is at an end.

(e) You may mention that Colin may plead the s. 5 defence although certainly you would *not* be expected to repeat matters discussed in part (a).

(f) The question says 'relevant law of divorce'. The facts would indicate s. 1(2)(e) but can Jill petition on other facts? For example, s. 1(2)(b). Colin has presumably committed a serious criminal offence. Is he therefore guilty of behaviour which Jill ought not reasonably to be expected to put up with? But remember that he has now been imprisoned for five years and it is only now she seeks to petition. Will she fall foul of s. 2(3)?

See, for example, *Stanwick* v *Stanwick* [1971] P 124 where the emphasis was on persistent criminal behaviour.

(g) Is Colin in desertion? Presumably not because he does not intend to bring married life to an end. We are told he does not want a divorce.

Remember to engage in a little lateral thinking. The unstated aspects are often the ones which will gain you the high marks.

Question 2

Each line of the question should be taken in turn:

(a)   Paul and Vera agree a course of action, i.e., that Paul will work abroad for a limited period. From this information you may note that there is at this stage no intention on Vera's part to regard the marriage at an end (*Santos* v *Santos* [1972] Fam 247). If anything the course of action is designed to support rather than weaken the marriage.

(b)   Note the date of leaving, January 1986. It may or may not have any significance but you should record it as an *aide-mémoire*.

(c)   You are told that he returned home periodically which is not consistent with Paul regarding the marriage being at an end. It may be evidence from which to suggest they have not 'lived apart'.

(d)   June 1986 — Vera committed adultery and this gives Paul the right to petition for divorce. You must in addition look for evidence of intolerability. You must raise the authority of *Cleary* v *Cleary* [1974] 1 All ER 498 and the judgment of Davies LJ in *Carr* v *Carr* [1974] 1 All ER 1193.

You are advising Paul in 1988 and of course it is not made clear in the question whether or not he knows of the adultery. Tell the examiner of the six-month absolute bar but that time only runs from the discovery of the adultery.

(e)   Vera's determination in July 1986 that she does not wish to live with Paul is an indication of when the two-year separation period might start to run. This is again a direct reference to the *Santos* case. Thus in order to petition any time after July 1988 she will have to bring evidence of this secret intention. You will also have to mention that she will need Paul's *positive* consent to the divorce. A comment on the ethics of Vera's actions may not go amiss but try to relate it to whether or not she *ought* to be allowed to succeed.

(f)   At this point the question concentrates on Alan's marriage to Maud. They have been separated for over five years. Alan may therefore petition but is left in no doubt that his wife does not want to divorce. The information given will allow you to advise Maud that she could use s. 5 in order to resist the petition. Three things are isolated — religious beliefs, her job and her age. As she has a full-time job she will presumably have her own pension rights. We are not informed of her husband's job or pension prospects. However, the net effect of divorce is that she will lose her job and with it her security at a time when teaching jobs are hard to obtain. Her age will not enhance her chances of a new job. Section 5(2)(b) says that the court *shall* consider the interests of the parties. On the one hand Alan wishes to remarry but is uncertain when that will be because Paul may not consent to the divorce in which case they would have to wait for three more years. That may be a point to convince the court that in the present circumstances the decree ought not to be granted at this stage.

(g)   In conclusion you could briefly summarise the advice that you would give to each party.

Question 3

Employ the same techniques as for Question 2.

(a)   The parties married in February 1986. Thus the one year absolute prohibition on petitioning will not apply in this case.

(b)   Before the marriage he had shown signs of depression. As the question does not confine you to divorce remedies you should mention s. 12 of the Matrimonial Causes Act 1973 as to whether he was capable of giving a valid consent and the level of understanding needed to satisfy the courts (see *Re Park* [1954] P 112). Reference should also be made to s. 2 of the Matrimonial and Family Proceedings Act 1984, which amended s. 13 of the MCA 1973. A court may grant leave to present a petition based upon any ground even though more than three years have elapsed since the marriage was celebrated. This is conditional upon the petitioner having suffered from a mental disorder recognised under the Mental Health Act 1983 at any time during the first three years of marriage and that it is just to do so.

(c)   From a divorce viewpoint I have raised the possibility of pre-marriage conduct being evidence upon which a petition might be based. This should be mentioned even though you would advise Jill that she may petition on other evidence.

(d)   The marriage is successful for a period of 18 months which suggests that Jack's illness is minor. However, things changed in August 1986. He pushed Jill out of his life and the question leads us on to the standard of behaviour required to satisfy s. 1(2)(b). In *Bannister* v *Bannister* (1980) 10 Fam Law 240 the husband stayed away at nights and exhibited total disinterest in his wife. The wife was granted a divorce. The greater impact of the respondent's behaviour on the petitioner the greater her chances of success. We are told that Jack hit Jill on two occasions. In *Bergin* v *Bergin* [1983] 1 All ER 905 the wife received black eyes and a cut face on three separate occasions. This was a magistrates' court application which had, said the Divisional Court, to apply the same test as for divorce on the fact of behaviour.

It would not appear that Jill will have too many problems.

(e)   Running through the question is the problem of Jack's mental illness. You should consider whether this will affect Jill's ability to petition on the ground of his behaviour. The violence is said to have occurred when he was 'very depressed'. In responding to this you would mention *Thurlow* v *Thurlow* [1975] 2 All ER 979 to the effect that negative behaviour can still count as 'behaviour'. Reference to the pre Divorce Reform Act position with the law on cruelty would not go amiss. In *Gollins* v *Gollins* [1964] AC 644 the House decided that the courts should concentrate on the effect of the conduct not whether it was intentional. This view was adopted by the House in *Williams* v *Williams* [1964] AC 698 when dealing with a respondent who suffered from a mental illness.

(f)   Jack has committed adultery. Remember to mention the intolerability and attendant case law. However, time would appear to be against Jill on this fact, unless you can show that they have lived apart. Certainly if they have lived in the same property for over one year then it will be hard for Jill to maintain that she finds it intolerable to live with him whether from the adultery or other factors.

(g)   Jack may be guilty of constructive desertion. Even though they live in the same house they may not for these purposes be in the same household (*Hopes* v *Hopes* [1948] 2 All ER 920). His conduct would have to be grave and weighty.

(h)   A diagnosis has determined that Jack is a manic depressive – hence his irrational conduct is likely to continue. An attempt might be made to petition under s. 12(d) of the Matrimonial Causes Act 1973 to the effect that he is suffering from a mental disorder making him unfitted for married life. Evidence is available to show he suffered from depression at the time of marriage. (See (b) above.)

(i)   It is submitted in conclusion that Jill ought to succeed in obtaining a divorce on the basis of Jack's behaviour, and from the range of possible options at the outset this is the one most likely to succeed. Alternatively the adultery fact would also appear to stand a good chance of being accepted.

Conclusion

Despite the special procedure, divorce questions remain popular, to test either application of the law or to elicit comment on the philosophy of the divorce laws. Make sure you categorise each fact clearly and in answering questions please keep an open mind as there is usually more than one 'fact' on offer.

In the very near future it is likely that the legislature is going to have to give consideration to revision of the existing ground for divorce and the facts which support it. The Law Commission Discussion Paper, *Facing the Future – The Grounds for Divorce* (Report No. 170 HC 479 £5.90, May 1988) has started the ball rolling and the outcome for students is that examiners are likely to include questions on their papers dealing with problems inherent in the present law and asking for a reconsideration of the current philosophy on divorce. Questions dealing with these issues are likely to be extended to cover procedural difficulties, requiring at least a working knowledge of the Report of the Matrimonial Causes Procedure Committee (The Booth Report) (ISBN 011 380004 5). Published in 1985 it is sad to reveal that it has not resulted in any changes to procedure, and one is left to conclude that its findings may well have been 'shelved'. This does not mean it should be ignored, however, because it is the only current report which deals with the vexed issue of divorce procedure.

There may therefore be questions dealing with divorce reform or those which deal with the demand for a family court. Whichever your examiner chooses these reports will be invaluable.

The Booth Committee sets its recommendations against the backcloth of encouraging parties to reach agreement on financial matters and the arrangements for children, thus reducing hostility and bitterness between them. One of the major proposals is that the applicant (the suggested replacement word for petitioner) who alleges adultery need not name the co-respondent and where behaviour is relied upon to support irretrievable breakdown there would no longer be the need to spell out details. These changes would, it is argued, mean divorce by consent but, runs the counter argument, that is what we in effect have at the moment in the vast majority of cases. The Report also places great emphasis on the need for effective reconciliation, in particular at the initial hearing, although the possibility of compulsory conciliation was rejected. A lot has been written about conciliation in the past few years and you may therefore be faced with a separate question on this topic. The major points would appear to be:

(a)   In-Court or out-of-court conciliation?

(b)   Voluntary or compulsory?

(c)   Funded by whom? Note that the Newcastle University/Lord Chancellor's Department study on conciliation services is due to report in late 1988/early 1989 after a three-year investigation.

(d)   Should communications made during conciliation be privileged?

(e)   Should conciliation only cover custody and access matters or should it be extended to allow conciliators to cover financial and property disputes?

There are numerous articles covering the topic. See: Bromley, footnotes to pp. 213-216; Hoggett and Pearl, 2nd ed., chapter 16, pp. 636-647.

The recent Law Commission Report — *Facing the Future* — recognises that there is no ideal route to divorce and concludes that most commentators would agree that the present law is unsatisfactory. The present system is also open to abuse, especially by practitioners using the adultery or behaviour facts to avoid a two or five year wait. It is also acknowledged that the present law creates bitterness, contributes to increased anxiety amongst children and discourages reconciliation. Given the two new options for discussion — fixed separation and the 'process over time' — one can conclude that whichever is chosen the demise of 'fault' in divorce has been achieved.

My suggestion is to approach the two reports and the question of divorce reform in the following ways:

(a)   Ascertain the defects in the present substantive law on divorce and also the procedural problems.

(b)   Examine in detail the 'fresh approach' and the *purpose* behind the procedural reforms in Part III (p. 17) of the Booth Report.

(c)   Take a wider view and try to ascertain what you would consider to be the most effective way of dissolving marriage, in the light of what one assumes are laudable objectives of conciliation and agreement.

(d)   Look closely at Law Commission Report 170 but bear in mind it is only a discussion document.

(e)   Always bear in mind other developments, in particular any movement towards the creation of a Family Court because selective changes in the law now covering divorce, child care, custody, etc. will need to be harmonised if a new court is created.

(f)   Try to obtain the latest divorce statistics in order to ascertain the underlying trend for divorce. It is probably better to look for the number of petitions presented rather than those granted to gain a clearer picture of demand.

SIX

ANCILLARY PROVISIONS AFTER
DIVORCE AND NULLITY

With the demise of judicial consideration of s. 1(2) of the Matrimonial Causes Act 1973 following the introduction of the special procedure for divorce, the emphasis moved to reviewing the working of the provisions of financial relief and property adjustment, in particular ss. 23, 24 and 25. That is not to say that the courts were not active in the area throughout the 70s as important cases such as *Wachtel* v *Wachtel* [1973] Fam 72 show, but latterly there have been many reported cases dealing with the *minutiae* which if anything is indicative of the acrimonious atmosphere in which these matters are often conducted. To this end the Family Law Bar Association launched an arbitration service in 1985, designed to give parties an assessment of the likely outcome of a financial dispute if the matter had to be decided by the court. In 1986 there were 109,788 applications to registrars or judges for financial relief, periodic payments, transfer of the matrimonial home or division of other assets. This indicates the scale of the problem and is a measure of the task facing the legal profession.

Law lecturers are therefore likely to set their discussion of ancillary provision against the background of high divorce rates, varying assets of the parties and as a result the options available to a court to settle any dispute. The development of 'ancillary' conciliation may be an area for future examination questions; our task is to consider what appears at present and how to prepare for success. The extent of the subject-matter can be gleaned initially by examining any law publisher's current advertising brochures, where you will discover an increasing number of books dealing with the subject.

With limited space available one has to be selective but having reviewed various examination papers I would suggest that the items covered in this chapter are those most likely to appear at examination time. It goes without saying that you should pay careful attention to the emphasis given to the subject by your tutor. It may well be that he would wish to concentrate on the wider issues of financial provision rather than the detailed application of the law in a problem question. Let us therefore begin by looking at the background to the changes introduced by the 1984 Act. This will involve a brief examination of the Law Commission Report No. 112, The Financial Consequences of Divorce (1981), which is relevant to the following questions which are illustrative of many which have appeared on family law papers.

1   Recently reported cases concerning ancillary proceedings reveal legal costs of £22,000, £10,000 and £24,000 (*R* v *Law Society ex parte Sexton* [1984], *Simpson* v *Law Society* [1987] and *Mason* v *Mason* [1986]). In virtually all cases payment of these costs will have to be met from the parties' assets accumulated during marriage. There must be a better way of ensuring a sensible division of matrimonial property.
Discuss.

2 'The family assets can be divided into two parts: (i) those which are of a capital nature, such as the matrimonial home and the furniture in it; (ii) those which are of a revenue-producing nature, such as the earning power of husband and wife. When the marriage comes to an end, the capital assets have to be divided; the earning power of each has to be allocated. (Lord Denning MR in *Wachtel* v *Wachtel* [1973] Fam 72.)
In light of this statement consider how successful the judges have been in offering a consistent approach to the problem of a fair distribution of family assets on divorce.

The wider issues

It would be helpful if you worked on the assumption that there have been two philosophies underpinning the reallocation of family assets, the first incorporated in the Matrimonial Property and Proceedings Act 1970 (later consolidated into the Matrimonial Causes Act 1973) and the second now contained in the Matrimonial and Family Proceedings Act 1984. In 1970 the legislature described the purpose as being:

to place the parties, so far as it is practicable and, having regard to their conduct, just to do so, in the financial position in which they would have been if the marriage had not broken down and each had properly discharged his or her financial obligations and responsibilities towards the other (1970 Act, s. 5(1), and 1973 Act, s. 25(1)).

The 1984 philosophy emphasises that the court is under a duty:

to have regard to all the circumstances of the case, *first consideration* being given to the welfare while a minor of any child of the family who has not attained the age of eighteen (1984 Act, s. 3, and the new s. 25 of the 1973 Act).

Having taken this stance you must now build up evidence primarily to show why the objective of 1970 was deemed inappropriate in 1984. The obvious answer is to say: 'In the light of experience!' The Law Commission mention the following points (Report No. 112, para. 17, p. 7):

(a) It is described as the 'primary objective' to ensure that the financial position of the parties so far as possible remains unaffected by their divorce.

(b) Those responding to the Law Commission's Discussion Paper (The Financial Consequences of Divorce: The Basic Policy, October 1980) took the view that the policy was no longer appropriate.

(c) It was said to be inappropriate because it imposed on the courts a task which was rarely possible of attainment.

(d) In many cases it was undesirable that the objective should be attained.

(e) These views came not only from those professionally concerned with the law but also from private individuals, i.e., a cross-section of those with an interest in divorce.

Move then from the 'authority' of the Law Commission to how the objective was viewed by the courts. There appear to be two major criticisms. First that those couples who have only limited resources cannot hope to come away from divorce without their standard of living being adversely affected and secondly it was maintained that the objective enshrined a principle of lifelong support usually for the wife. This in turn often had a dramatic impact where one spouse remarried. It was a common complaint that the creation of a new family unit was adversely affected because of the continuing obligation to the former spouse. Attention was focused upon the wife who in theory could demand lifelong support even though the marriage had been very short. Sir George Baker P received widespread publicity as a result of comments he made in *Brady* v *Brady* (1973) 3 Fam Law 78 when he saw 'no reason why a wife whose marriage has not lasted long, and who has no child, should have a "bread-ticket" for life'. It would be valuable to you in the examinations if you could refer to a couple of judicial statements on this matter. By 1976 Ormrod LJ, in *S* v *S* [1977] 1 All ER 56, was speaking in these terms of spouses whose marriage had broken down after only two years:

> While there is *no question* of putting her back into the position in which she was before the marriage, or performing any hypothetical task of that kind, these are all factors which are to be borne in mind in making an order which is *just in all the circumstances . . . which is the primary requirement of the 1973 Act. . . .*
>
> So the court has to do the best it can to do *broad justice*. (At p. 61, emphasis added.)

The importance of the Law Commission Report should not be underestimated. In one of the latest cases to reach the Court of Appeal, *Whiting* v *Whiting* [1988] 2 All ER 275, Balcombe LJ delivering the leading judgment quotes extensively from it (see pp. 279-80) before deciding the case in the context of the clean break provisions.

You do not need many such quotations, only sufficient to indicate judicial disapproval of this aspect of the legislation. For the sake of brevity you will find similar material in the following cases:

Case	Judge	Reference
Wachtel v *Wachtel*	Ormrod J	[1973] Fam 72 at p. 77.
Barrett v *Barrett*	Cumming-Bruce LJ	(1981) 11 Fam Law 178.
Scott v *Scott*	Cumming-Bruce LJ	[1978] 3 All ER 65 at p. 68.
Kokosinski v *Kokosinski*	Wood J	[1980] 1 All ER 1106 at p. 1115.

You do not need many such quotations, only sufficient to substantiate your argument that the judiciary found the objective unworkable in practice. Wood J's comment in *Kokosinski* would sum up the feeling: 'The function and duty of the court is to reach a physical and financial resolution of the problems of [the] family which is fair, just and reasonable as between the parties'. To list criticisms of the old test is one thing but how should it be changed? What ought to be the test for now and the immediate future? Indeed ought there to be any one overriding objective? Why not leave each and every case to be decided by the judiciary after consideration of all the circumstances? If you wish to detail objections to this approach you will have to read para. 18 of the Law Commission Report. These are the types of questions which should appear at the heads of sections in your revision notes with the appropriate evidence listed underneath.

The Law Commission's conclusion was that an evolutionary rather than revolutionary approach should be adopted. There ought, said the Commission, to be a 'clear indication of how the discretion should be applied' (para. 23). That 'clear indication' is now enshrined within the new s. 25, i.e., that first consideration be given to the welfare of any children of the family. Children are seen as the innocent parties in divorce and as such ought not to be regarded as being of secondary importance. In supporting this as the new objective the Commission saw two major benefits accruing. First, adequate recognition would be given to the value of the custodial parent's role and secondly to award a larger proportion of the overall maintenance provision for the children's benefit makes the maintenance obligations more acceptable to the payer. For more detail see the Report para. 24-30.

In the first edition of this book we speculated on how the courts would approach the new objective. The authoritative answer is to be found in the report of the very important case of *Suter* v *Suter and Jones* [1987] 2 All ER 336. The parties were divorced in 1986 and the wife had custody of the two children of the marriage, aged 14 and 8. The wife continued to live in the matrimonial home and the co-respondent also slept there each night. The judge ordered that the husband transfer to the wife all his interest in the matrimonial home subject to the mortgage. The wife was also to receive the surrender value of insurance policies and periodical payments of £100 per month until the youngest child reach 18.

The husband by his appeal sought a termination or reduction of the order to pay £100 per month and that his financial obligations to her should be terminated at once, or at least a date set which was substantially earlier than that ordered by the judge.

The basis of this contention was that the judge had taken the view that 'first consideration' meant that the welfare of the children was overriding and paramount *to the exclusion of other matters*, and the result was the judge had ignored cohabitation with the co-respondent.

Cumming-Bruce LJ had this to say on the issue (emphasis added):

> . . . I collect an intention that this consideration is to be regarded as of first importance, to be borne in mind throughout consideration of all the circumstances including the particular circumstances specified in s. 25(2).

But Parliament had not made it the overriding consideration:

> So I construe the section in requiring the court to consider all the circumstances, including those set out in sub-s. (2), always bearing in mind the important consideration of the welfare of the children, and then to try to attain a financial result which is *just as between husband and wife*. (p. 342 c).

Other changes

Certain further points require mention because of their continued relevance to ancillary provision and presence on examination papers.

Clean break

The Law Commission Report No. 112, *The Financial Consequences of Divorce*, made a number of recommendations for changing the law, one of the most important being the suggestion that a 'clean break' be imposed where practicable and appropriate. The clean break principle can be traced back to Lord Scarman's speech in *Minton* v *Minton* [1979] AC 593 at p. 608:

> There are two principles which inform the modern legislation. One is the public interest that spouses, to the extent that their means permit, should provide for themselves and their children. But the other — of equal importance — is the principle of 'the clean break'.

You therefore need to note that the philosophy was not something introduced by the Matrimonial and Family Proceedings Act 1984, rather it was clarified and put onto a clear statutory footing. The following are examples of the type of essay question you might face in an examination.

(a) 'The law now encourages spouses to avoid bitterness after family breakdown and to settle their money and property problems. An object of the modern law is to encourage each to put the past behind them and to begin a new life which is not overshadowed by the relationship which has broken down'. (Lord Scarman in *Minton* v *Minton* 1979).

Do you consider that the 1984 Act has promoted the above expressed object of the law? [1985]

(b) In the light of recent judicial comment critically consider the inter-relationship between s. 25(1) and s. 25A of the Matrimonial Causes Act 1973 as they apply to the 'clean break' concept. [1987]

Prior to the 1984 Act the Law Commission saw a 'technical difficulty' in imposing a clean break because it was felt that the court had no jurisdiction to dismiss a wife's claim for periodical payments without her agreement. Take a look at the following cases in order to understand the problem:

(a) *Dipper* v *Dipper* [1981] Fam 31.
(b) *Carter* v *Carter* [1980] 1 All ER 827.
(c) *Dunford* v *Dunford* [1980] 1 All ER 122.

The court can now dismiss an application for periodical payments if it considers that 'no continuing obligation should be imposed on either party'. (See s. 25A(3) MCA 1973.)

A useful way to approach this topic is to pose certain questions to yourself, seeking out the appropriate authorities to provide you with the answers:

(a) *What is the attraction of the clean break?* The Law Commission at para. 28 thought that finality should be achieved *wherever possible* as, for example, where there is a childless marriage of comparatively short duration between a husband and a wife who has an income or earning capacity. In the case of a longer marriage one would look to the adequacy of capital available for redistribution.

Another useful authority is the statement made by Waite J, in the unreported case of *Tandy* v *Tandy* [1986] CA Transcript 929, cited with approval by Balcombe LJ in *Whiting* v *Whiting* [1988] 2 All ER 275, at p. 281j:

The legislative purpose . . . is to enable the parties to a failed marriage, wherever fairness allows, to go their separate ways without the running irritant of financial interdependence or dispute. For better-off families that can and will normally be achieved by a capital lump sum paid in satisfaction or commutation of the right to be maintained on a periodic basis.

Interestingly Waite J goes on to say:

> The legislation clearly contemplates, however (and there is no dispute as to this), that there will be circumstances in which fairness to one side demands, and to the other side permits, a severance of the maintenance tie in cases where no capital resources are available.

A good example is the decision in *Seaton* v *Seaton* [1986] 2 FLR 398 where, although the husband was severely disabled, it was found as a fact that any financial contribution by the wife would not have any material effect in enhancing his lifestyle since his needs were already reasonably satisfied, in particular by a state disability pension. The Court of Appeal agreed, accepting that as there was no prospect of any change in the foreseeable future it would be wrong to impose a continuing obligation on the wife to support the husband.

An example of the childless marriage is *Lynch* v *Lynch* (1985) Lexis (PC). The marriage had lasted seven years. Since divorcing, the wife had qualified as a lawyer and had better financial prospects than her husband. Lord Scarman commented:

> But, if ever there was a case for a 'clean break' (*Minton* v *Minton*, 1979) and for limiting the provision for the wife to a sum which went no further than to meet her need and to compensate for her past contributions to the family life which sadly did not endure for very long, it is this case. The marriage has imposed no future burdens or responsibilities upon the wife. She is well placed to achieve a standard of living far higher than the husband is ever likely to attain.

(b) *Is it applicable to all divorces?* The prevailing thinking prior to the 1984 Act was that the principle could not be applied to all divorces. In *Moore* v *Moore* (1981) 11 Fam Law 109 Ormrod LJ said:

> where there are no capital resources . . . it is unrealistic to talk about a 'clean break' if there are children. It is not possible for the father and mother of dependent children to have a clean break from one another. . . . So, in my judgment, the so called principle of the 'clean break' has no application where there are young children.

However, this would appear no longer to represent the law because in *Suter* v *Suter and Jones* [1987] 2 All ER 336, at p. 340(h) Cumming-Bruce LJ said that the pre-Act cases have to be read subject to the new s. 25A. This section, he said 'imposes a mandatory duty on the court in every case to apply itself to the questions set out in s. 24A(2) whenever a court decides to make a periodical payments order in favour of a party to a marriage'.

So even though parties may have dependent children and still have to co-operate with each other over them:

it may be possible on the facts to recognise a date when the party in whose favour the order is made will have been able to adjust without undue hardship to the termination of financial dependence on the other party.

(c) *Does this mean that Parliament contemplated deferred clean break orders?* The answer is very plainly, yes. By s. 25A(2) the court is under a duty to consider making an order for a fixed term. Section 28(1A) empowers the court, when making a fixed term order, to consider whether the party shall not be entitled to apply under s. 31 for the order to be varied by extending the term.

What you must point out to an examiner is that the court has to consider the impact of making a limited term order. The key words are whether the party can adjust to the termination *'without undue hardship'*.

The Court of Appeal is likely to demand specific evidence, as was highlighted in *Morris* v *Morris* [1985] FLR 1176. (See also *M* v *M* [1987] Fam Law 195.) A good pre-Act example is *Attar* v *Attar* (No. 2) [1985] FLR 653 where the marriage was short and childless and the husband was extremely wealthy. Before the marriage the wife was earning £15,000 net p.a. but was unemployed at the time of the hearing, although she had been offered a job at £6,800 p.a. gross.

Booth J thought that a 'readjustment' period of two years was required to enable her to find employment and become self sufficient *and* to *re-establish* herself in society. A lump sum of £20,200 was ordered as a full and final settlement and in order to achieve a clear financial break.

In general terms, therefore, it has been said that the clean break principle may be most applicable where:

(i)   The marriage was of short duration and childless. See Sheldon J in *Soni* v *Soni* [1984] FLR 294 at p. 297 where he comments:

In all likelihood, moreover, the younger the wife may be and the shorter the marriage (particularly if there are no children) the more difficult it will be for her to persuade the court that she is unable to earn her own living and to order her husband to make any substantial continuing provision for her.

(ii)   Where sufficient capital exists to provide an adequate settlement. See *S* v *S* [1987] 1 FLR 71 where £400,000 was ordered to the ex wife of a pop star.

(iii)   Where there are no children.

(d) *How have the provisions worked in practice?* In practice the 'clean break' provision is equally relevant to applications to vary an existing order as it is to new orders. In *Morris* v *Morris* [1985] 1 FLR 1176 the parties had divorced in 1977 after 24 years of marriage and periodical payments of £75 per month were ordered. A variation was agreed and the order increased to £85. However, the county court judge, taking cognisance of the new Act which had come into force 10 days before the hearing, inserted a termination date for the payments, i.e., when the husband reached 65. The Court of Appeal felt the judge was wrong to make the order. It was felt that the situation would 'have to be looked at and monitored as it develops; as [they] grow older, and as they retire, or get fresh employment as the situation may be'. In the first edition of this book it was said that this decision against including a determination provision did 'not augur well for the clean-break provisions in the new Act to be extensively used'. Further support for this view is now to be found in the Court of Appeal decision in *Whiting* v *Whiting* [1988] 2 All ER 275. The parties divorced in 1975 and a consent order was made by which the husband paid the wife £83.88p per month. Four years later, after the wife had qualified as a teacher, the periodical payments were reduced to a nominal order for 5p per annum. Remember that at the time they could not have been discharged altogether without the consent of the wife. The husband subsequently remarried and later was made redundant. He now acted in a consultancy capacity and earned around £4,300 p.a. His ex-wife earned approximately £10,500 p.a. He applied for the nominal order to be discharged, with a direction that the wife should not be entitled to make any further application for maintenance.

The significance of this case is that it is a split decision to dismiss the husband's appeal against the refusal of the registrar to discharge the order. Here, therefore, is a case which must be studied closely.

Balcombe LJ dissenting took the view that, given the parties' respective incomes, the husband could have applied and obtained a nominal order against his ex-wife. However, and here is the crux of the matter:

> But to make mutual orders for periodical payments in nominal amounts just in case something should happen to either party, or, as the judge put it, as a 'last backstop', is to *negate entirely* the principle of the 'clean break' which, . . . was introduced by Parliament for sound policy reasons.

Thus, Balcombe LJ is saying that to leave an order open simply to allow the husband to endeavour to come to the wife's aid, if ever she should need it, is contrary to the whole philosophy of the 1984 legislation.

Of the majority Stocker LJ considered that the Court of Appeal could intervene only if the decision below had been 'plainly wrong' (see *G* v *G* (Minors: custody appeal) [1985] 2 All ER 225) and he could not conclude that the judge had misdirected herself with regard to the relevant statutory provisions. He felt there had to be 'compelling reasons' before an order should be varied and a clean break imposed. The problem with this judgment is that he candidly admits that 'my own inclination, on the facts of this particular case, would have been to hold that this was indeed an appropriate case for a "clean break" to be imposed'.

Slade LJ takes the same line as Stocker LJ and holds that the judge below was not plainly wrong in reaching her decision.

You may argue that full weight has not been given to the policy consideration enshrined in the Act and no consideration at all to how likely the ex-husband is to come to the wife's aid should she need it perhaps 10 years in the future. He had remarried in 1982 and the prospect of being under a legal obligation to support his ex-wife in the distant future is an extremely unattractive and impractical one. In conclusion look closely at Slade LJ's final comments at p. 287(g) where he urges judges, when considering this section, not to take the 'easier course of declining to order a clean break' because that may not in all cases be the right decision. One hopes that this case may go to the Lords for clarification on the application of the policy considerations and the role of the Court of Appeal in such cases.

For other determinations on the clean break principle see

(i)   *Seaton* v *Seaton* [1986] 2 FLR 398. This case would appear to suggest that a clean break can be ordered where no practical benefit will be achieved as a result of continuing a financial dependence.

(ii)   *Suter* v *Suter and Jones* [1987] 2 All ER 336. A clean break between husband and wife may be possible depending on the particular circumstances, even though there are dependent children.

Revision note   The great benefit of revising by posing questions is that almost subconsciously you are becoming mentally attuned to the major issues. If you can list the questions at an early stage then you should be able to recall the issues fairly easily in the examinations. Obviously this aspect of the law combined judicial decision-making with a review of the basis of the legislation by the Law Commission and as such is likely to be a popular source of examination questions for the foreseeable future especially as more cases are reported dealing with the new clean-break principle. (For a résumé of how the law stood prior to the Law Commission Report see Gillian Douglas, 'The clean break on divorce' (1981) 11 Fam Law 42.) (For a post-Act critique see Symes, 'Indissolubility and the clean break', 48 MLR 44.)

Conduct

Examination questions frequently appear on the subject of the parties' conduct and how much influence this should have on the eventual financial settlement. The following are examples:

Describe the present law in relation to the relevance of conduct in proceedings for matrimonial financial relief.

'it does seem to me that in ancillary proceedings it is right that by and large the court should, in the words of the statute, have regard to [the parties'] conduct' (Davies LJ in *Rogers* v *Rogers* [1974] 2 All ER 361, at p. 363).

To what extent has this view prevailed with regard to judicial interpretation of the 'conduct' element within s. 25 of the Matrimonial Causes Act 1973?

Remember that the subject may also form part of a problem question and you may have to decide what weight to give to one or both parties' conduct. In the event it may cancel itself out as in *Leadbeater* v *Leadbeater* [1985] FLR 789. As Balcombe J said:

. . . if I have to take the husband's conduct into account in bringing Miss D into the house, then equally I have to take the wife's conduct into account in her attitude over her son, her alcoholism, and indeed also the question of the adultery in Cyprus. In my judgment it is proper in this case not to give any effect to conduct. . . .

The 1984 Act specifically listed conduct as a factor within s. 25 to which the court must have regard.

Compare the new wording with that of the original 1973 legislation:

1984
The conduct of each of the parties, if that conduct is such that it would in the opinion of the court be inequitable to disregard it.

1973
(after listing specific matters) s. 25 concluded with the words:
and so to exercise those powers as to place the parties, so far as it is practicable, and having regard to their conduct, just to do so, in the financial position in which they would have been if the marriage had not broken down.

Your approach to this topic should be to look at the relevant law before 1984. Ask yourself how far the courts took conduct into account and what effect it had on financial provision. What did the Law Commission say about it? How has the 1984 Act changed, if at all, the previous position? The standard texts all deal quite extensively with conduct. A full review is contained in Cretney, 4th ed., pp. 797-806 and in Bromley, 7th ed., pp. 700-703 although it does not take into account the latest cases. Similarly Hoggett and Pearl went to press before the important recent case law but pp. 252-256 should still be consulted.

You are therefore taking a 'before and after' approach and this should ease the revision burden as you approach your final examination. Structured information in notes certainly helps you to carry out informed and constructive revision.

Before the 1984 Act

The starting-point in practice was *Wachtel* v *Wachtel* [1973] Fam 72 and *Harnett* v *Harnett* [1973] Fam 156 and you should consider and note the arguments put forward by Lord Denning MR in particular that led to the conclusion that only 'obvious and gross' misconduct by one spouse would leave the court free to decline to afford financial support to that spouse. Both parties, said the Master of the Rolls, usually shared responsibility for the breakdown of the marriage. As Bagnall J said in *Harnett*:

> obvious and gross in the sense that the party concerned must be plainly seen to have wilfully persisted in conduct, or a course of conduct, calculated to destroy the marriage in circumstances in which the other party is substantially blameless.

Having established the test to be applied you ought to seek out a couple of cases to illustrate 'obvious and gross' misconduct and others which indicated what the court refused to accept under that head. Examples of the former are *Cuzner* v *Underdown* [1974] 2 All ER 351 when the conduct of the wife in taking a half share of the house while she was committing adultery was 'obvious and gross' and *Robinson* v *Robinson* [1983] 1 All ER 391 when the Court of Appeal found that the wife who had deserted her husband was guilty of such conduct to entitle the court to reduce the maintenance. In the latter case the husband was described as 'completely blameless'.

In the latter category comes *Robinson* v *Robinson* (1973) 2 FLR 1. The judge found that the wife had lost all affection for the husband and this 'poisoned their personal relations for the rest of their married life'. As a result his health was affected yet nevertheless he continued to try to 'establish an intimate and satisfactory personal relationship with his wife'. The husband's unhappiness stemmed from her failure to give him the affection and love which he needed. Nevertheless the court held that she should have a standard of living reasonably comparable to that of her husband. Another example would be *Evans* v *Evans* (1981) 2 FLR 33 where the wife had a history of psychiatric disturbance. During the relevant period she committed adultery and was convicted of shoplifting. Wood J did not believe that her conduct should be taken into account in balancing the scales of justice between the parties. (However, see *M* v *M* (1982) 3 FLR 83.)

Having listed examples you then ought to consider whether or not conduct other than that during the subsistence of the marriage can be a factor for a judge to consider when dealing with financial provision. Thus in *Jones* v *Jones* [1975] 2 All ER 12 a month after the decree absolute the husband attacked his ex-wife with a knife and inflicted a number of wounds one of which severed the tendons of her right hand resulting in a 75% disability and in consequence affecting her ability to gain remuneration from her profession as a nurse. The Court of Appeal held that conduct was not limited to events which had taken place before the breakdown of the marriage or indeed before the decree was made absolute. In *Kokosinski* v *Kokosinski* [1980] 1 All ER 1106 the parties had cohabited for 24 years before marrying. Marriage proved to be their downfall and within months cohabitation ceased. Wood J held that the court could not do justice between the parties unless it took into account the wife's conduct during the 24 years they cohabited. Thus the case is authority for the proposition that conduct can be taken into account not only when the court is considering a reduction of maintenance but an increase. And in *West* v *West* [1977] 2 All ER 705 the Court of Appeal decided that the word 'gross' meant that conduct was of 'great importance in relation to the marriage', and did not mean gross in a moral sense.

All these factors are of importance because the key question is how the courts will approach the interpretation of the new conduct provision. To have a solid background of the previous law will help you to fully appreciate the post-Act stance of the judiciary.

Post 1984

It was suggested that Parliament was not intending to impose a radical change to the law. It was certainly not the intention that the conduct provision should act as a catalyst to copious litigation where spouses might air their mutual recriminations in public. Recent case law has tended to confirm this view. In *Kyte* v *Kyte* [1987] 3 All ER 1041 the Court of Appeal said that conduct in the context of s. 25(2)(g) included any relevant conduct during and after the marriage which might have contributed to its breakdown or which it would otherwise be inequitable to ignore, regardless of whether or not the other party's conduct was blameless.

Take a close look at what Purchas LJ says at p. 1047(h) where he poses questions which will ultimately have to be answered (emphasis added):

> It may well, therefore, be argued that the 1984 Act, being an amending Act, should in the first instance be read so as to give effect to the ordinary meaning of the words used. *These are not the test of gross and obvious conduct as developed in Wachtel v Wachtel* [1973] 1 All ER 829, [1973] Fam 72, or conduct such as to make it repugnant to ignore it as between the parties.

And:

> It may well be (that the new wording) may give a broader discretion to the court than that envisaged hitherto under the authorities.

He does not answer the questions posed because he concludes that the wife's conduct would satisfy any of the tests. The wife, who stood to inherit the husband's estate, knew that he wished to commit suicide and either did nothing or provided him with drugs and alcohol to facilitate the attempt. The husband failed and the parties eventually moved to divorce. As a result of her conduct a lump sum order in her favour of £14,000 was reduced to £5,000.

Note also that the court rejected counsel's submission that before conduct could be counted the other party had to be blameless. The section as worded did not envisage one or other being blameless. The judge also went on to express his opinion that there are no 'restricting words or meaning to be inferred in the wording of s. 25(2)(g)'. So the court can, according to Purchas LJ, look at conduct *during* the marriage and *after* the marriage which may or may not have contributed to the breakdown or which in some other way makes it inequitable to ignore.

The three other cases to which reference must be made are *Suter* v *Suter and Jones* [1987] 2 All ER 336, *Atkinson* v *Atkinson* [1987] 3 All ER 841 and *Duxbury* v *Duxbury* [1987] 1 FLR 7, which interestingly all deal with ex-wives who were cohabiting, on a relatively secure basis in the latter two cases. In *Suter* the court recognised that the wife's conduct was a relevant factor. Taking the cohabitation factor into account, together with an assessment of what her lover could reasonably contribute to her maintenance, a £100 per month maintenance order was reduced to a £1 p.a. nominal order. It must be stressed that in addition to these factors the husband had also made capital transfers.

In *Atkinson* the wife formed a long-term relationship with another man. She had been in receipt of £5,500 p.a. maintenance. Of course if she remarried then the payments would cease. It was accepted that a deliberate decision not to remarry because of the financial consequences of such a move had been taken.

The Court of Appeal accepted that in some circumstances such conduct could lead to a diminution of maintenance, but stressed that there was no statutory requirement that the court should give decisive weight to settled cohabitation. In the event the court agreed that a £1,000 p.a. reduction was appropriate, given that the wife's cohabitee earned very little by contrast to the ex-husband's high income as a successful businessman. What must be cited is the conclusion that there is no authority from legislation or case law which says that settled co-habitation should be equated with remarriage, with the consequential effect being to disentitle the ex-wife to anything more than nominal maintenance, irrespective of the financial circumstances of the other party. (For comments on these cases see [1987] All ER Annual Review, p. 134.)

Finally, in *Duxbury* the wife was living on a settled basis with a married man (and therefore could not at that stage remarry). She was the ex-wife of a millionaire, he earned under £5,000. The court refused to engage in a moral exercise; s. 25 was a financial exercise and as neither party wished the judge to have regard to conduct there was no basis for reducing the capital provision for the wife, which in this case was over £½ million. (For a discussion on the effects of cohabitation see [1987] All ER Annual Review, pp. 132-33.)

In the light of *Kyte* there are likely to be further cases to answer the question posed by Purchas LJ and thus the topic should continue to remain popular with examiners. Note that even though certain conduct may not have any decisive weight it can still be taken into account along with other factors, both when making an order or seeking a variation.

Effect of conduct

Usually it will be a reduction in maintenance as seen in *Robinson* (1983), *Atkinson* (1987) and *Suter* (1987). In *Robinson* the court ordered £15 per week and not the £45 the wife had demanded. In *Atkinson* a 20% reduction from £5,500 to £4,500 per year and in *Suter* the whole of the maintenance was lost. In *Cuzner* the impact of conduct was seen in the context of the matrimonial home. The court decided that it would be unjust for the wife to have a share in it. And in *Kyte* a lump sum payment of £14,000 was reduced to £5,000.

When reviewing the cases note the effect on financial provision in broad terms, e.g., 40% reduction in maintenance or 30% reduction in lump sum payment.

Law Commission

Read paras 36-39 in the Report at p. 13. The Commission did not recommend the inclusion of the words 'obvious and gross' and it was felt that 'any further elaboration can, in our view, best be left to case law development'.

Revision note 'Conduct' provides a discrete package of information. It is popular with examiners. Try to obtain past examination papers and attempt to answer any question on conduct in note form. Mapping out a strategy to answer such questions can be very beneficial as there are a very limited number of ways that examiners can express a question.

One-third rule

An examiner may set you a question on the allocation and redistribution of family assets, expecting you to discuss the s. 25 criteria and any other 'rules' which may help in reaching a final settlement. The so-called one-third principle discredited in the 60s was revived by Lord Denning MR in *Wachtel*. A wife should start with one-third of the combined resources of the parties, and if this at first appears unfair the court pointed out that the husband would have an obligation to maintain his children and also have further expense in setting up a new household.

However, since 1973 the courts have used the principle not so much as a starting-point but purely as an adjunct to the wide discretionary powers under s. 25. As with 'obvious and gross', 'one-third' is not a statutory creation and should not be allowed to deflect the court in its duty to examine s. 25 in order to achieve a fair and just settlement. This was emphasised in a series of cases in the late 70s and early 80s. In *Foley* v *Foley* [1981] 2 All ER 857 at p. 862 Eveleigh LJ said of the principle:

> it is in no way a rule of law. . . . It is an aid to the mental process when arriving at the appropriate figure and there are many cases where the 'one-third' figure would not enter the mind of the court, because it would be obvious from the start that the proportion would be nothing like that. For example the young marriage that lasts but a day or two.

See also Ormrod LJ in *Preston* v *Preston* [1982] 1 All ER 41 at p. 47.

However, despite criticisms of the principle it is extensively used in practice, most recently in *Bullock* v *Bullock* [1986] 1 FLR 372 and *Dew* v *Dew* [1986] 2 FLR 341. When compiling information on the principle it would be beneficial if you listed circumstances when it is unlikely to be used. One examination question put it this way:

> Consider the circumstances in which the one-third rule may be less than appropriate when making financial provision orders in matrimonial proceedings.

Not useful	Case	Comment
Where resources of the parties are small or very large.	*Slater* v *Slater* (1982) 12 Fam Law 153.	One-third guideline useful in cases of moderate means.
(a) Small income.	*Cann* v *Cann* [1977] 3 All ER 957.	Cases where neither party earning. One-third rule inappropriate.
	Scott v *Scott* [1978] 3 All ER 65.	One-third inappropriate in assessing periodical payments when dominating feature to provide a home for children.
(b) Large income.	*Preston* v *Preston* [1982] 1 All ER 41.	Assets £2 million. Wrong in principle to adopt arithmetical approach.
	O'Donnell v *O'Donnell* [1975] 2 All ER 993.	£¼ million. One-third 'ratio' may produce results that are too high.
Where husband is applicant for lump sum.	*Calderbank* v *Calderbank* [1975] 3 All ER 333.	Not applicable as this is not a usual case.
Marriage of short duration.	*Wachtel* v *Wachtel* [1973] Fam 72.	Lord Denning's judgment. Wife will not have 'earned' one-third of resources.
Where there has been 'conduct' which the court would find inequitable to leave out of the calculation.	(see discussion above)	

Revision note   Having mapped out the points and cases you can then expand them until you feel that you have a sufficient grasp of the issues. The aim is to understand why the courts have placed the one-third principle firmly in the background. However, it can be confidently asserted that the courts are not prepared to dispense with the principle (see *Bullock*) although, since the case of *Stockford* v *Stockford* (1981) 3 FLR 58, the so called 'net effect' approach has gained credence which involves making a hypothetical order, deducting the parties' tax liability and comparing the result with the reasonable needs of the parties.

Section 25

No review of ancillary provisions can be complete without consideration of the factors listed in s. 25. Demands for the limited space available make it impossible here to discuss each one in turn. However, the standard texts do this more than adequately (see Cretney, *Principles of Family Law*, pp. 768-810 and Bromley, *Family Law*, 7th ed., pp. 692-704). My task is to suggest a way to understand the material so that revision becomes a straightforward exercise.

First it is likely that the statutory provisions will be available to you in the examination room. There will be no point (or marks to be gained) in attempting to learn them by heart.

Secondly ask what is the purpose of s. 25. The answer is that the court can only make a fair and just decision if it considers all the circumstances of the marriage. A cursory examination indicates a very comprehensive list of factors. It is difficult to think of anything of significance which has been omitted. The subsections cover earning capacity, property, expenditure, standard of living, needs of the parties, age, infirmity, contribution to the welfare of the family, duration of the marriage and even loss of future benefits. If Parliament had not listed them the judiciary would certainly by now have invented them. The variations in the facts of cases make examination predictions a high-risk enterprise and you would therefore need to establish whether or not your tutor has emphasised any of the factors listed in s. 25.

Look at each factor in a broad way under separate heads and jot down what you consider important points. Let me take an example by way of illustration.

Section 25(2)(f)

Articles
K. O'Donovan, 'Legal recognition of the value of housework', (1978) 8 Fam Law 215.

Background information
To give the wife recognition and credit for maintaining a home and acting as a housekeeper, wife and mother.

1984 Act
Has amended the 1973 Act in the words 'or is likely in the foreseeable future to make' have been inserted.

Important cases
1973 Act

Wachtel v *Wachtel*
[1973] Fam 72.

Trippas v *Trippas*
[1973] Fam 134;
Preston v *Preston*
[1982] 1 All ER 41;
P v *P* [1978] 3 All ER 70.

1984 Act
Day v *Day*
[1988] 1 FLR 278

Type of contribution
Cumbers v *Cumbers*
[1975] 1 All ER 1.

Page v *Page* (1981) 2
FLR 198.

Hunter v *Hunter* [1973]
1 WLR 958.
Bateman v *Bateman* [1979]
Fam 25.

Comment
Parliament recognised that the wife who looks after the home contributes as much to the family as one who goes out to work.

Contribution to success of business can be taken into account. Not limited to 'housekeeping' function.

Confirms the view in *K* v *K* [1980] Fam 72 holding premarital conduct relevant when assessing financial provision. Regarding children before marriage as children of the family is also relevant to their maintenance provision.

Short marriage but wife had looked after child and had worked and made contribution to household expenses.

'There are those cases where she has participated in a family business project, whether in farming, industry or otherwise . . . she may be able to make out a case for a slice of that part of the family wealth which she helped to create.

Caring for children for over 10 years.

Three young children and maintaining responsibility for them.

Conclusion

Now to be read in light of changed wording in that the court must look to likely future contribution to the welfare of the child. This is in keeping with the philosophy that parents should be encouraged to continue that role after divorce and also with the new objective of the welfare of the child being first consideration. A more significant weighting is likely to be given to this factor especially if at some stage joint custody orders become the norm.

Revision note

You should adopt a similar pattern with the other factors until you feel you have a grasp of the significance attached to s. 25. From a mass of material and case law you *must* isolate the important principles to be gleaned from the cases. It is *not* important to make notes of the facts of each case. Perhaps in the examination you could explain the significance of a case in one sentence, therefore making copious notes redundant. Copying from law reports is no substitute for meaningful investigation.

The matrimonial home

Perhaps the most problematic matter in the financial equation. Often it represents the parties' only capital asset. In most cases it will also be the only home possessed by the spouses as well as being 'base camp' for the children.

As with the financial matters there is an abundance of case law from which you should endeavour to draw upon only those which are authoritative. Look at the problem from this standpoint: What options does the court have given the particular circumstances? Obviously the house could be sold and the proceeds divided, not necessarily equally. Another option is for one spouse to 'buy out' the other's share or for the court to transfer that share to the other party. In some cases justice may be achieved by allowing one spouse to live in the property for life or a specified period. Another course of action which found favour was the postponement of the sale of the property so that one party may continue to occupy usually for the benefit of the children. In such circumstances the court can determine when the sale should take place, e.g., on the youngest child's 16th birthday, and the other spouse can then realise his capital asset.

Therefore your revision can again take the form of a list of headings under which you can detail the key case and specify why they are important.

New cases will always be appearing in the reports so when working leave sufficient space in your table for cases to be inserted. Bear in mind what Dunn LJ said in *Mitchell* v *Mitchell* [1984] FLR 387 at p. 389E:

> . . . previous decisions are useful as an indication of how this court in particular has dealt with a particular factual situation, but the decisions are not binding as such because in this jurisdiction each case depends essentially on its own facts.

Therefore you are seeking to glean points of principle to which the court can have regard if necessary in reaching a decision.

I give below an example of how you may approach the task. I have chosen the postponed trust for sale example because the justification for its use is to preserve a home for the children and of course, the new primary objective is to give first consideration to the welfare of the children.

Category: Postponed trust for sale
NB. Often referred to as a 'Mesher order' after the case at [1980] 1 All ER 126.

Justification
To preserve the matrimonial home for the benefit of one spouse, invariably the custodial parent, yet not depriving the other spouse of all of his interest in the property. The parties thus retain an interest in the proceeds of the sale of the property at some future, discernible time.

Development via case law

Case and reference	Importance
Mesher v *Mesher* [1980] 1 All ER 126.	'What is wanted is that the wife and daughter should have a home, . . . rather than that she should have a large sum of available capital.' Sale at 17 or further order. Daughter aged nine at time of case.
Allen v *Allen* [1974] 3 All ER 385.	Matrimonial home in husband's name. Transferred to joint ownership on trust for sale postponed until younger child 17 or finished full-time education (joint custody).
Carson v *Carson* [1983] 1 All ER 478.	Comments of advisability of making *Mesher* order. Ormrod LJ: 'good example of chickens coming home to roost'. 'Dangers': wife will become homeless. Weak position to rehouse out of share of proceeds.
Harvey v *Harvey* [1982] 1 All ER 693.	Sale postponed not until it ceased to be required for children but until one of:

> (a) remarriage by wife
> (b) voluntarily left home
> (c) became dependent on another man
> (d) death.

But she should pay H occupation rent after she ceased to be responsible for children or had paid mortgage. NB: *Mesher* distinguished. See also *Tinsdale* v *Tinsdale* (1983) 13 Fam Law 148 and *Simmons* v *Simmons* [1984] 1 All ER 83.

Thompson v *Thompson* [1975] 2 All ER 243.   Contingency contained in property adjustment order not arisen when wife wished to sell. Court *had* power to make a further order.

It will have become obvious at this stage that the *Mesher* order has become discredited, although it may still be appropriate in certain cases. Pay particular attention to the following:

(a) *Mortimer* v *Mortimer-Griffin* [1986] 2 FLR 315. Lord Justice Parker at p. 319 comments that the *Mesher* order has 'been criticised since its birth; it is an order likely to produce harsh and unsatisfactory results. For my part, I hope that that criticism, if it has not got rid of it, will at least ensure that it is no longer regarded as the "bible".'

(b)   Picking up the point about harsh and unsatisfactory results look at the decision in *Greenham* v *Greenham* [1988] 138 NLJ 200. In this case the wife was 45 and the husband approximately 20 years older. When the marriage broke down he bought his wife a house and he continued to live in the former matrimonial home. She applied for ancillary relief and the judge ordered that she receive £2,500 and 20% of the sale price of the matrimonial home which should occur when the husband reached 70 years of age, thus effectively forcing him to sell irrespective of whether or not he wished to do so.

The Court of Appeal allowed his appeal. There was a loose analogy with *Mesher*. No good reason had been shown why it was justifiable to force the husband to sell. The commentary in the New Law Journal referred to the initial decision as being 'extraordinarily insensitive and inappropriate'. The net effect had been to subjugate the housing needs in favour of the wife's financial interests.

(c)   *Harman* v *Glencross* [1986] 1 All ER 545. Balcombe LJ at p. 556 states what can be regarded as the authoritative comment on *Mesher* orders:

> The *Mesher* type of order has fallen out of favour of late, since its result is to throw the wife onto the housing market at a time of her life when she is unlikely to be able to secure adequate accommodation for herself, and the modern practice is to make an order to postpone the sale of the house until her death, remarriage, voluntary removal from the premises or becoming dependent on another man, although sometimes requiring her to pay an occupation rent after the youngest child has attained the age of 18: see e.g., *Harvey* v *Harvey* [1982] 1 All ER 693, [1982] Fam 83.

Articles
J. G. Miller, 'The Mesher order today' (1983) 127 SJ 196; M. Hayes and G. Battersby, 'Property adjustment orders and the matrimonial home' [1981] Conv 40; S. Blake, 'The matrimonial home on divorce' [1984] Fam Law 45; M. Hayes and G. Battersby, 'Property adjustment: order or disorder in the former matrimonial home' [1985] 15 Fam Law at p. 213; Cleary, 'Icebergs and elephant traps' [1987] 17 Fam Law 43.

Textbooks
Bromley, *Family Law*, 7th ed., pp. 704-09; Cretney, *Principles of Family Law*, 4th ed., pp. 837-51.

Conclusion
The question of what to do with the matrimonial home will always be a difficult one to answer. This is one approach that has been favoured and then more or less abandoned by the courts for the reasons displayed in *Carson* above.

Now go on to consider other options in the same way.

Matrimonial orders

The final element of the chapter is concerned with the orders available to a court when disposing of the family assets. We have seen what it may do with the matrimonial home, what options does it have with available finance?

Therefore you should examine the merits of periodical payments and when they might be secured. When will the court award a lump-sum payment? Will it combine secured periodical payments and a lump-sum order? And so on. By posing your own questions you are in effect giving consideration to the application of the orders which may be the form required by the examiner. Recent judicial attention has been concentrated upon the issue of lump sum payments, especially as it overlaps with the problematical matter of costs. In *Collins* v *Collins* [1987] 1 FLR 226 the Court of Appeal was quite clear that when assessing the quantum of a lump sum, the right approach was to consider each particular case in strict accordance with the requirements of s. 25(1) of the MCA 1973 as amended. That of course is not controversial. However, Lloyd LJ emphasised that the court is not entitled to include costs in the lump sum. 'Nothing in s. 25 . . . would justify that course'. Anthony Lincoln J in *B* v *B* [1988] 138 NLJ 186 warned against lengthy enquiries involving expert witnesses in order to seek valuation of business assets' from which a lump sum order would eminate, especially if that business was not to be sold. Citing Dunn LJ in *Potter* v *Potter* [1982] 3 All ER 321 to the effect that only a general consideration of sources of income and capital, not a detailed one, was required. What people are prepared to spend contesting ancillary matters never ceases to amaze. In this case 'a substantial proportion of £50,000 has been spent by both spouses in an utterly sterile controversy, much of it detailed, as to the extent and value of the husband's assets'.

The Court of Appeal in *Davies* v *Davies* [1986] 1 FLR 497 cited Cumming-Bruce LJ in *Priest* v *Priest* [1980] 1 FLR 189 to the effect that it is the duty of the court to 'have regard not only to the property in possession and financial resources in possession, but to the property and financial resources which either party is likely to have in the foreseeable future'. Where there are substantial assets then a lump sum award is most appropriate in order to achieve a clean break as in *Duxbury* v *Duxbury* [1987] 1 FLR 7.

Conclusion

The major textbooks deal extensively with the type of orders available and when they are appropriate. From the student viewpoint you need to ascertain the general principles to be applied to what will in all probability be a problem question giving basic information about the parties' means and outgoings, coupled with some information about their respective futures.

The checklist approach advocated above can again be used for this topic. It may be worth mentioning that it is generally thought desirable that parties are encouraged to agree on the financial consequences of their divorce. Where this is achieved the court will recognise it in a consent order. However, note the important decision of *Livesey* v *Jenkins* [1985] 1 All ER 106 in which the House concluded that there must be a 'full and frank disclosure by the parties before a consent order is made' (Lord Brandon at p. 118h).

The Law Society statutory charge

The Law Society charge has become a major problem for those who are legally aided in their pursuit for a financial or custody ajudication. The Legal Aid Act 1974, s. 9(6) puts the Law Society under a statutory duty to recover costs by way of a charge over any property 'recovered or preserved' in the proceedings. The Act provides for certain exemptions, i.e., periodical payments and the first £2,500 for any lump sum or property transfer order. If one looks at the costs in some of the recent cases, then one immediately realises that the efficacy of a court order may be totally or partially undermined because of the liability to the legal aid fund. In *Clark* v *Clark* [1988] 138 NLJ 101 costs were over £20,000 and brought this comment from Booth J:

> At the end of the day it is a sad fact that a great deal of money has been wasted and the wife will have gained nothing at the conclusion of a long and tortuous legal process. The outcome emphasises yet again the care which must be taken by counsel and solicitor alike to ensure that such funds as are available to the parties are not dissipated by the costs of the actions they pursue.

In *Anthony* v *Anthony* [1986] 2 FLR 353 at p. 355 Parker LJ said:

> The divorce proceedings, in which both parties are legally aided, have been protracted, acrimonious and costly. . . . The combined cost . . . which the Law Society are entitled . . . to recover . . . already amount to some £8,000. . . . the family's only substantial asset is the matrimonial home in which the equity is some £18,000 or £19,000. In the result, nearly half of the family asset . . . has already been eaten up in costs . . . legal aid does not mean that they [solicitors] conduct litigation free of charge forever.

These comments will give you the gist of the problem. Solicitors wish to do the best for their clients, negotiations are lengthy and acrimonious, parties are reluctant to settle out of court, and if one is not careful costs totalling many thousands of pounds result — all to be paid for out of the relatively slender resources of the parties as will be the case for most people on legal aid.

There will be questions on this topic for the foreseeable future because not only does it deal with the Legal Aid Act requirements but also raises for critical scrutiny the whole process of divorce and pursuit of asset redistribution.

The following cases must be looked at and concise notes made indicating their importance. There are probably two leading cases, namely *Hanlon* v *Law Society* [1981] AC 124 and *Simpson* v *Law Society* [1987] 2 All ER 481 and I will use these to illustrate the sort of notes that you should make.

Hanlon

(a)   *Costs*
Total £8,025.
Property worth £14,000.
Costs as a % of total: 57.3%.

(b)   Costs covered main suit, injunction application, custody and access application and property adjustment order.

(c)   Court – House of Lords.

(d)   *Findings*

(i)   If the property had been 'in issue' between the parties in the proceedings then the Legal Aid Act applied.

(ii)   Totality of proceedings covered for cost purposes.

(iii)   The Law Society did have a discretion to postpone enforcing the charge (which in practice they tend to do in the vast majority of cases).

(iv)   Recommendation of the Royal Commission on Legal Services (1979) that the matrimonial home should be free of any charge ought to be adopted. Any reform should be radical. The registrar could be the final arbitrator except for an appeal on a point of law. This would have three advantages – speed and finality, saving in costs and adjudication by a group of experienced judicial officers who would soon establish a predictable pattern and thereby conduce to settlement between the parties.

(v)   See Lord Lowry, Lord Simon and Lord Edmund Davies who were all critical of the present position. For example, Lord Edmund Davies said 'the present unsatisfactory state of affairs could, if permitted to continue indefinitely, substantially erode our present pride in the legal aid system of this country'.

Simpson

(a)   Total costs 'Substantially greater than £10,784'.
Property sold for £33,431.10.
Court awards £30,000 to wife as settlement. As she was joint owner £16,715.55 is not recovered in the proceedings. £13,284.45 is the amount recovered and from this £2,500 is exempt, leaving £10,784.45.

Result: Whole of £10,784 'swallowed up by the legal aid fund instead of being available to the appellant . . . towards the purchase of a new home for herself'.

(b)   Court — House of Lords.

(c)   *At issue.* As this was money recovered from the sale of the property did the Law Society have the discretion to postpone the enforcement of their statutory charge or to allow the charge to be transferred to a new house purchased with the money?

(d)   *Comment.* Per Lord Bridge (as paraphrased in the headnote to the All England Law Report):

> It is grotesque that the Law Society should have a discretion to postpone enforcement of the statutory charge when the matrimonial home itself is recovered in ancillary proceedings but not when *proceeds* from the sale of the matrimonial home are recovered and any further delay in amending the 1980 regulations to remove this anomaly would be intolerable.

(e)   *Authority.* Interpretation of Regs 88, 91 and 93 of the Legal Aid (General) Regulations 1980.

Note: Even if the regulations are changed to bring a discretion to bear in this situation it does not affect the whole question of the amount of costs which are accumulated in this type of proceeding and whether the matrimonial home should be exempt.

I have used these cases by way of example. You should proceed on the same basis with the following:

(i)   *Curling* v *Law Society* [1985] 1 All ER 705. In particular see the comments of Oliver LJ at p. 715j.

(ii)   *Stewart* v *Law Society* [1987] 2 FLR 223. Wife was receiving periodical payments and sought an increase. H offered £7,000 in commutation of the wife's rights to future periodical payments. W's legally aided costs came to £4,600. Held that charge attached to £7,000.

Effect — W was receiving £1,820 p.a. by way of periodical payment. After costs she was left with £2,400 from the lump sum, and this represented the full and final settlement! Why did she bother?!

(iii)   *Collins* v *Collins* [1987] 1 FLR 226. Judge wrong to include in lump sum order an amount to cover legal costs.

(iv)   *Mason* v *Mason* [1986] 2 FLR 212. See in particular the comments by Purchas LJ on duty of lawyers to advise litigants as to costs (and presumably what is likely to be achieved by pursuing the case).

(v)   *Jones* v *Law Society* (1983) 4 FLR 733.

(vi)   *Simmons* v *Simmons* [1984] 1 All ER 83.

(vii)   *Van Hoorn* v *Law Society* [1984] 3 All ER 136.

Conclusion

It is ironic that a legal aid system which allows parties to have access to the higher courts ultimately penalises them by undermining the very basis of the order they have sought *and* according to *Collins* the courts cannot compensate for it. The courts are therefore left to seek to avoid making an order which brings the charge into play, e.g., by ordering periodical payments as opposed to a lump sum. Yet in doing so they may then be going against the basic philosophy of seeking to achieve a clean break. In the end the parties may achieve a clean break from each other but one party who has a charge placed on her property will only achieve a clean break from the Law Society when she *finally* sells the matrimonial home.

A current topic worth investing time and energy.

Sample question

Hywel and Winifred married in 1976 and their son Julian was born in 1977. Three years later they moved into the matrimonial home which was bought for £25,000. Each contributed £2,000 from their own savings and the remainder was raised on a mortgage. Title to the house and the mortgage were in Hywel's name alone.

Hywel subsequently met Jean and in 1986 he moved out of the matrimonial home. Winifred now seeks your advice about obtaining a divorce and financial provision for herself and Julian. The house is now valued at £60,000 with an equity of £34,000. Hywel is now living with Jean and their daughter Mary was born three months ago. They are living in Jean's house which she inherited from her father. Hywel earns £18,000 and Winifred £5,000 from her part-time job as a nurse. Jean does not have salaried employment. Hywel would like to have the matrimonial home sold so that the proceeds could be invested in a business he is establishing. Winifred is entitled to receive legal aid. Hywel and Jean intend to marry in the near future.

Advise Winifred.

Suggested approach

The facts listed are, one would imagine, fairly typical of many actual divorces. Your advice to Winifred would cover the following:

(a)   *Divorce.* Can Winifred divorce her husband and if so on what grounds? The most obvious would be adultery. They have not lived together since her husband committed adultery and presumably she would find it intolerable to live with him anyway.

(b)   *Conduct.* A side issue here is concerned with the responsibility for the breakdown of the marriage and whether or not his conduct might count against him when a court assesses financial provision. You should obviously have regard to and make mention of the key cases listed earlier in this chapter.

(c) *Ancillary provision.* The question is fundamentally concerned with ancillary provision. What can be done with the matrimonial home? Hywel would like it sold, Winifred would presumably like to stay. In all probability the house would not be sold especially as Hywel already has a roof over his head. Winifred on the other hand is likely to retain custody of Julian, who is, let it be said, a child of the family. At this point you would discuss the options available to the court. You are not told Winifred's age but might speculate that she is in her mid thirties having been married 12 years ago. So how appropriate is a Mesher or Harvey order? Could Winifred purchase Hywel's share of the home? Ought it to be transferred to her in lieu of or for a reduction in maintenance?

(d) *Sections 25 and 25A of the 1984 Act.* It is vital to refer to the new legislation and primary objective. How will the court approach the welfare of the child – also bearing in mind that Hywel has responsibility for Mary? Point to other s. 25 factors which may be relevant such as Winifred caring for the child of the marriage although we are told she has a salary and was thus working albeit in a part time capacity.

(e) *Clean break.* Despite the fact that Hywel has a son, is this a case for a clean break? Presumably not as there is no evidence of any large capital available and there will be a continuing obligation to Julian who is only 11.

(f) *Interest in property.* You are given enough information to decide if Winifred has a beneficial interest in the home, but this could be seen as a 'red herring' as the question is concerned with the redistribution of assets based upon the complete discretion of the court irrespective of interests of the parties.

(g) *Second marriage.* You are told that Hywel will marry Jean and thus have financial needs and obligations 'in the foreseeable future'. You ought to point out that a court may well take this into account.

(h) *Earning capacity.* Hywel has a good salary and prospects to develop a business. Winifred could move towards financial independence and at least appears to have a steady income which could be improved when Julian is older and she may have more free time. You may consider the option of a deferred clean break with the court putting a time limit on maintenance payments to Winifred.

You are also told that she is entitled to legal aid and may therefore speculate on how the costs may rise if litigation is protracted, with particular reference to the statutory charge.

(i) *Conclusion.* There is no need to try to ascertain the final settlement, only to consider her rights in the matter. This involves examining and applying the relevant legislation as well as other basic principles backed by case law. The question gives you enough information to bring in many aspects of the divorce and ancillary provision laws and good marks can be forthcoming for a structured and well argued answer. You should whenever possible refer to academic comment in your answer but not to the extent of giving a complete résumé of an article.

SEVEN

DOMESTIC VIOLENCE AND
EXCLUSION FROM PROPERTY

If you are ever asked to write a paper entitled 'Legal landmarks of the 1970s', I wonder exactly which examples you would choose to illustrate the title. It is a reasonable assumption that somewhere on the list of topics for inclusion would be domestic violence and the circumstances which led to the emergence of the Domestic Violence and Matrimonial Proceedings Act 1976. The decade began with media attention focused on the opening of the first women's aid shelter in Chiswick, the story of some of those women victims of domestic violence in *Scream Quietly or the Neighbours Will Hear* by Erin Pizzey which in turn led to reports being prepared by two House of Commons Select Committees (1974-75 and 1976-77). The Act soon followed.

The first piece of advice I would give to the student is not to ignore the background to the legislation and subsequent judicial involvement. To do so is to throw away a great chance of understanding the purpose behind the Act and the strength of feeling and sympathy within the country at the lot of those affected by violence within the home. You will then be able to appreciate why cases were decided in a particular way and perhaps more importantly to adopt a critical perspective to recent developments. However, do not fall into the trap of seeing the topic as one which has lost its interest more than a decade after the Act was passed. The following type of question may still be found on examination papers.

What appears to have been the intention of the legislature in enacting s. 1(2) of the Domestic Violence and Matrimonial Proceedings Act 1976? To what practical difficulties has the subsection given rise?

The key words in this question are 'intention' and 'practical difficulties' and one hopes that the information given in this chapter will be of assistance when seeking to answer this and questions of a similar kind.

Background

The reading list is extensive so remember that within the context of your family law course you are likely to seek only an 'overview' of the material rather than an in-depth study, unless of course you are looking at the topic with a view to writing a project. For a quick résumé of the literature you would be well advised to read chapter 9 in Hoggett and Pearl, *The Family, Law and Society*, entitled 'Dangerous families', and concentrate on sections 1, 2 and 3. There you will find brief examples of the types of violence experienced within the home expressed not only towards a spouse or cohabitee but also children. The authors give quite horrific examples of marital violence and make suggestions as to why violence in the home is so prevalent.

In addition you should direct your attention to the role of the criminal law. After all we are dealing with very serious assaults which if done outside the home context would merit serious charges being brought against the perpetrator. Yet the criminal law proved to be a singularly ineffective deterrent to marital violence. There were many reasons why this should have been so ranging from the police attitude that 'It's a domestic matter' to the unwillingness of the wife to testify in court against her husband.

The outcome of all the deliberations was that civil remedies were likely to prove more effective than criminal in combating domestic violence. Thus Parliament in 1976 passed the Domestic Violence and Matrimonial Proceedings Act. (A very full and comprehensive reading list is provided in Cretney, *Principles of Family Law*, 4th ed., pp. 234-5, nn. 7 and 8.)

In conclusion note only those points from the available literature which you feel help you to appreciate the concern that was felt in the 1970s over this problem.

The 1976 Act

The good student now needs to make a note of the crucial points in the Act and once this has been achieved will be in a position to look to the case law and be better able to understand the reasons why the court has become involved. You may decide to do this in list form:

(a)   Section 1 deals with *matrimonial injunctions* in the *county court*.

(b)   The words 'without prejudice to the jurisdiction of the High Court' would appear to warrant clarification.

(c)   The section gives the right to apply to 'parties to a marriage'.

(d)   It also says that the court may grant an injunction containing one or more of the following orders: *restraint, exclude* from matrimonial home or from specified area in which the matrimonial home is included, *require* to permit *entry* into and to *remain* within the matrimonial home.

(e)   The injunction *restraining* a persion is granted upon proof of *molestation.*

(f)   Application is *not* ancillary to other proceedings.

(g)   Section 1(2) makes it clear that the above applies equally to a man and woman *living with each other in the same household as man and wife.*

(h) Section 2 allows for arrest to take place of a person subject to an injunction who is in breach of its terms. The application has to be from 'a *party to a marriage*' (which covers cohabitees living as man and wife).

(i) The *restraint* in s. 2 relates to violence (not molestation) including that against a *child living with the applicant* (not child of the family).

(j) If a judge is satisfied that the other party has caused *actual bodily harm* and is *likely to do so again* a *power of arrest* may be attached.

(k) If a *power of arrest* is attached a constable may arrest without warrant if he has reasonable cause to suspect a person to be in breach of the injunction.

(l) A person arrested should be brought before a judge within 24 hours and he cannot except on the authority of a judge be *released* within that period. Nothing though shall authorise detention after that time has expired.

(This sort of format and approach can be adopted in relation to any key sections of legislation whether dealing with family law or any other subject.) Having underlined the words which may cause interpretational difficulties you ought to proceed to list the case law and supporting material under subheadings. I will be selective for the sake of brevity although virtually all things underlined have been examined by the judiciary since 1976.

Matrimonial injunctions

Generally, and matrimonial proceedings are no exception, a court could grant injunctions only if some legal or equitable right needed protecting. Thus in matrimonial cases a wife would have to commence proceedings, e.g., for divorce, and then seek the injunction as a matter ancillary to such action. In *Re W* [1981] 3 All ER 401 an interlocutory injunction was granted in order to support a custody order obtained under s. 9 of the Guardianship of Minors Act 1971.

Therefore the 1976 Act enhanced the power of the county court as it can now grant an injunction 'whether or not any other relief is sought in the proceedings'. The benefit of this is that as the existence of marital violence is not synonymous with the desire to divorce, a wife is not forced to contemplate the renunciation of her marriage in order to obtain emergency relief.

One favourite question is whether or not the Act is meant only to be applied by the county court and not the High Court. Rules of Court in 1977 suggested not (SI 1977 No. 532) but the decision in *Crutcher* v *Crutcher, The Times,* 18 July 1978, would suggest the opposite conclusion. There are dicta in *Davis* v *Johnson* [1979] AC 264 which could support both views and the question posed has never been satisfactorily answered. The case of *Richards* v *Richards* [1984] AC 174 has confirmed that applications for ouster orders must now be made under the provisions of the Matrimonial Homes Act 1983. Sir Roger Ormrod recently put it this way in *Baggott* v *Baggott* (CA 9 May 1985, Lexis transcript):

In my judgment there are two things about ... [*Richards* v *Richards*] . First, the jurisdiction to make orders regulating the occupation of a matrimonial home when divorce proceedings are pending, or even when they are not, now depends entirely upon the Matrimonial Homes Act 1967 as amended in 1983, and perhaps also on the Domestic Violence Act 1976.

The reference to the 1976 Act perhaps casts some doubt upon the effect of *Richards* but the judgment in *Baggott* is centred in its entirety on the Matrimonial Homes Act. Therefore whether or not the Domestic Violence Act confers jurisdiction only upon the county court is a question relevant now to non-molestation injunctions and not exclusion orders.

Parties to a marriage

At first sight this phrase would not appear to present problems. However the Court of Appeal in *White* v *White* [1983] 2 All ER 51 had the opportunity to consider the words in the context of s. 2 of the 1976 Act. Cumming-Bruce LJ felt that the 'true construction' of the words comprehended only a party to a *subsisting* marriage or a man and woman who were living with each other in the same household as husband and wife *at the time of the incidents* giving rise to the application under s. 2. However, if after decree absolute the parties cohabit as man and wife then they would fall within the terms of the Act. Thus the court refused the applicant's request for a power of arrest to be attached to an injunction some six months after the decree absolute. *Sharpe* v *Taylor* (1 May 1985, Lexis transcript) develops the thinking on the correct interpretation of the words from Lord Denning MR in *Davis* v *Johnson* [1978] 1 All ER 841 at p. 850 when he said that a literal meaning attributed to the words would deprive the subsection of much of its effect. He went on:

> They are used to denote the relationship between the parties before the incident which gives rise to the application. If they were then living together in the same household as husband and wife, that is enough.

Those words were later considered by Ormrod LJ in *McLean* v *Nugent* (1980) 1 FLR 16. He said:

> The fact that she is also complaining of subsequent acts of violence after the relationship had come completely to an end is not particularly important.

The next case of importance is *O'Neill* v *Williams* [1984] FLR 1 where the applicant brought proceedings under the 1976 Act eight months after the last incidence of violence and having since that date been living with her parents. The appeal against want of jurisdiction was dismissed. Cumming-Bruce LJ observed that a liberal construction had succeeded the literal interpretation of the words.

The Act was concerned with providing short-term relief in an emergency where a party alleged that he or she was being excluded from the quasi-matrimonial home by virtue of violence by the other party. He held the 'proper test' was that the 'condition precedent of judgment would be established if at the date of the alleged exclusion by violence the applicant and the respondent were then living with each other in the same household as husband and wife'.

This 'liberal interpretation' was adopted by Stephen Brown LJ in *Sharpe* v *Taylor*. As a revision aid this case is invaluable because it takes the 'historical approach' to the law and reviews the major authorities. Thus if you are referred in lectures to, say, *O'Neill* v *Williams* there is no real need to read all of its 10 pages noting simultaneously a précis of the case. The importance of *O'Neill* can be summarised in a few lines providing you place it into its proper context. A thorough reading of one recent case can save you a tremendous amount of time. In this last case the fact that they had not cohabited for seven and a half months proved fatal to the application (see also *Adeoso* v *Adeoso* [1981] 1 All ER 107).

Molestation

The word is not defined in the Act but it is obviously crucial to know exactly what types of conduct it covers. It goes without saying that violence is encompassed by the word but equally there is no need to prove violence in order to qualify for an injunction. Viscount Dilhorne put it this way in *Davis* v *Johnson* [1978] 1 All ER 841:

> Violence is a form of molestation, but molestation may take place without the threat or use of violence and still be serious and inimical to mental and physical health.

And in *Spindlow* v *Spindlow* [1979] 1 All ER 169 the Court of Appeal found it possible to *exclude* a cohabitee even though there had been no violence or molestation. The decision was severely criticised by Tom Harper (1979) 129 New LJ 207 and subsequently doubted in *Richards* v *Richards* [1983] 2 All ER 807 at p. 819. It has been said earlier in this book that *Horner* v *Horner* [1982] 2 All ER 495 concluded that harassment short of violence was sufficient to bring the case within the ambit of the county court jurisdiction under the 1976 Act. The point for the student to appreciate is that such a wide interpretation is within the ambit of the Act's philosophy to protect women, in particular, from the ravages of 'domestic hooliganism' as Sir George Baker P termed it in *Davis* v *Johnson* (CA) [1978] 1 All ER 841 at p. 857.

An interesting point arose in *Wooton* v *Wooton* [1984] FLR 871 where the respondent was an epileptic and was violent only when having a fit. The parties had cohabited for 18 years. The judge had dismissed the application because the respondent's violence was involuntary. However, the Court of Appeal felt that the judge had been wrong. It was the actual violence and the consequences to the applicant which were the important factors.

'What's so special about football hooligans?'

Exclude

The Court of Appeal has taken every conceivable opportunity to reiterate the point that the purpose of exclusion is simply to provide short-term emergency relief. In *Galan* v *Galan* [1985] FLR 905 the court, following *Spencer* v *Camacho* (1983) FLR 662, emphasised that an order under s. 1 of the 1976 Act should be of short duration, usually for a fixed period. It was considered inappropriate in the vast majority of cases to make the order limitless, although it was recognised that nothing in the Act specifically prevented this from occurring. In *Wiseman* v *Simpson* [1988] 1 All ER 245, another application under the Domestic Violence Act, the court spoke of the 'draconian nature of an ouster order' and in *Burke* v *Burke* [1987] 2 FLR 71 it spoke of the ouster order as being 'a drastic step to be used only in cases of real emergency and should normally take effect within a week or two'. As if to emphasise the point the Court of Appeal stressed that ouster orders should not have been seen as routine stepping stones to divorce and should not be granted *only* on the ground that the marriage had become a place of tension.

One of the earlier problems had centred around the question of whether it had been Parliament's intention that a property owning spouse could be deemed to have the right to enjoy his property. The House of Lords in *Davis* v *Johnson* [1978] 1 All ER 841 had absolutely no doubt that Parliament had used 'clear and unambiguous language', intended to allow the court to reach that conclusion.

Note that in *Masich* v *Masich* (1977) 121 SJ 645 it was determined that *ex parte* applications for ouster orders would only be granted in the most exceptional circumstances.

It will be convenient at this point to expand the discussion on ouster orders to include consideration of the decision of the House of Lords in *Richards* v *Richards* [1983] 2 All ER 807 because not only does it determine what factors need to be considered when seeking an exclusion order under the 1976 Act but it has determined which procedures ought to be used to obtain an ouster injunction. Thus in response to the question, what are the relevant principles and procedures to be adopted in seeking an ouster injunction?, I would suggest the following learning and revision approach.

Principles   An ouster injunction can be sought for tactical purposes as well as securing temporary relief from violence. A spouse in sole occupation of the matrimonial home is likely to have a stronger claim to remain in occupation after divorce, especially if she is awarded custody of the children of the marriage. In *Spindlow* v *Spindlow* [1979] 1 All ER 169 the Court of Appeal was prepared to see the matter as one of housing for the children and excluded the father even though there was no evidence to indicate that violence was an issue in the case. Rather, it was simply a case of the other party no longer wishing to live with her man. You could quote Ormrod LJ at p. 173 to substantiate the assertion:

> If this case is looked at rationally it is essentially a housing matter, housing for the children, and it should be looked at, in my judgment, mainly in that light.

However, it soon became apparent that judges were less than unanimous in assuming that this approach was the correct one to adopt when deciding whether or not to exclude. So in leading up to the case of *Richards* you must emphasise the conflict in judicial opinion and seek to illustrate that clash by reference to case law. Many of the cases in the 1970s were brought as an adjunct to divorce proceedings on the basis that under ss. 43 and 45 of the Supreme Court of Judicature (Consolidation) Act 1925 a court may grant an injunction in all cases in which it appeared just and convenient so to do. (The corresponding power is now contained in s. 37 of the Supreme Court Act 1981.) Therefore you should examine a line of cases decided under this procedure and ascertain the principles applied. Note the case name and jot down the factors in the following way:

Bassett v *Bassett* [1975] 1 All ER 513 (see also *Hall* v *Hall* [1971] 1 All ER 762 and *Phillips* v *Phillips* [1973] 2 All ER 423).

Factors:

(a)   Had the marriage already broken down?

(b)   Court should think of homes for children (cross-reference *Spindlow* and Domestic Violence Act).

(c)   Balance of hardship if exclusion approved as opposed to it being refused.

(d)   Difficulty in finding somewhere else to live.

(e)   Could a scheme be worked out to enable them to live together in the matrimonial home?

(f)   Did an 'impossible' situation exist? If so the sooner it ended the better.

Walker v *Walker* [1978] 3 All ER 141.

(a)   Exclusion should depend on whether in all the circumstances it was 'fair, just and reasonable'.

(b)   Regard to be had to behaviour.

(c)   Regard to be had to effect on children if husband excluded or if he stayed.

(d)   Personal circumstances to be considered.

(e)   The words 'impossible' and 'intolerable' should not be used in the context of applications for exclusion orders. What a party can tolerate and what is impossible differ according to the facts of the case.

Elsworth v *Elsworth* (1980) 1 FLR 245.

(a)   Wife had left — was there any prima facie good reason why she should not return?

(b)   Had the wife acted reasonably in refusing to return?

Conclusion

In this series of cases the courts have emphasised not only the interests of the children being important but also whether or not it is reasonable to expect the wife to live in the property with the other party or to return to the said property.

You should then embark upon a similar process with applications for ouster injunctions under the Domestic Violence and Matrimonial Proceedings Act 1976. By way of example you may cite the following cases:

Rennick v *Rennick* [1978] 1 All ER 817.

(a)   In determining an application under s. 1 *which involved children* their interest was the paramount consideration.

(b)   If mother had left with the children consideration should be given as to whether the father could take charge of them.

(c)   Should the wife return to 'take a chance' with husband?

Spindlow v *Spindlow* [1979] 1 All ER 169.

(a)   See notes above.

(b)   Cohabitee case, but where children present no difference in approach to that of married couples with children.

Conclusion
Strong emphasis given to welfare of children.

Having ascertained the background you are now in a position to understand the significance of *Richards*. In two cases reported consecutively in 1982 the opposing views were vividly illustrated. In *Myers* v *Myers* [1982] 1 All ER 776, an application under the 1976 Act, the Court of Appeal stressed that the test to be applied in deciding whether the husband should be excluded was whether or not the wife's decision not to return was reasonable. As the judge had not considered this matter he had erred in principle. However, in *Samson* v *Samson* [1982] 1 All ER 780 as an adjunct to divorce proceedings the wife who had left the home with the children sought to have the husband excluded. The court found her reasons for leaving were vague and that her attitude towards her husband was 'relentless and uncompromising'. The test to be applied, though, was that of the welfare of the children and then be guided largely by that. Accordingly the husband was excluded. Such inconsistency in approach needed to be resolved and the opportunity was first presented to the Court of Appeal in *Richards* [1983] 1 All ER 1017 in which the *Myers* line of cases was disapproved in favour of the *Samson* test. As a result the husband obtained leave to appeal to the House of Lords. Before reading the House of Lords decision you would be wise to consider the points which weighed heavily with the Court of Appeal, as this will help towards an understanding of the stance taken by the House in matters concerning ouster injunctions. The Court of Appeal had emphasised that the needs for the children were paramount and that despite an extremely 'flimsy' divorce petition presented by the wife, the husband had to be excluded from the home to allow the wife and children to return. Even if the wife would not show that she had any reasonable grounds for refusing to return to live with the husband, the court still had the power to exclude.

The importance of the *Richards* (HL) decision has been described by Ruth Deech in these words, 'The decision dominated all family law developments in the year under review' (1983 All ER Annual Review 212 at p. 213 for an extremely comprehensive review of the decision). Thus you ought to make special reference to it in your notes.

Richards v *Richards* (HL)

Important points:

(a)   A court's jurisdiction to make ouster injunctions is 'governed exclusively' by s. 1 of the Matrimonial Homes Act 1983.

(b)   A court was therefore obliged to follow the criteria listed at s. 1(3) of the Matrimonial Homes Act 1983.

(c)   *That subsection* made it clear that the needs of the children was only one factor to take into account and certainly no one matter listed was to be taken as being paramount over the others.

(d)   The court must try to produce a just and reasonable result.

(e)   The husband's appeal was allowed.

Having stated the outcome of the case you should then seek to list the *reasons* for the approach taken by the House.

Reasons

(a)   Two statutory provisions existed under which a party could be excluded from the matrimonial home. One, the 1925 Act (now the Supreme Court Act 1981), was essentially 'general' in nature, the other, the Matrimonial Homes Act 1967 (now 1983), deals with the 'special' situation under consideration. Litigants were not entitled to bypass the provisions of the 'specialist' legislation by resorting to the general Act because that meant that a different jurisprudence to that intended by Parliament to apply to such cases would be brought to bear.

(b)   By adopting this approach the House would not need to decide between the competing views.

(c)   The Matrimonial Homes Act was intended to codify and to make clear the jurisdiction of the High Court and county courts in ouster injunctions. This view came as a complete surprise to many (if not all) practitioners!

(d)   Note that Lord Scarman specifically dissented from the view that the jurisdiction of the High Court and county court was governed exclusively by s. 1 of the Matrimonial Homes Act.

(e)   The procedure in s. 37 of the Supreme Court Act 1981 has not been abolished and can be invoked in appropriate cases, e.g., molestation, for the *protection* of minors.

Comment

(a)   The Matrimonial Homes Act 1983 refers to spousal conduct but it was held in *Lee* v *Lee* [1984] FLR 243 that the factors listed in s. 1(3) of the 1983 Act apply also to cohabitees in the context of the Domestic Violence and Matrimonial Proceedings Act 1976. These factors are:

(i)   conduct of the *spouses*,
(ii)   respective needs and financial resources,
(iii)   needs of any children,
(iv)   all the circumstances of the case.

If confirmation of this point were needed one would cite Ralph Gibson LJ in *Wiseman* v *Simpson* [1988] 1 All ER 245 at p. 250b:

> It was not in issue that, in proceedings under s. 1 of the 1976 Act between an unmarried couple to whom the section applies, the court must apply the principles set out in s. 1(3) of the Matrimonial Homes Act 1983 (see *Richards* v *Richards* [1983] 2 All ER 807 at 829).

Indeed cohabitees are confined to applications under the 1976 Act or possibly in other proceedings, e.g., custody, and a court has no jurisdiction to deal with applications by cohabitees under the Matrimonial Homes Act 1983.

(b)   Consider the impact of the *Richards* decision on a council's responsibility to rehouse under the Housing (Homeless Persons) Act 1977. If, because of the 'new' criteria, a wife failed to obtain an ouster order then she may be regarded as intentionally homeless. As an example see the decision of the Court of Appeal in *Clarke* v *Clarke* (13 December 1984, Lexis transcript) where Stephenson LJ said:

> what really seems to be the case is that under the Homeless Persons Act a person who has left accommodation voluntarily has no hope of being rehoused under the Act . . . but if an order is obtained from the court . . . priority [is] very often . . . given to a person who has been ousted by the order.

In *Thurley* v *Smith* [1984] FLR 875 the Court of Appeal said that one of the factors to be taken into account when considering the needs of the parties was the duty of the local authority to provide accommodation for homeless persons under the 1977 Act. See also *Wooton* v *Wooton* [1984] FLR 871 where the essential problem was one of housing.

(c)   Despite changes to the Matrimonial Homes Act 1967 by the Domestic Violence and Matrimonial Proceedings Act 1976 which allowed for the total exclusion of an owner, the Act was in practice little used, probably because of the availability of injunctions under the 1976, 1978 and 1981 Acts.

(d)   You ought to analyse Lord Scarman's dissenting judgment and look to the events which led to the passing of the Matrimonial Homes Act, in particular the decision of the House in *National Provincial Bank Ltd* v *Ainsworth* [1965] AC 1175.

(e)   Another apparent problem resulting from *Richards* is the necessity to start separate proceedings under the Matrimonial Homes Act 1983 for an ouster order, even though a divorce petition has been presented to the court.

(f) Make a list of circumstances in which the Matrimonial Homes Act 1983 procedure will still not apply. Mention has been made of the position of cohabitees who have to apply under the 1976 Act. In *Re W* [1981] 3 All ER 401 the Court of Appeal confirmed that when making a custody order under the Guardianship of Minors Act 1971 the County Court has power to grant an interlocutory injunction under s. 38 of the County Courts Act 1984 in support of the order. *Re W* was reconsidered in *Ainsbury* v *Millington* [1986] 1 All ER 73. The applicant sought an injunction to oust a former cohabitee from a jointly occupied house. It was accepted that neither the Matrimonial Homes Act 1983 (because she was not married) nor the Domestic Violence and Matrimonial Proceedings Act 1976 (because they no longer lived together) was applicable. There was one child of the relationship and the mother subsequently married another man. She brought proceedings under the Guardianship of Minors Act 1971 seeking interim custody and an ouster injunction. The judge held he had no jurisdiction to grant the ouster relief sought. To exclude the former cohabitee would require jurisdiction under s. 37 of the Supreme Court Act 1981 (applied to county courts by s. 38 of the County Courts Act 1984) and this would only be found if the injunction could be granted in support of a legal right.

The appellant argued that proceedings under the Guardianship of Minors Act 1971 were an exception to the rule and cited *Re W*. The Court of Appeal held that the case was reconcilable with the speeches in *Richards* on the basis that the applicant in *Re W* was the sole owner of the flat, and therefore had a property interest capable of being supported by an injunction. *Re W* thus did not create an exception to the rule and the appeal was dismissed.

But in wardship proceedings where the custody and upbringing of the child and his welfare generally are the paramount consideration the court could exclude an occupant of the property in which the child lived. *Quinn* v *Quinn* (1983) 4 FLR 394 also indicates that the court has an inherent jurisdiction to exclude one parent from the matrimonial home if that was desirable in the 'interests of the children'. (See also *Montgomery* v *Montgomery* [1965] P 46.) A further problem concerns the exclusion of third parties, for example, a mistress whom the husband has brought into the matrimonial home. Neither the 1976 Act nor apparently the 1983 Act gives any remedy to the other spouse *against the third party*. There are some examples of the court granting injunctions against third parties and presumably these remain good authority. See in particular: *Adams* v *Adams* (1965) 109 SJ 899; *Jones* v *Jones* [1971] 2 All ER 737; *Pinckney* v *Pinckney* [1966] 1 All ER 121.

Revision note The impact of *Richards* has been enormous. It is likely to have an influence on examination questions for a long time to come. It is extensively discussed in the standard texts and in numerous articles. You should clearly see it as one of the major cases of the decade and engage in a thorough, structured and searching review of the background to and impact of the decision by the

House. It would be of advantage to search for post-*Richards* cases and then note how the decision has been applied and what judicial comments could be used in an examination in order to illustrate its effect. I list below some examples:

(a)   *Anderson* v *Anderson* [1984] FLR 566.

(b)   *Briscoe* v *Briscoe* (1984 Lexis transcript). Note that Dunn LJ said of the Act:

> like all orders under the Matrimonial Homes Act . . . [this order] is only a temporary measure so that the parties can have a breathing space to enable them to make permanent arrangements for their own accommodation. The order has no effect on property rights and will have no effect on the ultimate future of the matrimonial home and dispersal of the proceeds of sale.

(c)   *Harris* v *Harris* [1986] 1 FLR 12 where the court indicated that the court should have regard to the reasonableness or unreasonableness of the wife's conduct.

(d)   *Lee* v *Lee* [1984] FLR 243. A useful case. Dunn LJ said: 'and as we were told that the judge appeared to have been under some misapprehension as to what the House of Lords decided in *Richards* v *Richards*, it is desirable that I should explain that case'.

(e)   *Summers* v *Summers*, [1986] 1 FLR 343. An order ousting a 20-year-old father of three young children so as to 'allow the dust to settle' and thus lead to a possible reconciliation with his wife was held to be wrong in law. Although the judge at Merthyr County Court had regard to s. 1 of the Matrimonial Homes Act 1983 he had failed to give sufficient thought to an important consideration — the Draconian nature of making such an order and the effect of it on the person against whom it was made. In this case the judge had applied criteria not included in the statutory provisions and omitted other vital factors. As a result the order could not stand and a new trial was ordered before a different judge.

(f)   *Shipp* v *Shipp* [1988] 1 FLR 345. The Court of Appeal setting its face against interim ouster orders unless it was absolutely imperative to make one.

(g)   *Summers* v *Summers (No. 2)* (1987) 137 NLJ 611. Further support for the view that ouster orders should only be made in cases of real necessity.

(h)   *Wiseman* v *Simpson* [1988] 1 All ER 245. Proof of violence or conduct adverse to the applicant or child was not a necessary requirement to the making of an ouster order. It was insufficient to consider that just because the need for housing for one party was greater the order should be made. A judge should consider whether it was *just and reasonable* to make an ouster order. Case remitted to county court for consideration of whether it was just and reasonable to exclude.

Power of arrest

As a final example of the sort of points to consider when revising I shall look at the circumstances in which a power of arrest may be attached to an injunction. To obtain an injunction is one thing, to have it effectively enforced is a different matter altogether. It is not generally a criminal offence to breach an injunction and so the police were in the past reluctant to be involved. However, the Domestic Violence and Matrimonial Proceedings Act 1976 shows that Parliament was well aware of the problem. It has given the court the ability to attach a power of arrest to an injunction, although it only applies where the injunction is granted to restrain violence or where there is an ouster order.

The terms of the legislation seem to make it clear that a power of arrest is not to be attached automatically. You should note that two things have to be shown:

(a)   that actual bodily harm has been caused to the applicant or child by the respondent *and*
(b)   that it is likely that he will cause actual bodily harm again (see s. 2).

In *Horner* v *Horner* [1982] 2 All ER 495 the Court of Appeal decided that as nine months had elapsed since the husband had been violent to the wife it could not in all the circumstances attach a power of arrest. As a statement of principle you could cite Ormrod LJ at p. 498:

it has been said many times that to attach a power of arrest to an injunction is very serious because it exposes the husband to immediate arrest; it causes great problems for police officers who have to enforce it; it leads to the husband being kept in custody for a period up to 24 hours . . . and it often involves a committal order to prison. Anything in this sphere which operates more or less automatically is to be deprecated.

The latest example of this is the Court of Appeal decision in *Carpenter* v *Carpenter* [1988] 1 FLR 121. Here the wife had petitioned for judicial separation and had obtained a non-molestation injunction with a power of arrest attached. Later the wife alleged that the husband has assaulted her. The husband give the judge various undertakings and when the case was heard the judge doubted that the wife's allegations were true. Nevertheless the judge further extended the power of arrest. The husband appealed. The Court of Appeal allowed his appeal. It reiterated the point that a power of arrest could only be attached where there was proof of actual bodily harm and that it was likely to happen again. As the judge rejected the wife's allegations there was no basis for the power of arrest.

Note also that the point was left open as to whether a power of arrest which had already been attached could be extended and whether the finding of the original incident of assault could be relied upon as a ground for extending the power of arrest.

(See also *Lewis* v *Lewis* [1978] 1 All ER 729.)

Sample question

A review of recent family law question papers shows almost without exception that reference is made to the decision in *Richards*. A question may not necessarily refer to *Richards* by name as in the following:

How does the law seek to protect adult or child victims of 'family' violence?
Consider the adequacy, or otherwise, of the procedures and sanctions available.

This is an interesting question and one that can lead a student astray unless he is very observant. The use of the word 'or' between adult and child would indicate that separate treatment may be required. As the powers under the Domestic Violence and Matrimonial Proceedings Act 1976 apply to children of the applicant, it is pointless to repeat any earlier comments about the use of the Act to protect adults. It is correct to assume that Parliament and the courts have recognised that children deserve special protection because of their relatively vulnerable position in the household. Therefore this question is written in such a way as to allow you to mention in varying degrees of detail, depending on your course emphasis, the following:

(a)   Wardship proceedings where the welfare of the child is the first and paramount consideration.

(b)   An application under the Guardianship of Minors Act 1971 as in *Re W* [1981] 3 All ER 401.

(c)   The Children and Young Persons Act 1969 which allows the child to be removed from the hostile environment for his own protection rather than removing the source of the problem from the home. As we shall see later both the facts contained in s. 1 of the Act and associated procedures have come under severe criticism from the judiciary. (See for example the comments of Dunn LJ in *Re E (Minors)* [1984] 1 All ER 21.)

(d)   Criminal law sanctions where the action is severe. Unfortunately the criminal law's intervention is often too late to help the child.

All these points are in addition to factors mentioned in connection with adult protection by injunction in particular under the three pieces of legislation the Domestic Violence and Matrimonial Proceedings Act 1976, the Supreme Court Act 1981 and the Matrimonial Homes Act 1983. The more one thinks about the spread of the question it soon becomes apparent that given adequate preparation one could write for two hours or more on the subject rather than, in this case, the 45 minutes allowed. This means that you would have to be very selective in the information you use. One big saving to be made when answering such a question is to determine in advance that you will refrain from detailing the *facts* of cases unless it is *absolutely imperative* that they are included to illustrate some point that you are making. A further complication is that the question refers to *'adults'* as opposed to, say, 'married women'. Therefore it is quite legitimate to include discussion of cohabitees and the difficulties experienced by the courts in deciding whether or not for the purposes of the 1976 Act the couple are living together as man and wife. The question also puts the word *family* into quotation marks thus implying that the examiner does not wish the answer to be confined to the married family.

So the impact of *Richards* would undoubtedly be part of the answer but only one part. Many students aware of the importance of *Richards* would, I am convinced, have answered the question set purely by reference to ouster injunctions under the Matrimonial Homes Act 1983 and the Domestic Violence and Matrimonial Proceedings Act 1976 thus denying themselves perhaps as much as 40% of the marks for that question. The moral is to read the question very carefully, then seek to place an interpretation on particular words or phrases. In this question, why is the word 'family' in quotation marks, and why is 'or' used instead of 'and' between 'child' and 'adult'? A little lateral thinking is not a bad thing when faced with essay questions of this nature.

Other questions refer to *Richards* by name: 'Consider the effect of the decision of *Richards* v *Richards* on the law relating to ouster injunctions'.

Here your context is a little more clearly defined. You must obviously make clear to the examiner that you are aware what the decision is and some background to the problem would not go amiss. You have then to assess its impact on the ability of a court to grant ouster injunctions. I have stated previously that *Richards* affects established procedures as well as establishing which criteria have to be taken account of in reaching a decision on an application to exclude.

Finally you should point to those categories of persons not covered by the Matrimonial Homes Act 1983 such as cohabitees and thus illustrate that if the Matrimonial Homes Act 1983 was intended to be the all-embracing legislation that the House asserted it to be, why was it necessary for Parliament to pass the Domestic Violence and Matrimonial Proceedings Act 1976 other than to make specific reference to cohabitees?

Let us analyse the following question:

Mary and Gordon were married in 1980 and there are two children of the family, Katherine aged 10, being Gordon's daughter from a previous marriage, and Ben, born to the couple in 1985. Mary and Gordon's relationship has since 1986 been less than cordial and many arguments have ensued, although there has only been one occasion when aggression was shown, when as a result of a disagreement Mary threw a saucepan at Gordon hitting him on the arm. In January this year Mary left Gordon taking the two children with her and went to live with James until May when their relationship ended. She and the two children are now living with her mother in overcrowded conditions. Mary wishes to reoccupy the matrimonial home, a council house, rented in the sole name of her husband. She also realises there is little future in the relationship and is prepared to contemplate divorce although she wonders about the effect this may have on the children. Throughout the period of separation Katherine has made it clear she wishes to be with her father and although Gordon would like this he cannot see how he can continue to work and look after his daughter.

Advise Mary on whether or not she can successfully occupy the matrimonial home with the children and exclude Gordon from it.

You are specifically asked whether or not Gordon can be excluded. By way of analysis let us take each line in turn.

(a)   You are told that there are two children of the family but that the elder is from a previous marriage. This raises a question of who has the legal custody of the child and in the absence of any evidence of step-parent adoption it would appear that Gordon is in a stronger position than his wife, subject always to the welfare principle.

(b)   The relationship is briefly described. They appear, as Ormrod LJ put it in *Adeoso* v *Adeoso* [1981] 1 All ER 107, to be a couple whose 'marriage . . . is in the last stages of break-up'. However, there is no real evidence of violence and the facts stand comparison to those in *Spindlow* v *Spindlow* which were sufficient to warrant a non-molestation order although not exclusion. Note in this case that Mary is the one causing harm.

(c)   There is no evidence of any unreasonableness by Gordon and it appears that Mary is the one taking the initiative in the demise of their relationship.

(d)   Although it is not overtly stated the motivation for her leaving in the first place is her relationship with James which has presumably been in existence while she was still living with her husband. It is reasonable to assume that adultery has been committed by Mary with James. Unfortunately things have not worked out resulting in the position where she has to take refuge with her mother. There are obvious parallels with the *Richards* case and its predecessors such as *Myers* and *Samson*. You are therefore invited to explain the dilemma faced by the courts as to whether the overriding principle was homes for the children or reasonableness of the wife's action and the justice of excluding the husband. From there you would discuss in some detail how the House resolved the problem. It would be incumbent upon you to make reference to *Wiseman* v *Simpson* [1988] 1 All ER 245 which is authority for the proposition that it must be just and reasonable before a party is excluded from property.

(e)   Does it make any difference that the property is council-owned rented in the sole name of her husband? Under the 1983 Act a tenant's wife has rights of occupation during the currency of the marriage and under s. 1(2) she can make application to the court for her rights with regard to the property to be declared. Naturally there will be the question of whether or not she has made herself intentionally homeless and thus not qualify for rehousing under the Homeless Persons Act or, if Gordon is excluded, whether the council would rehouse. Reference would ordinarily be made to the cases of *Thurley* v *Smith* and *Wooton* v *Wooton* which both have something to say about rehousing.

(f)   The matter of divorce being contemplated by Mary raised the possibility of a divorce petition being presented. Since *Richards* the proper procedure for exclusion of the other party is via the Matrimonial Homes Act 1983. This would appear to duplicate proceedings connected with the breakdown of marriage. If the court can order maintenance pending suit, why not allow it to readjust the living arrangements without separate proceedings being commenced?

(g)   As Katherine wishes to be with her father this would be taken into account under s. 1(3) of the Matrimonial Homes Act 1983. However, it may be possible for the father to seek sole interim custody of the children and in proceedings under the Guardianship of Minors Act 1971 seek to have the children returned and Mary excluded. Wardship is perhaps not a practical suggestion but could be called upon if needed. The success of an application for custody would very much depend on the day-to-day arrangements that could be made. As it is doubtful whether Mary has any custodial rights over Katherine proceedings to secure custody may be unnecessary. However, the child's welfare will always be regarded as paramount.

Conclusion

The question has given you an opportunity to look at different proceedings with regard to ouster injunctions. Custodial issues loom large as well and in the end you are probably aware of how difficult it must be for a judge, when considering competing claims for the matrimonial home, to do what is best for the welfare of the children and to attempt to do justice between the spouses. For another worked example on exclusion from property see chapter 2 on assessment techniques.

EIGHT

COHABITEES

Much has already been said in the previous chapter about those couples living together as man and wife and their legal rights as far as ouster injunctions are concerned. Suffice it to say that in this chapter we will be looking at other aspects of cohabitation which may have given undergraduates more than a few headaches as they sat their finals paper in family law. In the last two decades much has been written on the subject especially in the context of what legal rights should be possessed by those persons who have a relationship akin to that of husband and wife. On the one hand there are those who would argue that an extension of legal rights for cohabitees would seriously undermine the status of legal marriage. If people wanted the legal 'security' gained by entering marriage then the remedy was simple, they should get married.

The contrary view relates to the present law in that it is illogical and arbitrary for cohabitees, especially those who are parties to a stable relationship akin to marriage. The problem has been recently highlighted by the provisions relating to financial provision for children, whether born in or out of wedlock, contained in s. 12 of the Family Law Reform Act 1987. Either parent may apply for an order transfering to the other 'such property as may be specified' *for the benefit of the child.* So the 'illegitimate' child is now catered for, but there is still an absence of any legislative provision allowing a court to transfer property between cohabitees for their own benefit after a relationship has folded. It has been argued by Robert Johnson QC that the present law does not do anything to reduce the inherent insecurity of such a relationship. In *Thomas* v *Fuller-Brown* [1988] 1 FLR 237 at p. 247 Slade LJ highlighted one of the problems when dealing with a plaintiff who had done work valued at over £12,000 to the defendant's property: '. . . this case illustrates . . . that a man who does work by way of improvement to his cohabitee's property *without a clear understanding* as to the financial basis on which the work is to be done does so at his own risk'.

These arguments may reflect the discussion of cohabitee relationships encountered on your course. On the one hand is the general question of what sort of recognition should be given to a stable family unit and what rights and duties should accrue to the parties. In many cases the cohabitee relationship will be much stronger than many marriages and yet the cohabitees are certainly at a legal disadvantage. This major area could be raised in many ways in an examination. One of the most popular is to use a quotation and then to ask for

a suitable commentary. In chapter 1 I referred to the case of *Burns* v *Burns*
[1984] 1 All ER 244, a most significant case dealing with the principles to be
applied in determining whether or not a long-term cohabitee had a beneficial
interest in the 'matrimonial' home. At the end of his judgment Fox LJ said:

> Nevertheless, she lived with him for 19 years as man and wife, and, at the end
> of it, has no rights against him. But the unfairness of that is not a matter
> which the courts can control. It is a matter for Parliament.

In similar vein May LJ said:

> When one compares this ultimate result with what it would have been had she
> been married to the defendant and taken appropriate steps under the
> Matrimonial Causes Act 1973, I think that she can justifiably say that fate has
> not been kind to her. In my opinion, however, the remedy for any inequity
> she may have sustained is a matter for Parliament and not for this court.

The quotations indicate not only that at least two members of the judiciary feel
that an application of the present principles can lead to unfairness but also that
any change must come from Parliament via new legislation – the very point
Robert Johnson appears to be making. A 1985 examination question quoted
Fox LJ (above) and asked the student:

> In light of the above statement comment critically on the legal position of
> cohabitees and suggest what parliamentary reforms are necessary to remedy
> the 'unfairness' to which Lord Justice Fox refers.

This type of question is very wide-ranging and you are entitled, because of the
inclusion of the words 'legal position of cohabitees', to go further than merely
concentrating on beneficial interests in property. The discussion in the first part
of this chapter will be centred around the problems faced by cohabitees and how
you can use this information in examinations, especially from the point of view
that change in this area of law is long overdue.

The other type of issue that may be raised in the course is to test your *knowledge* and *application* of the general principles to an examination problem. A
large body of case law has built up in particular areas especially:

(a)   Exclusion orders and the Domestic Violence and Matrimonial Proceedings Act 1976 generally (see chapter 7).

(b)   Trust and trustee – and the principles applicable in determining beneficial
interests in property.

(c)   Occupation of the home, e.g., licence to remain.

(d)   Inheritance – especially where one party is dependent.
(e)   Rights to succeed to a protected tenancy.

In addition there are problems connected with the status of any children of the relationship but this can best be left until the chapters dealing with children, although the changes contained in the Family Law Reform Act 1987 are indeed radical and very welcome.

Wider issues

The first thing your tutor is likely to mention is terminology. There does not appear to be one phrase that will cover a relationship other than the married state. The books refer to unmarried couples, common-law wives, cohabitees, mistresses, paramours; any one of which is precise enough to describe a particular relationship but each would appear inadequate as a generic title. Note also that Parliament when seeking to bestow rights on cohabitees has used different terminology. The phrase preferred in the Domestic Violence and Matrimonial Proceedings Act 1976 refers to a quasi-marital state – 'living together as husband and wife'. The Inheritance (Provision for Family and Dependants) Act 1975 – dubbed the mistresses' charter – makes dependence in whole or in part the criteria for financial provision from the deceased's estate. The Consumer Credit Act 1974 refers to the 'reputed husband and wife', while the Pneumoconiosis (Workmen's Compensation etc.) Act 1979 refers to 'reputed spouse'.

So, when analysing statutes and cases be extremely careful in choosing your words and always make sure that you are aware of the statutory context of the words under review and in addition the purpose of the legislation.

Secondly it would be valuable if you could gauge the reaction   the judi ary as evidenced by reported cases to the idea of the 'illicit union'. Have the judges attempted to deny cohabitees certain rights because of their prejudices against such relationships or would the opposite be a truer reflection of what has happened? Certainly where Parliament has made it clear that it was bestowing rights upon unmarried couples then the judges would have appeared to have given recognition to Parliament's intention. A good example was when the House of Lords in *Davis* v *Johnson* overruled the decisions of the Court of Appeal in *B* v *B* [1978] 1 All ER 821 and *Cantliff* v *Jenkins* [1978] 1 All ER 836 when that court by its decisions had threatened to drive a coach and horses through s. 1 of the 1976 Act as it applied to cohabitees living together as husband and wife.

Undoubtedly the view held by many is that by giving further legal recognition to unmarried couples then the institution of marriage is threatened. Yet on the available evidence the judiciary has responded positively to the fact that many people are choosing to live together rather than marry, providing in the main that the relationship reflects a 'family' rather than a 'casual' state. However, the case of *Harrogate Borough Council* v *Simpson* [1986] 2 FLR 91 shows that the court is not yet prepared to extend this reasoning to homosexuals living together as 'man and wife'. To make this sort of assertion in an examination is risky unless it can be supported by authority. You might quote from government statistics showing that on average fewer people are getting married now than 10 years ago. Judicial authority is not hard to find. In a Rent Act case in 1980 (*Watson* v *Lucas* [1980] 3 All ER 647) Stephenson LJ said at p. 652:

> Holding this man to be a member of this woman's family will not promote the support of marriage or the reduction of illicit unions. . . . But, though these objects might have influenced the judges who decided *Gammans* v *Ekins* [1950] 2 All ER 140, they had lost their relevance to the interpretation of this provision [s. 2(5)] of the Rent Acts a quarter of a century later. Their irrelevance in other fields has been recognised by Parliament.

Ormrod LJ in *Re Evers's Trust* [1980] 3 All ER 399 at p. 401 commented:

> This [cohabitation] is a situation which is occurring much more frequently now than in the past and is a social development of considerable importance with which the courts are now likely to have to deal from time to time.

Griffiths LJ in *Bernard* v *Josephs* [1982] 3 All ER 162 at p. 169 said:

> The judge must look most carefully at the nature of the relationship, and only if satisfied that it was intended to involve the same degree of commitment as marriage will it be legitimate to regard them as no different from a married couple.

And finally May LJ in *Burns* v *Burns* [1984] 1 All ER 244:

> This appeal raises a question which arises nowadays with increasing frequency . . . it is becoming increasingly frequent that couples live together without being married, but just as if they were so. . . . In the case of an unmarried couple . . . there is no statute which gives a court similar power to those which it has as between husband and wife [on divorce].

So there is ample authority to assert that judges do not seek to penalise unmarried couples although in many areas the law as it stands cannot be extended to cover cohabitees. For example, the marriage relationship imposes obligations upon the parties, the most obvious of which is the duty to maintain. With cohabitees there is no corresponding obligation. Thus when the relationship breaks down one cohabitee cannot, in the absence of any contractual agreement to the contrary, seek to be maintained in the future, whereas, say, a married woman may have maintenance awarded in her favour for the rest of her natural life. (This last statement though must be read in light of the guidelines contained in the Matrimonial and Family Proceedings Act 1984.)

Again, as a preliminary to further study you would be well advised to compare and contrast the rights and obligations that accrue to married couples with those recognised as attaching to, or stemming from a cohabitee relationship. (For a very brief review see M. Parry, *Cohabitation,* pp. 5-9.) Such investigation will help you to formulate your own views as to whether or not, on the breakdown of an established union, married or otherwise, there should be similar principles applied with equal consistency. Yet, as has been implied, those wanting greater rights which stem from marriage can always subscribe to the institution. Unfortunately it is not always as easy as that. Some parties may genuinely wish to marry but it is impossible because they cannot obtain a divorce from their existing spouse. *Johnson* v *Johnson* (1982) 12 Fam Law 116 is a good example of the problem with Mr Johnson having no opportunity to marry again unless his financial circumstances changed so as to allow him to make adequate provision for his wife, thus relieving the grave financial hardship likely to be experienced by her if divorced.

Revision note

As we examine in more detail some of the areas where cohabitees have come to court seeking to have their dispute resolved try to crystallise your thoughts on precisely what approach you would wish to see adopted in the future. Is the law about right as far as it affects cohabitees, given limited recognition by Parliament in some circumstances, but totally ignored in others or is there a need for a review of the existing law and together with the determined policy on cohabitation, for Parliament to create radical and innovative legislation so that individuals can make an informed choice as to whether or not to marry?

An examination question reflecting this appeared on a 1987 paper.

In July 1985 *The Times* quoted Booth J as saying that for rights of cohabitees to be contained in a single law would 'seriously undermine the status of legal marriage'. However, in *Burns* v *Burns* [1984] 1 All ER 244 Fox LJ, commenting on a woman who had lived with a man for 19 years and had no rights against him, said that any unfairness should be remedied by Parliament not the courts.

Assume you have been given the task to draft legislation entitled *'The Cohabitee Bill' 1987*. Prepare up to six clauses backed by reasons which you would think vital to include in such legislation.

OR

State with reasons why you believe it would be impractical or impossible to draw up such legislation.

Principles determining beneficial interests in property

As Godfrey Gypps tells us in his articles, 'Unmarried couples – legal problems when the relationship ends', 3 Lit 194 and 241, there are over half a million couples living together as man and wife, for a variety of different reasons. As with married couples it is rare for the law to be involved in their relationship until things begin to turn sour. Then, and this is an important point in the context of this discussion, they face exactly the same practical problems as their married counterparts, i.e., custody of and access to the children, property and financial matters and possibly some element of domestic violence or molestation. The major pieces of legislation concerning property and financial redistribution and exclusion from property, the Matrimonial Causes Act 1973 and the Matrimonial Homes Act 1983, do not apply to an unmarried couple. Property in particular can be very important not only as regards any share of the proceeds of sale but also as a home for any children of the relationship. The position of children in regard to property was given prominence in *Re Evers's Trust* [1980] 3 All ER 399. Here the parties cohabited for five years and had one child, later joined by the man's two children from his marriage. They purchased a house which was conveyed to them on trust for sale as joint tenants. The female partner remained in the house with the three children when they separated in 1979. The plaintiff sought an order under s. 30 of the Law of Property Act 1925 for the sale of the house. The Court of Appeal saw this situation as a 'family' case. Its approach was to consider both the *primary* purpose of the trust (i.e., sale) and its *underlying* purpose (i.e., to provide a home for the parents and children). It was decided that the interests of children, both legitimate and illegitimate, were a circumstance to be considered. In conclusion as the plaintiff had no great need to realise his investment the court dismissed his application. *Re Evers's Trust* was subsequently applied in *Dennis* v *McDonald* [1981] 2 All ER 632. You may note that this latter case was successfully appealed but not on the children point ([1982] 1 All ER 590). In this latter case the court considered the purchase of property for the family was the 'prime object' of the trust for sale.

Part of your tuition on cohabitees will undoubtedly concentrate on what ought to be their legal position if and when the relationship ends. If the parties are married, who actually owns the home or the respective interests of the couple are virtually irrelevant when the court comes to redistribute the family assets on divorce. That is because the philosophy underpinning the share-out is based primarily upon future needs and expectations, combined with the fact that the Matrimonial Causes Act 1973 gives the court an absolute discretion over such matters. The court does not have a corresponding power with cohabitees although individually their expectations may be precisely the same as a married couple. Thus as far as cohabitees are concerned it becomes increasingly important to establish their respective interests in the property which in practice means falling back on principles developed from cases decided under the Married Women's Property Act 1882. This is made even more surprising as there have been no cases reported in the *All England Law Reports* for the last six years under this legislation.

Therefore in your preparation of material you ought to consider and list the factors which will be relevant when applied to ascertaining whether a cohabitee has an interest in the property. The following is an example:

(a)   Look to the title deeds. What do they indicate? Do they make any express mention of the beneficial interests?

(b)   Is the property in joint names? Is it thus owned equally?

(c)   Was the property purchased in the sole name of one party?

(d)   If so, did the other party make a direct contribution to the purchase price or any indirect contribution?

(e)   Can the court impute from the conduct of the couple a common intention that the woman/man was to have a beneficial interest in the property?

(f)   Has the woman/man made a substantial financial contribution towards the expenses of the household which could be related to the acquisition of the property?

(g)   Had the claimant acted to his or her detriment on the basis of the common intention and in the belief that by so acting he or she would acquire a beneficial interest?

Once you have listed points which are relevant to help determine the issue you then need authority to illustrate the weighting given to each one. You can accumulate such information by ploughing through the textbook or by taking the latest case of significance and noting the cases referred to in the judgments. Thus you may care to examine *Grant* v *Edwards* [1986] 2 All ER 426 or *Turton* v *Turton* [1987] 2 All ER 641. In the former 12 cases are listed and in the latter 13. It is suggested that the most important are:

Bernard v *Josephs* [1982] Ch 391.
Cooke v *Head* [1972] 2 All ER 38.
Goodman v *Gallant* [1986] 1 All ER 311.
Eves v *Eves* [1975] 3 All ER 768.
Gissing v *Gissing* [1971] AC 886.
Hall v *Hall* (1981) 3 FLR 379.
Burns v *Burns* [1984] 1 All ER 244.
Pettit v *Pettit* [1970] AC 777.
Pascoe v *Turner* [1979] 2 All ER 945.
Walker v *Hall* [1984] FLR 126.

Undoubtedly the basic principles stem from the cases of *Pettit* and *Gissing*.

Goodman v *Gallant* [1986] All ER 311 is authority for the proposition that the doctrines of resulting, implied or constructive trusts could not be invoked where there was an express declaration which comprehensively declared what were the beneficial interests in the property or proceeds of sale. Similarly in *Turton* v *Turton* [1987] 2 All ER 641 the Court of Appeal applied *Goodman* and held that where there was an express declaration of trust regarding an unmarried couple's beneficial interests in property that declaration was conclusive.

In the absence of such a declaration the courts will look to see whether or not an implied resulting or constructive trust has been established. In *Burns*, Fox LJ said:

> If . . . the plaintiff is to establish that she has a beneficial interest in the property she must establish that the defendant holds the legal estate on trust to give effect to that interest. That follows from *Gissing*. For present purposes I think that such a trust could only arise (a) by express declaration or agreement *or* (b) by way of a resulting trust where the claimant has directly provided part of the purchase price *or* (c) from the common intention of the parties.

On the last point the court confirmed that in determining whether a common intention exists it is normally the practice to look at the intention when the property was purchased. Similarly in *Grant* v *Edwards* [1986] 2 All ER 426 the Court of Appeal confirmed that a constructive trust would be established if there was evidence that it would be inequitable for the legal owner to claim sole beneficial ownership. This could be demonstrated by showing a common intention that they both should have a beneficial interest. In turn this could be proved by direct evidence or inferred from their actions, including indirect contributions to the purchase such as mortgage payments, housekeeping expenses, and crucially that the claimant had acted to her detriment on the basis of that common intention. (See Sir Nicolas Browne-Wilkinson at p. 437.)

These comments by Fox LJ and Sir Nicholas Browne-Wilkinson would appear to represent statements of principle and by adopting the method so far used you are able to pose the correct questions, seek relevant authorities and then accumulate statements of principle which can readily be applied to a problem in the examination concerning the property interests of cohabitees. I have stressed elsewhere that facts of cases are of limited value to the student. However, this is probably one area where it is useful to note briefly the facts of the important cases in order to establish whether the relevant common intention was present. You may decide to do it in the following fashion:

Cooke v *Head* [1972] 2 All ER 38
Acquired land. Intended to build bungalow. Eventually hoped to marry. Conveyance in his name. No cash contribution made by Miss C. Did a lot of heavy work – mixed cement, wielded sledge-hammer, helped in construction work. Separated when bungalow nearly finished. *Held:* Contributions sufficient to give her one-third interest in proceeds of sale. Seemingly an application of Lord Denning's idea of a constructive trust – e.g., to be applied whenever justice and good conscience require it.

Eves v *Eves* [1975] 3 All ER 768
Again a contribution by way of work done on property. Stripped wallpaper, painted woodwork, used 14 lb sledge-hammer, prepared front garden for turfing, did work in back garden, helped demolish a shed. *Held:* one-quarter of equity for the plaintiff. Case important for different approaches by judges. Lord Denning MR – constructive trust – in all fairness. Browne and Brightman LJJ – resulting trust applying accepted principles.

You can continue in this way until you reach the most recent decisions.

Bernard v *Josephs* [1982] 3 All ER 162
Couple engaged. Purchased property for joint occupation. Whole purchase price borrowed on mortgage. Each made an initial contribution to the expenses

'I thought being a cohabitee meant I didn't have to accept the obligations of marriage'

of purchase. Assumed joint liability for mortgage. As they had pooled their incomes, then equal shares in the house. Lord Denning and Kerr LJ thought regard could be had to post separation events; Griffiths LJ preferred to emphasise the intention of the parties at the time of the purchase by reference to their respective contributions then and subsequently.

Walker v *Hall* [1984] FLR 126
Began living together in man's house. Later sold and new premises purchased in joint names. £1,000 bank loan for which they were equally liable. Man remained in property after 'mistress' left and continued to repay loan. *Held:* Matter rightly decided by reference only to the financial contributions of the parties. No wide discretion given to the court. The relevant law was the 'general law of trusts'.

Burns v *Burns* [1984] 1 All ER 244
Parties lived together for 19 years as man and wife. Woman's contribution was to buy consumer durables for the house (which she took with her when she left), did some decorating – also brought up couple's two children. *Held:* Court had *no* jurisdiction to make an order on the basis of the fair and reasonable division of property. To obtain a beneficial interest there would have to be evidence of a common intention which depended upon a substantial financial contribution which could be related to the acquisition of the property. The court would not impute a common intention just because they had lived together for 19 years, had looked after the family's well-being, or from the fact that she had bought chattels for the house out of her earnings.

Young v *Young* [1984] FLR 375
Plaintiff had contributed £4,000 towards purchase of property, the defendant less than £200. The respective interests of the parties had to be determined by the application of the law relating to trusts. In the circumstances defendant not entitled to any share in the beneficial interest in the property. (*Bernard* v *Josephs* [1982] 3 All ER 162 followed.)

Grant v *Edwards* [1986] 2 All ER
Defendant told Plaintiff her name could not go on title deeds. Once joint intention proved, then it could be inferred that any act done to her detriment which, of course, related to their association together was done in the belief that she could take an interest in the house. Brown-Wilkinson VC said contributions made by claimant may be relevant for four purposes:

(a) Evidence from which parties' intentions could be inferred.
(b) Corroboration of direct evidence of intention.
(c) To show claimant had acted to her detriment in reliance on the common intention.
(d) Quantify extent of the beneficial interest.

Turton v *Turton* [1987] 2 All ER 641
Unmarried couple. Conveyance contained joint declaration of trust that property held on trust for sale as beneficial joint tenants. Couple separated in 1975. Order for sale only dealt with in 1986. Judge directed that relevant date for valuing

shares was date they ceased to live together, i.e., 1975. Appellant appealed, contending date of sale should be date for valuation. *Held:* As there was an express declaration of trust the shares fell to be valued on the date they were realised. Note that *Hall* v *Hall* [1982] 3 FLR 379 was disapproved on this point.

Revision note

As a result of the foregoing you should now clearly understand that the court does not possess the power to reach a fair and just settlement for cohabitees unless there is some evidence of a constructive trust as in *Grant* v *Edwards*. When purchasing property cohabitees ought to have the matter of beneficial interests drawn to their attention by solicitors. It was suggested in *Walker* v *Hall* that solicitors acting for joint purchasers should take steps to find out and declare what the beneficial interests were to be. The courts might, it was said, soon have to consider whether a solicitor acting for joint purchasers was not guilty of negligence if he failed to do so.

It is undoubtedly true that the Court of Appeal under the guidance of Lord Denning MR had striven hard through the use of the trust to achieve an equitable solution. In *Hall* v *Hall* (1982) 3 FLR 379, Lord Denning said:

if a man and a woman have been living together as husband and wife, and the woman has been contributing towards the establishment of a joint household, although the house is in the man's name, there is a resulting trust as a *matter of ordinary common justice for her.*

And later when discussing the appropriate share he said:

It depends on the circumstances and how much she has contributed – not merely in money – but also in keeping up the house and, if there are children, in looking after them.

The result of the decisions in *Burns* and *Grant* v *Edwards* is surely that this approach has been firmly rejected and the onus put upon Parliament to achieve 'ordinary justice' rather than leave it to the courts to strive to develop ground rules to remedy any unfairness inherent in the law of trusts. For students, this particular area of law should appear regularly on examination papers whether in trusts or family law. It is a fairly discrete topic which has case law in abundance and as such one must treat it with caution. As suggested your approach ought to be one of ascertaining principles from the case law whilst at the same time recognising that the courts have endeavoured whenever possible to do justice to the parties. If further evidence of this latter point is required then one need look no further than Lord Denning's invocation of the concept of the contractual licence in the case of *Tanner* v *Tanner* [1975] 1 WLR 1346 although the deve-

lopment of such an idea in the context of cohabitees was shown in *Horrocks* v
Foray [1976] 1 WLR 230 to have severe limitations. Based as it is upon proof of
a contract then all the necessary legal incidents of contract will have to be
proved — consideration, consensus, intention to create legal relations. In the
atmosphere of an intimate relationship that may not be an easy thing to do. This
has recently been shown in *Coombes* v *Smith* [1986] 1 WLR 808. The defendant
bought a house with the intention that they should live together. When the
plaintiff became pregnant she moved in. They never lived together. Subsequently
he bought a second house and she moved in there with the child. He offered her
£10,000 to vacate the house. She claimed she had a contractual licence to occupy
for life in consideration of her moving to the defendant's property. The contractual licence claim failed, as the evidence didn't justify the conclusion that a
contract entitling her to be accommodated for the rest of her life had come into
existence. The courts also appeared ready and willing to achieve justice in
Pascoe v *Turner* [1979] 2 All ER 945 through the use of proprietary estoppel.
There was nothing in the facts from which to infer a constructive trust, and at
best all she could show was a licence revocable at will. Yet the court had to
decide what 'was the minimum equity to do justice to her, having regard to the
way in which she had changed her position for the worse with the acquiescence
and encouragement of the plaintiff'. In the end the house was transferred into
her name! Cited in *Greasley* v *Cooke* [1980] 3 All ER 710, *Pascoe* v *Turner* and
the principles of proprietary estoppel found favour in the Court of Appeal in
Grant v *Edwards* (see Browne-Wilkinson VC at p. 439a and b).

Before we go on to consider the *application* of the legal principles I will
briefly examine two other areas from which questions are often drawn, namely
the reasonable provision from a deceased cohabitee's estate and rights to succeed
to a protected tenancy. As with beneficial interests both areas have attracted
judicial attention but the difference here is that statutory rights have been
bestowed on cohabitees and it is a matter of interpratation rather than seeking
to lay down ground rules which involved the attention of the judiciary.

Inheritance

The Law Commission Report No. 61, Family Provision on Death (1974) ought
to be your starting-point as it outlines the deficiencies in application of the
Inheritance (Family Provision) Act 1938. The Inheritance (Provision for Family
and Dependants) Act 1975 introduced a new category of applicant — any
person who immediately before the death of the deceased was being maintained,
either wholly or in part, by the deceased. There can be no doubt that Parliament
intended to allow cohabitees to claim reasonable financial provision and with
typical press over-reaction this clause was dubbed a 'mistresses' charter' when
the original Bill was published.

As I suggested with the Domestic Violence and Matrimonial Proceedings Act 1976, it is an aid to understanding the subsequent interpretation of the legislation if you have some appreciation of why such a provision was inserted into the Inheritance (Provision for Family and Dependants) Act 1975.

Once you have done this make a note of the relevant wording so you will be aware of which words are likely to give rise to difficulties in interpretation. Some help can be gained from reading the short judgment of Ormrod LJ in *Harrington* v *Gill* (1983) 4 FLR 265 at p. 272. In it he warns of the Act which 'was designed to deal with a comparatively simple situation . . . [being] . . . in danger of becoming a mass of technicalities. In my judgment this is very unfortunate and undesirable.'

He goes on to give his opinion of the purpose behind the relevant sections:

Section 1 defines the conditions which the applicant must fulfil to qualify for relief under the Act. One condition is that the testamentary disposition or the law relating to intestacy 'is not such as to make reasonable financial provision for the applicant'.

Section 2 gives the court power to make various orders if the conditions of s. 1 are satisfied. The *object* of the orders is clearly to remedy the deficiency which arises from a will or from the law of intestacy.

Section 3. To make reasonable provision for the applicant in the light of the express provisions in s. 3.

Conclusion. That it ought to be possible to arrive at a conclusion without getting involved in a mass of legal technicalities and complicated questions of construction of the various other provisions of the Act.

You will now be in a position to examine the relevant case law in order to ascertain the points of difficulty which have arisen in practice. You may decide to list the cases with brief notes as to their importance, as shown above when dealing with beneficial interests. For example:

Layton v *Martin and Others* [1986] 2 FLR 227. This is an interesting case which deals not only with the 1975 Act but attempts by a former mistress to establish a claim to the deceased's property in equity. On the former matter she failed because the relationship ended two years before her former cohabitee's death. The court acknowledged that if she had continued to live with him until his death she would have been entitled to claim under the Inheritance (Provision for Family and Dependants) Act 1975. On the latter point she failed because there was no evidence of a common intention that the claimant should have a beneficial interest in specific assets. Sadly Scott J concluded that it was a matter of regret that the case had been brought because it was 'hopeless from the start'.

Stead v *Stead* [1985] FLR 16. Case dealing with married couple. But extensive referencing to *Harrington* v *Gill* (1983) 4 FLR 265. Mistresses only entitled to maintenance rather than capital distribution. Sir John Arnold P at first instance referring to *Harrington* v *Gill* said that the fact she was a mistress did not seem to have any particular impact on the amount of the award.

Re Cairnes (deceased) (1983) 4 FLR 225. Deceased's pension scheme required that he nominate a beneficiary — he nominated wife. Later divorced and he lived with plaintiff. *Held:* Death benefit could not be construed as part of net estate. See s. 25(1)(a) of the 1975 Act. He had no power to dispose of funds — only trustees. No important statement of principle on mistresses.

Kourkgy v *Lusher* (1983) 4 FLR 65. Intermittent relationship. Deceased left wife and went to live with plaintiff in 1969. Contributed to maintenance. Plaintiff divorced but deceased would not divorce wife. He maintained contact with wife, paid wages and maintenance and all outgoings on matrimonial home. 1972-9 relationship with plaintiff deteriorated and immediately prior to his death he had committed himself to return to his wife. Deceased had been reluctant to continue financial responsibility for plaintiff. *Held:* Not entitled to provision. Failed to satisfy court that it was unreasonable that she had received no financial provision. Case useful as a detailed analysis of provisions including statement that the Law Commission Report No. 61 could be examined to find the 'mischief' behind the legislation. Important also for reaffirmation, if such be needed, of the statement in *Re Beaumont* [1980] Ch 444 to the effect that what is necessary is evidence of an assumption by the deceased of responsibility for the maintenance of the applicant. The degree of maintenance being whatever 'normally and habitually existed under the assumption of responsibility which was then in existence'. This passage was approved by the Court of Appeal in *Jelley* v *Iliffe* [1981] Fam 128.

Jelley v *Iliffe* [1981] Fam 128; [1981] 2 All ER 29. Elderly couple. Companionship relationship. No provision made in deceased's will for applicant. He claimed that immediately before her death she was maintaining him. *Held:* Concept of maintenance in the 1975 Act similar to concept of matrimonial maintenance, i.e., financial provision for spouse and provision of accommodation. In practice this meant that the deceased had to be making 'a substantial contribution in money or money's worth towards the applicant's reasonable needs immediately before his death'. This would be determined by taking a 'broad common-sense view of the relationship between the parties and had to strike a balance between the benefits received by the applicant from the deceased against those provided by the applicant to the deceased'. If the applicant's contribution was equal to or greater than the deceased there was no dependence. The benefit of rent-free accommodation was a substantial contribution to reasonable needs.

Conclusion

There are other cases which should receive similar treatment including *Harrington* v *Gill* (1983) 4 FLR 265; *Malone* v *Harrison* [1979] 1 WLR 1353 and *Re Coventry (deceased)* [1980] Ch 461. The object of cataloguing cases is to extract points from the judgments which will help you to gain a complete picture of how the legislation has been interpreted and applied. They highlight the arguments put forward by plaintiff and defendant which may prove valuable when you seek to interpret the facts of a problem in the examination. What you must always remember is that you are seeking to extract basic principles from the cases backed up by authority. To take a couple of key sentences from the judgment is far more valuable than laboriously copying out masses of factual detail which unfortunately many students tend to do. On many occasions I have seen half a page in a candidate's script devoted to the facts of one case and once the decision has been quoted he has patently nothing of any legal significance to add. How much time must have been spent on learning these irrelevancies is anyone's guess but it certainly does not help in achieving a decent pass mark.

Statutory tenancies

The Rent Act 1977 provides that if a statutory tenant dies then in the absence of a surviving spouse a member of his family residing with him at the time of death and for six months prior to his death may become a statutory tenant by succession. In the 1975 Inheritance (Provision for Family and Dependants) Act the key words were 'wholly or partly' maintained by the deceased. For the purposes of the Rent Act 1977 it is vital to establish that the applicant was a member of the tenant's 'family'. The important case for you to examine here is *Dyson Holdings Ltd* v *Fox* [1975] 3 All ER 1030, where the Court of Appeal were much taken by the so-called 'popular concept of family unit', even though there was earlier authority in *Gammons* v *Ekins* [1950] 2 All ER 140 to the effect that cohabitees for 20 years did not in the absence of chidren constitute a family. I said earlier when discussing the concept of 'child of the family' that the Court of Appeal in *M* v *M* (1981) 2 FLR 39 found that the word 'family' was a 'popular, loose and flexible expression, not a technical term' and that husband and wife could even in the absence of children constitute a family. Similarly in *Dyson* it was held that 'family' should not be construed in a technical or legal sense 'but in the sense that would be attributed to it by the ordinary man in the street at the time relevant to the decision of the particular case'. Note also that James LJ emphasised that not every mistress should be regarded as a member of the man's family. Relationships of a casual or intermittent character and 'those bearing indications of impermanence' would not fall within the meaning of family.

Having noted the last point you ought then to seek out an example. So in *Helby* v *Rafferty* [1978] 3 All ER 1016 the Court of Appeal discussed the degree of permanence and stability needed to justify the view that a person was a member of a single family unit. The statutory tenant, Miss T, had cherished her independence and according to the Court of Appeal had not 'adopted the character of a wife'. As a result the defendant had not become a member of her family, even though they had lived together for five years and he had nursed her and assumed great responsibility for her as her health had deteriorated. If you read the judgment of Stamp LJ at p. 1018 you will discover that he doubts the construction put on the word 'family' by the majority in *Dyson*. However, he is content to 'loyally follow the decision'.

Whether or not seven years on this view of 'family' is likely to change must be in doubt but note Cretney's comment in *Principles of Family Law*, 4th ed., at p. 684:

> In practice it remains difficult to predict the outcome of cases, and the authority of the decision which favours a more liberal approach to the problem is regrettably not unquestioned.

Revision note

I have considered some of the more discrete areas of the law relating to cohabitees. My intention has been to urge you to look both generally at mistresses' or cohabitees' rights and to ponder what reforms may be needed while at the same time examining the present law in some detail. All that now remains is to consider the application of some of the principles mentioned above.

Sample questions

This question is fairly typical of the type of problem which deals with cohabitee rights:

> Eve has been Adam's mistress for the past five years, and they have a daughter, Amy, who is four years old. Ever since they have been together they have possessed a joint bank account, but Eve has not earned any money during this time, since she has busied herself caring for the home and her family. As a result she never paid anything into the account. The balance today is £900.
>
> Last year they decided to buy a home for themselves to live in. The house today is valued at £25,000; the amount outstanding on the mortgage is £10,000. The legal title was conveyed into Adam's name. The house is in an extremely dilapidated condition and Eve spent a great deal of time replastering and redecorating it; she also put up a garden shed.

Unfortunately, the situation has now changed suddenly because last week Adam collapsed and died. In his will, Adam, a lifelong animal lover, left all his property to the RSPCA.

Advise Eve as to any property rights she may have, and as to any claim she may make against Adam's estate.

As before, each point will be taken in turn.

Suggested approach

(a)   You are told in the first line that Eve is Adam's 'mistress' which raises the matter of terminology. Are we meant to infer that she purely provides sexual services and companionship as and when Adam requires it or is she more a 'cohabitee'? In fact the first paragraph is ambiguous because it tells you that Eve has busied herself caring for *the* home and *her* family, but then we are told they decide to buy a home. Therefore the following possibilities arise:

(i)   They live together in rented accommodation and the family is constituted by Adam, Eve and Amy; or

(ii)   She already has a home and family completely independent from Adam and she has spent time looking after it and her family, implying that she has a husband and other children.

The fact that you are told that they have 'been together' would tend to lead one to the former rather than the latter conclusion. Reference could be made to the case of *Richards* v *Dove* [1974] 1 All ER 888 where cohabitees moved from rented accommodation to private property but did not change their various responsibilities towards household and other expenses.

(b)   You ought to note the fact that they would appear to constitute a 'family' and that throughout this period of living together Eve has been dependent upon Adam for everything. This point will become more relevant later when we discuss her rights under the 1975 Inheritance (Provision for Family and Dependants) Act.

(c)   What are we meant, if anything, to conclude from the information that they had a joint bank account? When dealing with beneficial interests we are looking for common intentions but this evidence may only indicate practical convenience, not a desire that she should share in property. In all probability it is in the question so that you may discuss whether or not she is entitled to any of the money currently residing in the account. (See Cretney, *Principles of Family Law*, 4th ed., pp. 659-60 and Bromley, 7th ed., pp. 508-10 for a discussion on entitlement to monies in joint bank accounts. The query, of course, is whether principles applicable to married couples will apply equally to cohabitees – see Parry, *Cohabitation*, pp. 38-40.)

(d)   The second paragraph tells you that they decide to buy a house for *themselves* to live in. What they are going to do with Amy remains a mystery. Is the examiner trying to tell us that the *prime object* of the purchase is *not* to provide a home for the family although in practice that is bound to be inevitable? Also the fact that the house is conveyed into Adam's name hardly seems consistent with the view that they were acting for themselves, with a common intention that both should benefit from the property.

(e)   It is suggested that the student's response ought to centre on the conveyance. At least here is a written document which gives some indication of the parties' original intention. We are not told whether the conveyance seeks to apportion the beneficial interest in the property so let us assume that it doesn't. This will lead you neatly into a discussion of the type of contributions that equity demands of the mistress and obviously as she has not made a financial contribution you would have to discuss the line of cases on indirect contributions from *Pettit* v *Pettit* [1970] AC 777 to *Grant* v *Edwards* [1986] 2 All ER 426. In answer to the question about property rights it is unlikely that you will have much good news for Eve given the line taken in *Burns* v *Burns* and *Grant* v *Edwards* although given the presence of Amy you could seek to tap the *Re Evers's Trust* line of cases and argue that she should be allowed to remain in the property. The difficulty here is that in *Re Evers's Trust* [1980] 3 All ER 399 the co-habitees were joint tenants and the Court of Appeal saw it as a 'family' case neither of which would appear to be the case with our friends Eve and Adam.

(f)   Given that her property rights are tenuous in the extreme, is she likely to fare any better under the Inheritance (Provision for Family and Dependants) Act 1975? The first point to consider is whether or not the court has jurisdiction. It has to be shown that Eve was being maintained either wholly or partly by the deceased, and that is achieved by establishing that the deceased was making a substantial contribution in money or money's worth towards the reasonable needs of that person. Thus the greater the dependence the greater the likelihood of success. On the facts of this case it would appear that she was totally dependent upon Adam and therefore ought to succeed. It would be valuable if you make reference to s. 3 of the 1975 Act and indicate which of the factors the court would find useful in evaluating the amount of financial provision. One irony is that if Eve had been making a claim as a spouse or former spouse then because of s. 3(2)(b) the court would have to consider the contribution Eve made to the welfare of the family of the deceased (Amy), including any contribution made by looking after the home or caring for the family. Unfortunately the court is under no duty to have regard to these factors in the case of cohabitees.

(g)   One final thought. If at the time of death the parties were still cohabiting in rented property because you are not told that they have actually moved into the new house and (although we are not told) if that property was one to which the Rent Act applied, thus making Adam a statutory tenant, then Eve may be able to succeed to the tenancy. A lot of assumptions need to be made as the evidence in the question is virtually non-existent. It is worth mentioning but not something upon which you should spend a lot of time.

Having given an outline of an answer to the above question perhaps you could use the following question to test your own analytical ability. It appeared on a 1988 final degree paper.

Michelle and Phillip met when students at University. They moved into rented accommodation but after a short time decided that it would be financially expedient to buy a house. This was done and the property conveyed into Phillip's name. Michelle helped redecorate the house but did not help financially towards the purchase. Michelle stayed on at University to study for a PhD while Phillip gained well paid employment. He met all the outgoings relating to the property, although Michelle bought the food and occasionally items of a domestic nature.

After gaining her PhD they decided to start a family and for the past five years Michelle has stayed at home looking after the children. Phillip has often suggested that Michelle should have a half share of the property but nothing has been done to give effect to this suggestion. Recently Michelle has been showing signs of anxiety and clinical depression and Phillip has taken a greater role in looking after the children, twin girls aged 5. Phillip has met and fallen in love with Hannah and has decided to sell the house and move in with her. Being concerned for the welfare of the children he wishes to take them with him. Hannah has one child of her own, a boy aged 8. Michelle would prefer to stay in the house.

(a) Advise Michelle as to whether she has any interest in the property or proceeds of sale and whether she will be able to remain.

(b) Advise Phillip on whether or not he can obtain custody of the children.

(c) How, if at all, would your advice differ if Michelle were married to Phillip?

Conclusion

A subject which is likely to remain 'current'. As such, information by way of articles and new cases should be much in evidence. While there are other aspects of cohabitee rights that I have not considered in this chapter it is arguable that what is here represents the 'topical' material and the approach to study adopted is likely to remain valid for other matters. Remember to look at chapters 4 and 10 which deal with the position under the new law of children born out of wedlock and new parental rights, especially for the father.

Further reading

Hoggett and Pearl, 2nd ed., chapter 8.
Freeman and Lyon, *Cohabitation without Marriage*.

NINE

CHILDREN I: WELFARE OF THE CHILD

Introduction

The final part of the divorce equation relates to children. How will a court settle a custody dispute, what principles will guide it in its attempt to reach a fair solution to a problem which affects over 150,000 children under the age of 16 each year? I have already intimated elsewhere in this book that the welfare of the child is the paramount consideration in trying to settle the issue. Yet the welfare of the child is relevant to other areas of child law although as will be seen, it does not always assume the overwhelming importance that it has in custody and access cases. It thus forms a useful thread for an examination of wardship, adoption and parts of the law relating to the duties of local authorities, although more will be said about the general duties and responsibilities of those bodies in chapter 10.

Child law is assuming a greater importance within the context of family law teaching than it did in the past. To my knowledge at least one institution has decided to create two syllabuses out of its existing family law course. Thus one syllabus deals with matrimonial law and the other with aspects of the law relating to children. Neither is there any shortage of materials to support such a course, one of the latest being the third edition of Hoggett's book, *Parents and Children: The Law of Parental Responsibility* (Sweet and Maxwell, 1987). However, the definitive text is *The Law Relating to Children* by Professor Hugh Bevan, and students should look out for a new edition in the near future (published by Butterworths). In addition there are other books which deal with specific areas of the law. Susan Maidment's *Child Custody and Divorce* is a comprehensive and informative study of the problems facing divorcing parents and how the legal system responds to their needs and expectations. Professor Michael Freeman's *The Rights and the Wrongs of Children* also demands attention especially as it considers the responsibilities of the state towards children through the workings of local authority social services and legal departments. Bevan and Parry's *The Children Act 1975*, published in 1979, contains a thorough review of the law on adoption although with the passage of time and the normal output of the Court of Appeal certain parts of the text are in need of revision, though this does not detract from the overall worth of the book.

Any consideration of the allocation of custody of children must of necessity take into account the psychology of children and their likely reaction to the trauma of their parents' divorce. As perhaps may be expected there is far more American than British literature available. You would be well advised to refer to:

(a)   Goldstein, Freud and Solnit's two books entitled *Before the Best Interests of the Child* and *Beyond the Best Interests of the Child*, and

(b)   Wallerstein and Kelly's highly acclaimed book *Surviving the Breakup*.

You may find it interesting to read Richards' article *'Behind the Best Interests of the Child: An Examination of the Arguments of Goldstein, Freud and Solnit Concerning Custody and Access at Divorce'* [1986] JSWL 77.

Add to all this numerous articles in *Family Law* and other related journals and one gathers that an extensive amount of literature is available to you. As a result you will need to seek the guidance of your tutor as to precisely what you should be reading and *why*. It is not a matter, for example, of reading the whole of Wallerstein and Kelly. As with reading judgments you need to be highly selective. Thus you could in your work and revision, list key points under the authors. For example:

Wallerstein and Kelly
Inter alia make the following important points:

(a)   Critical of conditions and restrictions imposed by the courts which 'encumber a relationship which under the best of circumstances is fragile and needs encouragement' (p. 123).

(b)   That what was seen by a court as 'reasonable' access was perceived by the youngsters in the study as inadequate. Five months after separation two-thirds were seeing their fathers at least twice a month – yet this was a severe cause for complaint about 'insufficiency of parental visits' (p. 134).

(c)   Some women attempted to use 'the child's symptomatic behaviour as proof that the visits were detrimental to the child's welfare and should therefore be discontinued' (p. 126).

(d)   'The best interest of the child' has more often been a matter of the perceived best interests of each parent, as negotiated by his or her attorney (p. 133).

(e)   A parent's divorce does not necessarily diminish the importance of the psychological link between non-custodial parent and child, and therefore both parents are necessary for the child's future psychological development (p. 308).

(f)   'The adversary nature of the proceedings by definition implies that each client, through his attorney, anticipates being a winner, not a loser, "winning" has encompassed not just property settlement, but the issue of who shall own the children' (p. 133).

(g) Joint custody orders are likely to encourage greater and more successful access and this in turn may influence the financial responsibility of the non-custodial parent (p. 310).

The above represents an example of how to deal with information contained in an extended study and is not meant to reflect all the findings contained in *Surviving the Breakup*.

In order to simplify the approach it will be preferable to take each topic in turn beginning with custody and access.

Recent developments

The amount of attention focused on marriage breakup during the 1980s is destined to lead to substantial changes in the law relating to children. The Law Commission has taken the opportunity to mount a major review of child law, culminating in a series of working papers between 1985-87. The first full Law Commission Report based upon these papers was published in July 1988 (Law Com. No. 172, *Review of Child Law – Guardianship and Custody*, HMSO £8.90).

However, whatever changes may be imminent, your task is to deal with the law as it stands and you must become thoroughly conversant with the principles and cases. But it is likely that your examiner will wish to question you on probable developments in the law and so there is much to be gained from spending some time on both the working papers and the Report mentioned above.

Custody of and access to children

In preparing for a study of custody and access you ought to become familiar with two things – procedures and terminology. Custody may be sought in the following ways:

(a) In matrimonial proceedings – most often, of course, in divorce under the Matrimonial Causes Act 1973.

(b) In wardship proceedings, the application for which is now covered by s. 41 of the Supreme Court Act 1981. (If successful legal custody will rest in the court.)

(c) Under s. 9 of the Guardianship of Minors Act 1971 of which s. 1 embodies the 'welfare principle' (includes an application for access). The original Guardianship of Minors Act 1971 has been amended on many occasions and most recently by the Family Law Reform Act 1987. The full text of the Act is listed at Schedule 1 in the 1987 Act. It is now clear that, irrespective of whether the child was born in or out of wedlock, any dispute about custody is to be settled by reference to the 'welfare principle', i.e., his welfare is the first and paramount consideration (s. 1). Section 9 of the Guardianship of Minors Act had directed the court to have 'regard to the welfare of the minor and to the conduct and wishes of the mother and father'. However, these words have now disappeared and the s. 1 principle will clearly apply in all cases.

(d)   As was mentioned in chapter 4 in an application under the Domestic Proceedings and Magistrates' Courts Act 1978.

Terminology

Examine here ss. 86 and 87 of the Children Act 1975 which introduced the concepts of 'legal' and 'actual' custody always bearing in mind that the sections are seeking to define parental rights (see s. 85). However, do remember that these definitions are contained in the Children Act and do not specifically apply to the divorce court where, as yet, no statutory definition exists.

Having established in your mind the various procedures upon which you may have to advise and being aware of the terminology we can proceed to consider the principles and general factors taken into account by a court. However there is one point which deserves emphasis and that is the role of the Court of Appeal in cases dealing with the welfare of children. Two conflicting approaches had been recognised. In *D* v *M* [1983] Fam 33 it was held that there was no statutory restriction on the power of the appellate court, nor were they subject to limitations because the court below was exercising discretionary powers. Therefore the appellate court had a duty to review the way the court below had conducted what was referred to as the 'balancing exercise'. Thus one had the impression that a very positive role was being advocated for the Court of Appeal in such cases.

The opposite view was endorsed in *Clarke-Hunt* v *Newcombe* (1983) 4 FLR 482 where Cumming-Bruce LJ put the question for the Court of Appeal in these terms: 'Had it been shown that the judge's decision had been plainly wrong?'

It appeared therefore that the chief purpose of the case was to show the limited role of the Court of Appeal in custody appeals. The difficulty for practitioners was therefore obvious and it needed a case to go to the House of Lords to resolve the matter. In *G* v *G* [1985] 2 All ER 225 the House approved the question posed by Cumming-Bruce LJ. The Court should only interfere when:

(a)   It considered that the judge at first instance had exceeded the generous ambit within which judicial disagreement was reasonably possible, and

(b)   Was plainly wrong, and

(c)   Not merely because the Court of Appeal preferred a solution which the judge had not chosen. The following cases must be examined, as statements from them were applied by the House: *Bellenden* v *Satterthwaite* [1948] 1 All ER 343 (dicta of Asquith LJ at p. 345); *Re F* [1976] 1 All ER 417 (dicta of Brown and Bridge LJJ at pp. 432, 439-40); *B* v *W* [1979] 3 All ER 83 (dicta of Lord Scarman at p. 96).

After this decision by the House of Lords one would have thought that the subject would have been laid to rest. However, nothing could have been further from the truth. *May* v *May* [1986] 1 FLR 325 is a good example of how difficult it will be to meet the *G* v *G* criteria and *Re W* (a minor) [1987] 137 NLJ 16 by contrast can be cited to show the sort of circumstances where the Court of Appeal would be inclined to say the judge was plainly wrong.

Three cases have particular significance. *M* v *M* [1988] 1 FLR 225 should be used in order to establish the point that the judge at first instance *must* make findings of fact. He had given custody, care and control of four children to their mother and had made an ouster order against the father. The parents' evidence had conflicted over several issues but, nevertheless, the judge had failed to make findings of fact on all of the important areas of conflict. The Court of Appeal allowing the appeal said it was not sufficient for him to rely merely on the overall impression he had formed. The importance of so doing is that it would help the Court of Appeal to determine whether the conclusion was correct. There have to be findings of fact in order to know if the initial decision was plainly wrong.

The second case is *A* v *A* [1987] 137 NLJ 768 where the Court of Appeal was prepared to accept fresh evidence to prove that supervening events had cast doubt on the basic premises upon which the judge had decided the case. No doubt it was a course of action considered to be in keeping with the 'welfare principle' as the custodial parent was shown to have behaved in a violent and uncontrolled manner towards social workers and had used foul language.

Finally reference should be made to the decision in *R* v *R* [1987] 137 NLJ 688 and, in particular, the very telling words of May LJ which may represent the last word on the subject:

> This is yet another appeal against the exercise by an experienced judge of his discretion in respect of children which, with respect to counsel, I think was well-nigh unarguable. . . . The principles of law applicable are quite clear and were recently re-emphasised in *G* v *G* [1985] 2 All ER 225. . . . In circumstances such as obtained in the instant case it is essential that the parties' advisers should consider the position in law and on the facts very carefully before advising that an appeal is arguable.

This particular topic would seem to possess many of the hallmarks which would make it attractive to examiners. It is a discrete topic, there is a relatively large amount of case law and it is easy to integrate it into a problem question. Part of your advice to a client would be on the feasibility of an appeal in a custody case.

Principles

At the risk of labouring the point there is in reality only one principle to apply, that contained in s. 1 of the Guardianship of Minors Act 1971. Note that the section refers to *any* proceedings before *any* court and therefore the 'welfare' principle is equally applicable to wardship proceedings as it is to actions under the Guardianship of Minors Act. The point to remember is that referred to in *Richards* v *Richards* [1984] AC 174 to the effect that the principle enunciated in s. 1 of the 1971 Act applied only to proceedings in which custody, upbringing or the proprietary jurisdiction implied by s. 1(b) fell to be decided as a matter *directly* in issue. In consequence s. 1 of the 1971 Act had no application to ouster injunctions, where those matters arose only incidentally.

The section 1 test is therefore that the child's welfare is the 'first and paramount consideration'.

Your first task as a student is to seek to give some meaning to these words. The Act is of no assistance and therefore you must look for judicial authority. This is to be found in the case of *J* v *C* [1970] AC 668 which is probably the most important case dealing with this area of law. Look at it first and foremost in order to obtain information to quote in an examination in order to show the examiner that you understand how the words 'first and paramount' are meant to apply in practice. The words most often quoted are from Lord MacDermott's speech which have been seen as illustrating the *'first view'* approach. Thus (at pp. 710-11):

it seems to me that they must mean more than that the child's welfare is to be treated as the top item in a list of items relevant to the matter in question. I think they connote a process whereby, when all the relevant facts, relationships, claims and wishes of parents, risks, choices and other circumstances are taken into account and weighed, the course to be followed will be that which is most in the interests of the child's welfare. . . . That is the first consideration because it is of first importance and the paramount consideration because it rules upon or determines the course to be followed.

The first serious attempt to challenge the validity of this principle is to be found in *Re KD (a minor)* [1988] 1 All ER 577 (HL). This was a wardship case concerning parental access to the ward. The House held that the first and paramount consideration is the welfare of the child and the parent's right or claim to access is subservient to the child's welfare. *J* v *C* was applied, as was Lord Scarman's dictum in *Re E (SA)(a minor) (wardship)* [1984] 1 All ER 289 at p. 290 (h). Counsel had argued that there was a legal right to access (s. 5 of the Guardianship of Infants Act 1886 and in some English authorities) and that right was recognised by the European Court of Human Rights as a fundamental element of family life protected by a convention to which the United Kingdom was a party.

In light of this the House was asked to reconsider the approach to such cases as emerges from Lord Macdermott's speech in *J* v *C*. In finding no conflict between parental 'rights' to access and the welfare approach, Lord Oliver said:

> . . . an examination of Lord Macdermott's reasoning in *J* v *C* discloses that it was in fact based on a recognition of the natural, or 'basic', right of parents over their children.

Lord Macdermott had quoted from Fitzgibbon LJ in *Re O'Hara* [1900] 2 IR 232 who stated:

> In exercising the jurisdiction to control or to ignore the parental right the court must act cautiously, not as if it were a private person acting with regard to his own child, and acting in opposition to the parent only when judicially satisfied that the welfare of the child requires that the parental right should be suspended or superseded.

So there is support at the highest level for the continued application of the welfare principle. The fact this was in wardship proceedings does not diminish its authority in the custody context. In addition to *Re O'Hara* you may find it worthwhile to dip into *Ward* v *Laverty* [1925] AC 101 where Viscount Care LC was of the opinion that:

> It is the welfare of the children, which, according to rules which are now well accepted, forms the paramount consideration in these cases.

Now *Ward* v *Laverty* was decided prior to the passing of the Guardianship of Infants Act. In a more recent case, *A* v *Liverpool City Council* [1981] 2 All ER 385, Lord Wilberforce, in giving a 'potted' history of the welfare principle, said (at p. 387):

> the word 'paramount' [was] clearly taken from the opinion of Viscount Cave LC in *Ward* v *Laverty* [1925] AC 101 at p. 108 . . . [and] so clearly not intended as a new or even talismanic word. The speeches in *J* v *C* provide authoritative guidance which I should not wish to repeat or to gloss.

The benefit of this wider approach is obvious. First it allows you to assert that the judges ought to be familiar with the relevant principles — as it is hardly a new concept. Secondly it shows the strength of the principle, and of *J* v *C* both of which received endorsement in *A* v *Liverpool City Council* and *Re KD*. Thirdly it will be evidence presented to the examiner of wider reading and research which has been used in order to add to the quality of your answer.

J v *C* can also be cited to the effect that the 'welfare' principle applies as much to disputes over custody and upbringing between parents and strangers as it does between parents, although ironically a third party would not have *locus standi* under the Guardianship of Minors Act.

Possible reforms

Although the House had given its approval to the longstanding welfare principle, the Law Commission has been posing the question of whether paramountcy is the right rule. The Law Commission Working Paper No. 96 which reviewed the law on custody (June 1986) recognised that the present rule gives absolute priority to the welfare of the child. The Commission was concerned in that seeking to give absolute priority to the *particular* child other children may be adversely affected. Paragraph 6.16 of the Report states:

> Nevertheless, whereas a child's interests may be paramount over those of all adults there can be no justification for making the interests of one child paramount over those of any other.

The conclusion was that the welfare of *each* child in the family should continue to be the paramount consideration. This suggestion has now been incorporated into the Law Commission's final report on this matter entitled *Review of Family Law: Guardianship and Custody* (Law Commission No. 172 HC 594, 25 July 1988). At para 3.14 the recommendation on this matter is stated in the following way:

> We recommend, therefore, that in reaching any decision about the child's care, upbringing or maintenance, the welfare of *any* child likely to be affected by the decision should be the court's only concern. Where the decision relates to the administration or application of the child's property, however, the court should only be concerned with the welfare of *that child*.

The draft Children Bill appended to the Report deals with the welfare of the child in clause 1. Clause 1(1) states that a court making an order under the Act must only do so if it is the 'most effective way of safeguarding or promoting the child's welfare'. Sub section (2), adopting the Commission's recommendation, indicates that when determining any question under the Act the welfare of *any* child likely to be affected shall be the court's *only concern*. But when determining any question under this Act or any other in connection with the administration of a child's property or the application of any income arising from such property, the welfare of that child shall be the court's *only* concern. This topic is therefore likely to command the attention of family law teachers in the next couple of years.

Factors

As may be imagined many factors are relevant when seeking to allocate the custody of a child. The standard texts will catalogue these quite adequately with supporting authority and there is no need for me to list them all here. (See Bromley, *Family Law*, 7th ed., pp. 322-33; Cretney, *Principles of Family Law*, 4th ed., pp. 329-37 and S. Poulter, 'Child custody – recent developments' (1982) 12 Fam Law 5, and generally Maidment, *Child Custody and Divorce*.) However, there are certain matters with which the judges tend to experience difficulty in custody disputes and examination questions will in all likelihood concentrate on them. You should therefore pay particular attention in your studies to the following points:

(a)   Continuity of care and control (or the status quo).
(b)   Mother or father?
(c)   Parental conduct.
(d)   Child's wishes.

Continuity of care and control (or the status quo)   When a relationship breaks down arrangements are usually made between parents as to who should look after the children until the divorce proceedings are completed. Maidment in an article for the National Council for One Parent Families (1981) entitled 'Child custody: what chance for fathers?' shows that most court orders simply preserve the arrangements existing at the time of separation leading to divorce. In two studies at Oxford and Keele the findings showed that the residential status quo was maintained in approximately 99% of cases. However, the article revealed that contested custody decisions in the appellate courts only confirmed the status quo in about 63% of the cases.

The reasons for maintaining the status quo are very strong. As Ormrod said in *D* v *M* [1982] 3 WLR 891 at p. 897:

In the first place, it is generally accepted by those who are professionally concerned with children that, particularly in the early years, continuity of care is a most important part of a child's sense of security and that disruption of established bonds is to be avoided whenever it is possible to do so.

A reversal of existing arrangements could be traumatic for a child at a time when he might already be feeling insecure. It could mean an upheaval from not only the existing home but also from school and friends calling for many other new adjustments in the child's life. The notion of continuity is supported by Goldstein, Freud and Solnit: that custody should safeguard the child's need for continuity of relationships. They argue that: 'Continuity of relationships, surroundings, and environmental influence are essential for a child's normal development' (*Beyond the Best Interests of the Child*, pp. 31-2).

The status quo was maintained in *Pountney* v *Morris* [1984] FLR 381 where the Court of Appeal dismissed the mother's appeal against the award of custody to the father of the two daughters of the marriage aged 10 and 7. They had been with the father for nearly two years when the mother applied for custody. The judge had found a strong bond between the father and his daughters and that as a result they should not be moved from their present home. However, any decision is set against the 'welfare' principle but there appears to be a strong desire to maintain, whenever possible the status quo. As such case law can only really serve as examples of the response of the judiciary and many of the cases are merely illustrative. The list of such cases is soon added to as new decisions are reported. Of the many cited in the footnotes to the standard texts perhaps the following are worth listing with a brief summary:

Allington v *Allington* [1985] FLR 586.
Short separation. No time for 'status quo' to be established.

Re L (Minors) (Interim Custody) [1987] Fam Law 130.
Transfer of custody as an interim measure to be avoided especially if receiving parent, in this case the mother who had a drink problem, was unsuitable.

Edwards v *Edwards* [1986] 1 FLR 187.
If child has been snatched the status quo ante *may* prevail — subject to the best interests of the child at that time.

It is a useful device to seek a case where the continuity concept has not been followed, which eventually confirms the point made by Cumming-Bruce LJ in *B* v *Y* (1981) 11 Fam Law 82 that: 'There is nothing much in the law books to help a judge dealing with a question of disputed custody'.

In *Re W* (1983) 4 FLR 492 despite a happy family relationship and the fact that the child was happy, custody was transferred to the mother although the little girl had been with the father for 18 months. *Family Law* commented that it was 'unusual' for the status quo not to be maintained after 18 months. They also offer reasoning to the effect that if the father had been seeking custody against the mother who had cared for a young baby for 1½ years then he would have failed. This leads on to a second factor, which has occasionally cropped up on examination papers — that of role stereotyping and what arguably appears to be an innate bias against fathers especially where young children are the subject of the dispute.

Mother or father?   In *Re K* [1977] 1 All ER 647 at p. 651 Stamp LJ tells us:

that effect should be given to the dictates of nature which make the mother the natural guardian, protector and comforter of the very young.

A century before Cotton LJ in *Re Agar Ellis* (1883) 24 ChD 317 at p. 334 felt:

> by birth, a child is subject to a father, it is for the general interests of families, and for the general interests of children . . . that the court should not . . . interfere with the discretion of the father, but leave to him the responsibility of exercising that power which nature has given him by the birth of the child.

Sir John Pennycuick in *Re K* at p. 655 comments:

> the welfare of these children requires that they should be in the charge of their mother who, not as a matter of law but in the ordinary course of nature, is the right person to have charge of young children.

This view that young children are better off with their mother has been widely challenged in recent years. Michael Rutter (1976) 6 Fam Law 125 has argued from his research that it:

> seems to be incorrect to regard the person with whom there is the main bond as necessarily and generally the most important person in a child's life. That person will be the most important for some things but not for others. . . . The father, the mother, brothers and sisters, friends, schoolteachers and others all have an impact on development but their influence and importance differs for different aspects of development. A less exclusive focus on mothers is required.

In similar vein Goldstein *et al.* comment:

> The role can be fulfilled either by a biological parent or by an adoptive parent or by any other caring adult — but never by an absent, inactive adult, whatever his biological or legal relationship to the child may be. (J. Goldstein, A. Freud and A. J. Solnit *Beyond the Best Interests of the Child,* 1980, p. 19.)

More recently French J in *Plant* v *Plant* (1983) 4 FLR 305 at p. 311 opined:

> But in the course of nature, as a matter of good sense, not of law, children who must be deprived . . . of one parent or the other, usually suffer the least if left in the care of the mother. . . . The advantages of the mother's care, in the ordinary case, are obvious.

So obvious that he doesn't tell us what they are!

You would be well advised to examine closely the judgment of Cumming-Bruce LJ in *Re W (a minor)* [1983] 4 FLR 492 where he seeks to play down the prominence given to the mother's position in cases where there are young children.

A statement such as the one made by Buckley LJ in *Ives* v *Ives* [1973] 4 Fam Law 16 to the effect that 'other things being equal . . . small children should be in the care of their mother' was dismissed as a 'generalization'. He would put it no higher than 'probably it is right for a child of tender years to be brought up by his mother' (if other factors are 'nicely balanced').

The survey carried out by Priest and Whybrow reported as a supplement to the Law Commission Working Paper No. 96 recognises the existence of the common beliefs about the award of child custody:

> that younger children, particularly girls, are better raised by their mother after divorce and that fathers are more appropriately caretakers of boys (particularly when they are older) than of girls (para 4.25, p. 40).

The cases are littered with similar statements and prompted one examiner to set a question in the following terms:

> The following comments regarding fathers have recently been voiced by judges of the High Court and Court of Appeal:

> > However good a sort of man he may be he could not perform the functions which a mother performed by nature in relation to the little girl. (Stamp LJ in *M* v *M* (1979) 9 Fam Law 92.)

'just my luck to be married to a judge'

> > a man ought not to give up work and turn himself into a mother figure or nanny and devote himself to bringing up a little girl at the expense of the state. (Payne J in *Bradley* v *Bradley* (1979) unreported.)

the value of knowing one's father is purely academic. (Ormrod LJ, May 1979.)

In light of the above comments critically analyse the principles upon which a court acts in determining a custody dispute paying particular attention to the position of the father in such a dispute.

Judges seem very conscious of the fact that they ought not to encourage men to give up work to look after their children. Nevertheless it is apparently fine for a woman to stay at home, possibly because the judges do not recognise any expectation that a woman should go out to work. Ormrod LJ in *Plant* said of a father who had given up his job to look after the child:

> I only hope he can get it back because it is a totally artificial situation to bring about to have a father giving up his work, which is his career and will certainly be something which he will need to follow for the rest of his working life, to live on social security to look after two small children when the mother is fully available to look after them.

As a final point on what appears to be the mother's pre-eminent position read the case of *L* v *L* (1981) 2 FLR 48 where the daughter was given to the mother for what appeared to be therapeutic reasons.

It must not be thought that fathers have no chance of obtaining actual custody. In the following cases fathers were successful:

May v *May* [1986] 1 FLR 325.
B v *B* [1985] FLR 166.
B v *B* [1985] FLR 462.

Parental conduct   Generally, the conduct of the parents is not a relevant factor except in so far as the court believes it might or will affect the future relations between parent and child. In *Re L* [1962] 3 All ER 1 Lord Denning MR considered that 'while the welfare of the child is the first and paramount consideration the claims of justice cannot be overlooked'. And in *J* v *C* it was said *obiter* that the wishes of the unimpeachable parent as a matter of justice must be taken into account but are not an overriding consideration. Subsequently in *S (BD)* v *S (DJ)* [1977] 1 All ER 656 the Court of Appeal said that even though one parent may claim to be 'unimpeachable' and therefore it may seem desirable that the justice of the case demanded that they be granted custody, nevertheless, the wishes of such a parent must give way to the 'guilty' party if the circumstances were such that it was in the best interests of the child.

In examination problems students will probably find themselves faced with assessing the allocation of custody against a background of a mother whose life-style and conduct may at first sight lead one to conclude that the child's interests could not be served by going with her. In one university examination question this factor was extended to cover the life-style and habits of the person with whom the mother wished to live:

> Josephine wants to take the children and live with Marvin, a social worker with 'Trotskyite' political views, atheist beliefs and unconventional views about teenage sex and the use of drugs.

It should be added that the father in this problem was a clergyman of the Church of England and that he recognised that Josephine had been, despite all her shortcomings, an exemplary mother to the children. Most custody disputes will have to be settled against a background of competing parental strengths and weaknesses. It is up to the judge to decide what weight he will give to those factors. But ultimately you are concerned only to indicate that the proper balancing exercise has been carried out against the background of the 'welfare' principle. Many would disagree with the outcome of the following three cases but the Court of Appeal confirmed in all three that the judge at first instance had not erred in principle and was certainly not plainly wrong in coming to the conclusion that he did. In *Re K* [1977] 1 All ER 647 the father was a parish curate. The mother met M and began an adulterous relationship with him. The mother intended to leave the father and, taking the two young children with her, go to live with M. The father took the view that if the children were to remain with the mother then spiritual harm would result since they would be brought up in an environment where the mother was living in adultery. This case is also useful to note from a procedural point of view in that the mother's application to a magistrates' court for custody, under the Guardianship of Minors Act 1971 was stultified by a subsequent application by the father to have the children made wards of court.

The decision, subsequently confirmed by the Court of Appeal, was to grant care and control to the mother. The judge found that the mother was an excellent mother, that the children liked M and that one of the two children was being adversely affected by the unhappy situation in the matrimonial home.

A slightly different problem arose in *Re P* (1983) 4 FLR 401 when the mother left the father in order to start a lesbian relationship. She took with her the two children aged 6 and 14 but subsequently the father took them back. When the custody matter came for adjudication the father did not seek custody so the choice was between the children staying with the mother or being committed to the care of the local authority. The judge found the mother to be 'a sensitive and understanding' woman who was discreet as to her homosexuality. The father appealed against the award of custody to her contending that in no circumstances should a child be brought up in a homosexual household since it would expose the child to corruption and adversely affect the child's reputation. As in the previous case the appeal was dismissed, on the grounds that the judge had carefully weighed all the evidence and concluded there was a perceptible advantage to the child in leaving her with the mother.

Finally in *L* v *L* (1981) 2 FLR 48 the mother left the matrimonial home leaving the daughter aged 2, with the father. She went to live with another man and after that affair broke down, lived at various addresses, attempted suicide, suffered from depression, received anti-depressant treatment and also drank heavily for a time. The father obtained a divorce on the grounds of the mother's adultery. The mother applied for and was granted custody of the child despite the very traumatic experiences she had gone through. Berkovits, 'Towards a reappraisal of family law ideology' (1980) 10 Fam Law 164 criticises the case and comments:

> The decision illustrates once again the scant consideration currently given to questions of justice and equity. . . . The decision amounts to a judicial licence to commit adultery, and then to claim the home from the other spouse, in almost all cases where young children are involved. . . . [T]he concept of granting custody in order 'to give the mother the chance of remaining stable' appears a novel and startling development.

Conduct is a factor to be taken into account where it is likely to have a direct impact on the future well being of the child. In *May* v *May* the Court of Appeal confirmed that the wife's behaviour could be taken into account because it affected 'the future permanence of the relationship which was currently existing between the mother and the cohabitee'.

Child's wishes   The Law Commission suggested in Working Paper No. 96 that, in contested custody cases, the court should be under a duty to ascertain the 'wishes and feelings' of the child and although they would not be bound to give effect to them, they would have to be given full consideration. The impact of this process would be to at very least pay lip service to the decision in *Gillick* v *W Norfolk and Wisbech Area Health Authority* [1986] AC 112 which emphasised that the relative maturity and understanding of a child were major factors in allowing him or her to act independently of parents, in that case with regard to the provision of contraceptives and whether parents had any right to be informed if contraceptive treatment was planned.

There have been plenty of examples of where the wishes of children have been disregarded in custody cases, e.g., *Doncheff* v *Doncheff* (1978) 8 Fam Law 205 and *Re DW* [1984] Fam Law 17, but in practice the court will be aware of a child's views although may not necessarily believe they accord with the course of action which will best serve his welfare. Children may be susceptible to parental influence and may not necessarily be articulating their own views on the custody problem. The key point is that as the law stands the court is not bound to pay any regard to the child's wishes. As a result the Law Commission in its Report on *Guardianship and Custody* (No. 172) recommended that the child's views should be included as part of a statutory checklist which in practice will be limited to contested cases (see paras 3.22-3.25, p. 20). More will be said about the 'checklist' at p. 182.

Revision note

I have given some examples of custody issues to which it is reasonable to expect examiners to have regard. Of course there are others. May I suggest that you make a list with supporting cases and brief comment in the way adopted in chapter 5 where I listed types of behaviour relevant to divorce proceedings under s. 1(2)(b) of the Matrimonial Causes Act 1973. Your list may include some or all of the following matters listed in tabular form:

TOPIC: Religious beliefs

Case	Reference	Comment
Hewison v *Hewison*	(1977) 7 Fam Law 207	Exclusive Brethren sect. Teachings harmful to children.
Re B	(1977) 7 Fam Law 206	Father obsessed by Calvinism. Court held religion not a crucial factor in case.
Re H	(1980) 10 Fam Law 248	Mother Jehovah's Witness. No evidence of risk to child. Custody to mother.
Re T (Minors)	(1981) 2 FLR 239	Court should not pass judgment on parental beliefs, if consistent with socially acceptable norms.
Re B and G (Minors) (Custody)	[1985] FLR 493	Scientology immoral, pernicious, obnoxious and sinister cult.

TOPIC: Parent or stranger?

Case	Reference	Comment
Re DW	[1984] Fam Law 17	Child strongly attached to stepmother. Nevertheless custody to mother after eight years. Severe criticism but decision upheld.
Re E (O)	(1973) 3 Fam Law 48	Care and control to foster parents. Child well integrated with them.

Re O	(1973) 3 Fam Law 40	Care and control to foster parents.
J v *C*	[1970] AC 668	Child to remain with foster parents. 'Psychological' evidence importance.

TOPIC: Children's wishes

Case	Reference	Comment
Marsh v *Marsh*	(1978) 8 Fam Law 103	Wishes of children in no way paramount.
Doncheff v *Doncheff*	(1978) 4 Fam Law 205	Children's expressed wishes held to have been influenced by father.
Cossey v *Cossey*	(1981) Fam Law 56	Court more concerned with long-term planning than satisfying immediate wish of daughter to live with father.
Adams v *Adams*	[1984] FLR 268	Responsibility for deciding between parents should not be cast on child.

As may be imagined there are any number of cases which may be chosen for inclusion in your list. Try wherever possible to include only those which make some significant contribution to illustrating the approach taken by the courts. Attitudes change and the view of the courts will ultimately follow suit. The above matters are not meant to be prescriptive and you should examine *Family Law* regularly to keep up to date on new cases in this area.

It has been shown how wide ranging a custody dispute may be with many factors potentially to be taken into account. Yet the court is not placed under a statutory duty as to which factors are deemed to be important. The Law Commission has therefore recommended that a statutory 'checklist' of factors relevant to custody and similar decisions might be of assistance to the courts. The idea is to have something similar to the 'checklists' which already exist for other discretionary powers of the courts in family matters, e.g., for financial provision and property adjustment in the Matrimonial Causes Act 1973 (s. 25). One interesting feature is that the existence of such a list might go some way in assisting parents and children to understand how judicial decisions are made. The parties' legal advisers would also be advantaged by having something definite with which to work. The factors recommended for inclusion into new legislation are listed at para 3.20 (p. 19) of the Law Commission Report No. 172 and the court, it is suggested, should have regard to all the circumstances of the case including:

(a)   The ascertainable wishes and feelings of the child considered in light of his age and understanding.

(b)   Child's physical, emotional and, where relevant, educational needs.

(c)   Effect on the child or any change of his circumstances, having regard to their duration and his separation from any person with whom he has been living.

(d)   Child's age, sex, background and other relevant characteristics.

(e)   Any harm which the child has suffered or is at risk of suffering.

(f)   How capable each parent and any other relevant person is of meeting the child's need.

The list is not meant to be prescriptive and therefore the court will be free to consider any other factors recognised as significant in the case before them.

Joint custody

As we approach the conclusion of our very brief look at custody, you ought to be aware of the current thinking towards joint custody orders rather than the traditional custody to one parent with reasonable access to the other. Pressure groups such as 'Families Need Fathers' have long advocated a greater use of joint custody orders on the basis that it gives the non-custodial parent a continuing voice in the future decision-making concerning the child. In addition it is believed that the non-custodial parent is more likely to adopt a positive attitude towards his child and as a result is less likely to default on maintenance payments for the child.

A 1984 examination question reflected this development:

'Unless continuing inadequacy is proven in one parent, joint custody should routinely be awarded to emphasise the need for the joint responsibility of both parents to continue for the children after separation or divorce.'
    Discuss.
    (Extract from a discussion document prepared for 'Families Need Fathers', September 1983.)

The call for joint custody to be ordered as a matter of routine had been strengthened by the Booth Committee's Consultation Document, the result of deliberations into ways in which reforms might be made:

(a)   to mitigate the intensity of disputes;
(b)   to encourage settlements; and
(c)   to provide further for the welfare of the children of the family.

At p. 54, para. 7.7, the Committee writes:

that the concept of joint custody has much to recommend it and should be the starting-point for the parties and the court in considering the arrangements for the chidren. Joint custody emphasises that both parents continue to be responsible for the children after divorce and it removes the idea of 'awarding' custody to one or other of them together with the concepts of 'winning' and 'losing'. . . . The Committee is, therefore, of the provisional view that custody should be granted jointly to both parents unless the court decides that on the particular facts of a case it is not in the interests of the children to make that order.

However, the Final Report (August 1985) while still supporting strongly the principle of joint custody is not prepared to recommend that there should be a presumption in favour of such orders. Those commenting on the interim proposal felt that the court should be more willing to make joint custody orders, but because in custody proceedings the welfare of the child was the first and paramount consideration any bias in favour of joint custody might detract from this 'overriding principle'. The committee believe that if there was in divorce proceedings 'an expectation that a joint custody order would be made, this would reinforce the idea of continuing joint parental responsibility and would thus help parents to agree satisfactory arrangements' (para. 4.130-2, pp. 63-4).

The latest study of joint custody orders is by Priest and Whybrow, published as part of the supplement to the Law Commission Working Paper No. 96 entitled 'Custody Law and Practice in the Divorce and Domestic Courts' (1986 No. 96). The authors found a wide regional variation showing that the percentage of joint custody orders made in the Western and South Eastern Circuits is over three times greater than that in the North and North Eastern Circuits. Overall the number of joint orders had increased from 5.2% of all custody orders in 1974 to 12.9% in 1985. They conclude that the reason for higher percentages in some areas is because judges endeavour to promote such orders, even if the parties had never considered the issue previously. At the opposite end of the spectrum some judges remain to be convinced that sufficient harmony exists between parents *before* they will pursue the matter. Solicitors also often seemed unwilling to take the initiative and suggest joint custody.

Therefore, if your tutor concentrates on the use of joint orders then it is imperative that you read this particular report (see Part V, pp. 41-65).

The current judicial attitude is very different from that expressed by the Booth Committee. The lead was given by Wrangham J in *Jussa* v *Jussa* [1972] 2 All ER 600. This case indicated that joint custody should *not* be ordered unless it was likely to promote the welfare of the child, and that the important matter to be taken into consideration is whether the parents can be expected to cooperate if an order for joint custody is made. Judges tended to express the view that joint custody orders should only be made in exceptional circumstances.

The current position is that with the growth of out-of-court conciliation services more parents are pressing for joint custody orders. A practice direction [1980] 1 All ER 784 urges courts not to make orders inconsistent with a provisional agreement reached by parents as to joint legal custody.

A more recent statement of principle has come from the Court of Appeal in *Caffell* v *Caffell* [1984] FLR 169 where it was said that in many cases joint custody should only be ordered if there was a reasonable prospect that the parents would cooperate. Nevertheless such an order might be equally appropriate to recognise the responsibility and concern of the parent who did not have the day-to-day control of the child and might ease bitterness between the parties. And in *Stanley* v *Stanley* (1983, Lexis transcript) an appeal against a refusal by a county court judge to make a joint order was allowed. Sir David Cairns said, 'I accept that the proper approach to the question, is "Is it in the interests of the child?" and, in particular, "Is it a case where there is a reasonable expectation of cooperation between the parents?"'

Revision note

The pertinent issues concerning joint custody are fully explored in Maidment, *Child Custody and Divorce*, pp. 257-68. In addition to noting the various points on joint custody, give some consideration to the wider issues of mediation and conciliation being a better way than the present adversarial system in helping to ease the problem of how to respond to the needs of the children at the time of divorce. Much has been written of late on the subject and students can gain much assistance from reading the many articles published in *Family Law* and from scouring the footnotes in Cretney, *Principles of Family Law,* 4th ed., pp. 188-204 and Bromley, *Family Law*, 7th ed., pp. 210-16. Further information is to be found in the Inter-Departmental Committee on Conciliation Report published in 1983.

Once you have covered the relevant material give thought to whether or not you could answer the following question:

'Whether the rarity with which joint custody is ordered is a matter of policy or indicative of a lack of imagination by the courts and the parties' legal advisers is unclear. The fact that they were slightly more common after a contested case suggests that they may be used as a compromise solution to a serious contest rather than as a constructive measure to maintain relative harmony between cooperative parents.'

Discuss.

(J. Eekelaar, *Family Law and Social Policy* (1978, p. 228.)

For an example of when joint custody was found to be inappropriate see *Jane* v *Jane* (1983) 4 FLR 712.

The future

Given the recommendations contained in the Law Commission Report No. 172 on *Guardianship and Custody* (July 1988) it is unlikely that we shall be discussing 'custody' or 'access' orders in the near future. The Report urges Parliament to accept a new legal concept of parenthood, recognising that parents have responsibilities for bringing up their children and stating that the courts are there to help rather than interfere. Custody should not be awarded as a prize between warring parents and therefore it is proposed that new orders of 'contact' and 'residence' be introduced to replace 'access' and 'custody'. It is considered of great advantage to seek to distinguish the role of parent from that of spouse, in effect drawing a clear distinction between child law and matrimonial law. The result is that it is proposed that the legal status of parents in relation to the care and upbringing of their children should be termed 'parental responsibility'. Parents with parental responsibility should have equal status and each should be able to act independently in carrying out the responsibility.

The true major orders, i.e., residence and contact, are defined thus:

Residence – an order settling the arrangements to be made as to the person with whom the child is to live.

Contact – an order requiring the person with whom a child lives, or is to live, to allow the child to visit the person named in the order, or for that person and the child otherwise to have contact with each other.

The major reasons why the Law Commission recommend replacement of the existing orders are listed at paras 4.2-4.4, pp. 22-23 of the Report. Essentially the difficulties may be stated to be:

(1)   The orders available differ according to the proceedings brought.

(2)   The effect of orders is not clear or well understood. For example, if a sole order is granted that parent thinks that he has sole control – but see *Dipper* v *Dipper* [1981] Fam 31.

(3)   The views and practices of courts differ considerably, largely, it is suggested, because of differences of opinion amongst judges, legal practitioners and clients about the merits of joint custody orders.

It would appear that the role of the law in future should be to encourage the child to maintain a good relationship with his parents. Where parents can cooperate then the law should interfere as little as possible. Where there is difficulty between them the law should seek to 'lower the stakes' and reduce the possibility of the dispute being seen on a winner takes all basis. Finally, any orders made should seek to reduce the possibility for future conflicts. Therefore, a residence order is designed to encompass a much wider range of situations than the existing custody order, e.g., the child may live with both parents even though they do not share the same household, and the order may specify the periods during which the child is to live in both households. The effect of the residence order is simply to settle the question of where the child is to live.

The contact order is designed to replace access. Where for practical reasons the child has to spend more time with one parent than the other, the contact order will provide for the child to visit and in many cases stay with the 'non-custodial' parent. While the child is with him he may exercise all his parental responsibilities. The court may also attach conditions if there are specific issues which need to be clarified. Although, at the time of writing, this Report has only just been published, it is likely to form the basis for legislative reform in the next couple of years. It should therefore demand your full attention as it, together with the Working Paper on custody, provides an invaluable amount of information on what the law is at the moment and how a new approach may soon be ushered in.

Wardship

As Sir George Baker says in his foreword to Lowe and White's *Wards of Court* (1st ed.), 'the days have gone when the Chancery judge could have all is wards to tea annually, and Family Division Judges in London alone are hearing 800-900 wardship summonses each year'. The book represents the most authoritative text yet written on the subject. This fact alone presents us with a dilemma: how in a few pages can one hope to represent in anything like adequate fashion a jurisdiction which originated in the Middle Ages and which is today as strong if not stronger than it has ever been? The answer, I suspect, is that I must endeavour to limit my discussion to those aspects of the jurisdiction which may trouble you, the student, in examination papers in the next few years. However, its popularity may diminish if the reform of statutory procedures, both public and private, regarding children, as recommended by the Law Commission (Report No. 172) and the Child Law Review (1987 Cm 62) is implemented. The Law Commission's stated aim, at para 1.4, p. 1, is to 'incorporate the most valuable features of wardship into our recommendations for a new statutory system . . . this should reduce the need to resort to wardship proceedings save in the most unusual and complex cases'.

You are unlikely to be asked about the history of wardship but you should know a little about its development from a jurisdiction based upon 'the estate not the person' (Sir George Baker). Today it is very much based upon the person not the estate, the transformation occurring mainly in the 19th century although there is some evidence of judicial concern for the child at an earlier stage. To gain an impression of how and why this transformation occurred you would be well advised to read *Wellesley* v *Duke of Beaufort* (1828) 2 Bli NS 124, sub nom. *Wellesley* v *Wellesley* [1824-34] All ER Rep 189. From 1660 it had been asserted that the power of the court over infants derived from the delegated powers of the monarch as 'guardian of the nation'. Lord Redesdale in *Wellesley* referred to judgments of previous Chancellors — Nottingham, Hardwicke and Somers — as to the basis of the jurisdiction. 'They all say, that it is a right which devolves to the Crown as *parens patriae* and that it is the duty of the Crown to see that the child is properly taken care of.' Today the jurisdiction is exercised by judges of the Family Division of the High Court upon the familiar principle of the welfare of the child being first and paramount described by Dunn J in *Re D* [1977] 3 All ER 481 at p. 486 as:

the golden thread which runs through the whole of this court's jurisdiction, the welfare of the child, which is considered in this court, first, last and all the time.

And Lord Scarman in *Re E (SA) (a minor) (wardship)* [1984] 1 All ER 289 at p. 290(h) described the 'fundamental feature' of the jurisdiction as non-adversarial and went on to say:

> Its duty is not limited to the dispute between the parties: on the contrary, its duty is to act in the way best suited in its judgment to serve the true interest and welfare of the ward. In exercising wardship jurisdiction, the court is a true family court. Its paramount concern is the welfare of its ward.

Until recently the jurisdiction has been exclusively vested in the High Court. However, s. 38 of the Matrimonial and Family Proceedings Act 1984 allows for transfer of the proceedings to the county court, but not applications that a minor be made, or cease to be, a ward of court. (See *Practice Direction* at [1988] 2 All ER 103 which supersedes the *Practice Direction* at [1987] 1 All ER 1087.)

The scope of the jurisdiction is considerable and it would appear that the only limitations are those imposed by statute or where there is conflict with the public interest. Lord Justice Roskill in *Re X* [1975] 1 All ER 697 at p. 705 said that 'no limits to that jurisdiction have yet been drawn and it is not necessary to consider here what (if any) limits there are to that jurisdiction'. In a more recent case, *X County Council* v *A and another* [1985] 1 All ER 53, Balcombe J at p. 57(b) said 'I am satisfied that I have the jurisdiction to make an order which is binding on the world at large'. This theme was pursued by Booth J in *Re L (a minor)* [1988] 1 All ER 418 at p. 421 (a):

> In the exercise of its wardship jurisdiction the powers of a court are sufficiently wide to enable it to make an order which operates against the world at large . . .

Of course the vital question in all this is to decide whether or not to exercise that power. Where press freedom is concerned (as in all these cases) it is a balancing exercise between the need to protect the child from harm and the importance of maintaining freedom of the press.

From 4 April 1988, when the Family Law Act 1986 came into force, an order of the High Court exercising its wardship jurisdiction which gives care and control of a child to any person, or giving access to the child or relating to his education is a 'custody order' for the purposes of the Act. The Act was passed in order to prevent conflict between different jurisdictions in the United Kingdom. However, s. 2 of the Act specifically preserves the jurisdiction of the High Court to deal with a ward if he is present in England or Wales and the court considered that the *immediate* exercise of its powers is necessary for his protection. At the time of writing there have not been any reported cases on the working of these provisions. A wardship order which does not cover custody, access or education is outside the scope of the Act.

As a student of family law you are likely to be invited to consider wardship in the following contexts:

(a)   Advising those who have an 'interest' in a child but who are neither mother or father. For example, foster parents, grandparents or other relatives may wish to seek care and control of the child but are prevented from applying under the Guardianship of Minors Act 1971. *J* v *C* [1970] AC 668 was of course a wardship case brought by foster parents. For an example of the potentially damaging effect of grandparent intrusion in a child's upbringing and the use of wardship to resolve the dispute see *B* v *W* [1979] 3 All ER 83. The examiner would now expect you to decide whether wardship or an application for custodianship under the provisions of the Children Act 1975 would be the more appropriate course of action. (For more detail on custodianship see p. 196.) The point must be made, however, that *anyone* with an interest in the child may apply, one of the most significant interventions being that of the educational psychologist in *Re D* [1976] 1 All ER 326 who would have faced significant costs if her application had been unsuccessful. See also *Re JT (a minor)* [1986] 2 FLR 107 where the guardian *ad litem*, being opposed to the local authority's attempt to rehabilitate the child with his mother, took the action. The judge commended his 'very brave' action in warding the child.

(b)   To deal with the unusual or unique cases which arise from time to time and for which no other jurisdiction seems a suitable venue. Examples of such cases are relatively easy to find. *Re X* [1975] 1 All ER 697 I have already mentioned. The others to which you ought to have regard are:

(i)   *Re F (in utero)* [1988] 2 All ER 193. The interesting and unique question in this case was whether the court had the power to make an unborn child a ward of court. The pregnant mother who was suffering from a mental condition had disappeared and concern was expressed for the well being of the unborn child. Had the court the jurisdiction to grant a wardship order? To help the unborn child the court would have to restrict the mother's liberty. If medical problems arose regarding the child the mother might wish for one course of action, the court another. It appeared to the court that there was 'an inherent incompatibility between any projected exercise of the wardship and the rights and welfare of the mother' (p. 194 h). May LJ thought that if there was to be jurisdiction in such a 'sensitive situation', it was a matter for Parliament and not for the court. See also Staughton LJ at p. 201 (f). He said:

> We were urged by counsel to extend the wardship jurisdiction; but, in my judgment, we are being asked to create a new, perhaps similar, jurisdiction to care for mother and foetus. . . . I do not think that it is for this court to create that jurisdiction.

(ii)   *Re B (a minor) (Wardship: sterilisation)* [1987] 2 All ER 206. Before reading this case study the judgment of Heilbron J in *Re D* [1976] 1 All ER 326. In that case the mother of an 11 year old mentally retarded child wished to have her sterilised, fearing that if she wasn't her daughter might be seduced and give birth to an abnormal child. The judge, giving full weight to the gravity of the case, spoke about the operation depriving the girl of a basic human right, i.e., to reproduce, and to carry out the operation for non-therapeutic reasons and without her consent would violate that right. The child remained a ward and the operation did not take place.

The House of Lords had the opportunity to review the powers of the wardship court when sterilisation was at issue in *Re B*. In this case a mentally handicapped and epileptic 17 year old girl who had a mental age of 5 was in the care of a local authority. She had no understanding of the connection between sexual intercourse and pregnancy. She was exhibiting signs of normal sexual drive and the expert evidence clearly indicated that it was vital that she didn't become pregnant. The local authority, supported by the minor's mother, wished to have her sterilised. It was held that, having regard to all the evidence and acting in the best interests of the minor, the operation should be authorised. Do note also that Lord Templeman issued a clear warning to the medical profession that a decision to sterilise a child should *only* be made by a High Court Judge. Any doctor carrying out such an operation with leave of the wardship court *not withstanding parental consent*, will be liable in criminal, civil or professional proceedings.

Re D and *Re B* can be distinguished on the basis:

(a)   Of age. The girl in *Re D* was only 11 and unlikely at that stage or in the near future to be seduced or become pregnant.

(b)   In that period a regime of 'protection' could be worked out.

(c)   In *Re B* the girl was 17 and sexually aware and after 18 would be outside the wardship jurisdiction when it would have been extremely difficult to keep legal control of her. (Although on this point see the decision of Wood J in *T* v *T* [1988] 1 All ER 613 where he urges that the inherent jurisdiction of the court as *parens patriae* should be reinvoked to cover such a situation.)

(iii)   *Re C (A Minor)* [1985] FLR 846. Unique in the sense that it was the first surrogacy case to come before the courts, in the full glare of publicity. When the child was born the local authority took a place of safety order. The natural father issued wardship proceedings and the court, acting in the best interests of the new born baby, gave the child to the father and his wife. The court was seemingly unconcerned about the method of procreation. (But see *A* v *C* [1985] FLR 445 for a similar case with a different outcome.)

(iv)   *Re B* [1981] 1 WLR 1421. A baby girl born with Down's Syndrome needed an operation in order to survive. The parents took the view that the kindest thing in the interest of the child was for her not to have the operation. The Court of Appeal reversing the first instance judge ordered the operation to proceed. It was felt that at this early stage in life there was no evidence that her life would be intolerable and she should be given a chance to live. A case such as this brings home the importance of the jurisdiction when judges are faced with making life and death decisions. Templeman LJ certainly contemplated the possibility of a court deciding that it was in the best interests of a child for it to be allowed to die:

> There may be cases, I know not, of severe proved damage where the future is so certain, and where the life of the child is so bound to be full of pain and suffering that the court might be driven to a different conclusion.

So it can be seen that these cases, together with the ones already cited, do introduce difficult questions for a court to answer. It is suggested that eventually this will be the only role for the wardship court as its present jurisdiction will be increasingly subsumed by new statutory procedures.

(c)   In the past decade the wardship jurisdiction has been closely associated with the statutory provisions relating to children, in particular the exercise by local authorities of powers contained in the Children and Young Persons Act 1969 and the Children Act 1948 (now the Child Care Act 1980). In essence parental dissatisfaction with the apparent lack of rights bestowed upon them by the provisions has meant that they have turned to the prerogative jurisdiction in an attempt to challenge the extent of those powers and often as a means of appeal where no statutory right to do so exists. This topic together with a fuller discussion of local authorities powers is to be found in chapter 10. Suffice to say that the court has seemingly decided that it has little or no role to play when decisions of local authorities are under challenge, an opinion most recently endorsed by the House of Lords in *Re M and H (Minors), The Times,* 29 July 1988. This case was a challenge by the putative father of two minors to be allowed access to his children who were in the care of the local authority by reason of a resolution passed under the Child Care Act 1980. Very simply, the House dismissed the applications by reason of the principle that if Parliament has entrusted to local authorities the powers and duty to make decisions about the welfare of children, the court had no power to review the merits of those decisions. (More will be said about this case in chapter 10.)

Revision note

Wardship undoubtedly has many uses in addition to those highlighted. For a comprehensive review see *Butterworth's Family Law Service,* Division E. The following represent the type of question likely to appear on examination papers (see chapter 10 for greater detail on the statutory code):

1 Despite recent statutory changes, which have improved the position of parents whose children are in care, there are few ways by which parents may

successfully challenge a decision made by a local authority which directly affects their children.

Discuss.

Obviously in the next question there are other issues but certainly the use of wardship is relevant especially to the final part:

2   Carol and Alan were married in 1979 when they were aged 34 and 40. Although their marriage was initially happy, there was increased discord due to Carol's inability to conceive. Despite medical assistance and treatment with fertility drugs, Carol had still not conceived by January 1987. The couple then approached an agency called Wombrent which specialised in putting prospective parents in touch with surrogate mothers. They agreed to pay the agency £5,000 upon the birth and they were put in touch with Beryl, who agreed to bear Alan's child for £4,000. Beryl was artificially inseminated and conception occurred in September 1987. Beryl is due to give birth next week. The media have taken a substantial interest in the case and Carol has agreed to sell her story to the *Daily Nonsense* for £20,000. The local authority social services department is also concerned as to whether Carol and Alan are likely to be suitable parents. However, unknown to all parties, Beryl is seriously considering keeping the child once it is born.

Consider the legal issues likely to arise from the above facts. What additional advice might be necessary if the child was at birth found to be suffering from Down's syndrome and was rejected by the natural parents, Beryl and Alan, but Carol still wished to have care and control of the child?

3   Amy aged 17 is the mother of an illegitimate daughter, Priscilla. Her school has persuaded her to continue her full-time education with a view to taking the Oxbridge examinations. The child is being brought up by Amy's mother Carol aged 51. As a result of the amount of school work that Amy has to do she has little contact with the child, and Priscilla, now aged 2, has always regarded Carol as her mother. Carol, realising that Amy is likely to go to university, is keen to have legal control of the child. Amy is reluctant to relinquish her legal rights in case she subsequently marries and wishes to look after the child herself. The local authority is also concerned in case the grandmother cannot adequately respond to the demands of bringing up a young child.

Advise all parties as to their respective legal positions.

Remember that wardship is only one option available and it is fairly unusual for a whole question to be devoted to the subject.

For the most up to date, comprehensive review of the wardship jurisdiction see the Law Commission Working Paper No. 101, *Wards of Court*, published in March 1987.

Adoption

The issue of adoption is being raised under the chapter title of 'welfare and the child' because it is an important consideration although not first and paramount. This is usually explained on the grounds that as the natural parent is expected to divest himself of all legal rights over the child then his interests should have a standing in the proceedings at least equal to that of the child's welfare. The Adoption Act 1976 which contains the relevant law on adoption puts it in this way in s. 6 (emphasis added):

> In reaching any decision relating to adoption of a child, a court or adoption agency shall *have regard to all the circumstances, first consideration* being given to the need to safeguard and promote the welfare of the child throughout his childhood.

For comment on the scope of the first-consideration test (the wording of course now used in the Matrimonial and Family Proceedings Act 1984) see Bevan and Parry, *The Children Act 1975*. Recent judicial comment on the test is to be found in *Re W* [1984] FLR 402 where Cumming-Bruce LJ, discussing the distinction between 'first and paramount' and 'first consideration', said:

> What precisely the distinction is I find it unnecessary, fortunately, to define. It is manifestly an extremely fine distinction. But the difference in language does have this effect, that in custody . . . welfare becomes paramount in the weighing exercise over all other considerations, including the interests of all the grown-ups. Parliament evidently decided . . . that though the welfare of the child should be the first consideration, it is the first among a number of considerations which will themselves depend upon the particular circumstances of the individual case, both as to the number of those considerations and, of course, their weight.

A similar test to s. 6 is to be found in the Child Care Act, s. 18(1) relating to the future planning for children in care. By way of contrast it is worthwhile looking at the case of *R* v *Avon CC ex parte K and others* [1986] 1 FLR 443 where the council in deciding to close a community home had not considered the welfare of *each* individual child and had not considered the views held by the children.

The case law on adoption tends to centre on the issue of dispensing with parental agreement and step-parent adoptions although the interrelationship between adoption and custodianship is now topical. The following are taken from examination papers:

1 (a) 'Two reasonable parents can perfectly reasonably come to opposite conclusions on the same set of facts without forfeiting their title to be regarded as reasonable. The question in any given case is whether a parental veto comes within the band of possible reasonable decisions and not whether it is right or mistaken.' (Lord Hailsham LC in *Re W* [1971] 2 All ER 49 at p. 56.)

In light of the above statement consider how a court will approach the issue of whether or not to dispense with the natural parent's consent to adoption.

(b) Jamie had been placed in local authority care by his mother Katherine soon after his birth in 1985. The local authority had placed him with foster parents who allowed Katherine to maintain contact with the child. Two months ago the foster parents, Mr and Mrs Wilson, indicated their desire to adopt Jamie. They have the backing of the local authority. Katherine, however, opposes the adoption but is prepared to consent to a custodianship order.

Advise Mr and Mrs Wilson as to the likely outcome of the case in the following alternative situations:

(i) the judge decides that Katherine is not unreasonable in withholding her consent to the adoption;

(ii) Katherine consents to the adoption or alternatively a custodianship order.

2 Christopher and Rebecca divorced in July 1986. Custody, care and control of their two children, Heather and Peter, aged 4 and 11, were granted to Christopher with reasonable access given to Rebecca. Christopher remarried in September 1987 and his new wife, Hannah, who cannot have children, wishes together with Christopher to adopt the children. Rebecca is currently living in a commune for single women in London and has had intermittent sexual relationships with a number of the residents although no permanent attachment has materialised. She regularly visits her children, and while Peter has responded well to seeing his mother, Heather becomes very upset when Rebecca has to leave. Rebecca hopes in the near future to establish a permanent relationship with her friend Ann and would like at some stage to resume caring for her daughter whom she has missed dreadfully since the divorce. Rebecca has made it clear that under no circumstances will she agree to the adoption of either Heather or Peter.

Advise Christopher and Hannah on their chances of succeeding in adopting the children.

Dispensing with agreement

For an adoption to proceed a child must be 'freed for adoption'. Section 18 of the Adoption Act 1976 allows the court, on application by an adoption agency, to make an order freeing the child. Once this order has been obtained no further parental consent is necessary. The order may be obtained at a very early stage, before prospective adopters have been chosen: see *Re PB (A Minor)* [1985] FLR 394. If a child is born to a married couple then both parents will have to consent. At present if the child is born to unmarried parents then only the mother's consent is necessary unless the father is a 'guardian', which means he has custody by virtue of s. 9 of the Guardianship of Minors Act 1971. When s. 7 of the Family Law Reform Act 1987 comes into force the legal position of a father of an illegitimate child will change. The section provides that before a child can be freed for adoption the court must satisfy itself that, where a father is not a guardian, he has no intention of applying for a s. 4 order under the 1987 Act (seeking a parental rights order) or applying for custody, or, if he did so, his application would be likely to be refused. 'Guardian' in s. 72(1) of the Adoption Act 1976 is redefined to include a father who already has a s. 4 order or has a right to custody by virtue of any enactment. The net effect of all this is that where he is a 'guardian' his agreement or the dispensing with it, becomes a pre-requisite to the making of an adoption order.

A court may dispense with parental agreement on any of the grounds mentioned in s. 16(2) of the Adoption Act 1976, the most popular being s. 16(2)(b) that the parent is withholding agreement unreasonably. It will come as no surprise that courts have on many occasions had to consider the construction to be given to this subsection. In *Re V* [1985] FLR 45 Sheldon J said that the question to be considered when agreement to adoption was withheld was 'what a reasonable mother in her place would do in all the circumstances . . . and that presupposed a reasonably mature mother regardless of age'.

In *Re A (minor) (adoption: parental consent)* [1987] 2 All ER 81 the Court of Appeal found that no useful purpose would be achieved by repeating the passages in *Re W* [1971] AC 682; *O'Connor* v *A and B* [1971] 2 All ER 1230 and *Re D* [1977] AC 602 which defined the test to be applied in deciding whether a parent's refusal of consent was unreasonable. However, the judgment of Purchas LJ in *Re H, Re W (adoption: parental agreement)* (1982) 4 FLR 614 at p. 625 was cited with approval:

The chances of a successful reintroduction to, or continuance of contact with, the natural parent is a critical factor in assessing the reaction of the hypothetical, reasonable parent. . . .

That dictum was also applied in *Re M (a minor) (custodianship: jurisdiction)* [1987] 2 All ER 88 where the Court of Appeal held that the proper test of whether natural parents had unreasonably withheld their agreement was whether, on all the evidence but having regard to the fact that there was room for two reasonable attitudes which were mutually conflicting, a hypothetical, reasonable parent would have refused agreement.

You will of necessity have to check the three cases cited above. Basically *Re W* is authority for the proposition that the test is objective – what would a reasonable parent, placed in the position of the natural parent, do in all the circumstances?

In *O'Connor* v *AB* [1971] 1 WLR 1227 the House of Lords dispensed with the consent of both parents and it appeared that their unstable relationship was a crucial factor in coming to that decision. *Re D* [1977] 1 All ER 145 is significant, if only for the wide divergence of judicial opinion expressed as the case travelled upwards to the House. The Court of Appeal ([1976] 2 All ER 342) had refused to dispense with the consent of a homosexual father who wished to continue to see his son after the marriage had broken down. The Court of Appeal believed there would be no immediate danger to the son if he continued to see his father. The House disagreed and Lord Wilberforce spoke out quite vehemently against current attitudes to homosexuality, reminding one of the opinion expressed in *Shaw* v *DPP* [1962] AC 220 to the effect that the courts of law were to be viewed as the guardians of the 'moral welfare of the State' (Viscount Simonds). The House reasserted, if that was necessary, that the assessment was by reference to an objective standard. The fact that the father was a practising homosexual was only one factor to consider. The House considered that the trial judge had taken account of all the factors and thus reinstated his order to dispense with the agreement of the father.

One thing is quite clear, however, and it is that the child's welfare is only one of many factors to take into account. This is well illustrated by *Re V (a minor)* [1986] 1 All ER 752 where the mother's wish to reunite her family, plus the fact that it might be conducive to his development for the child to grow up with his sisters, were relevant factors which the court had overlooked. The Court of Appeal allowed the mother's appeal against the dispensing with her agreement.

Finally note that applying this test at the 'freeing' stage may present difficulties, especially if the adoption agency has not determined who the prospective adopters are likely to be or if there has not been any contact between prospective adopters and child.

Regard should be had to the other factors in s. 16 but the case law is not extensive.

Step-parent adoption

Mine, Yours or Ours? A Study of Step-parent Adoption, by Judith Masson et al. (produced for the DHSS), tell us that in 1980 step-parent adoption accounted for 60% of all adoptions. With divorce continuing to run at record levels then it is likely that the figure for step-parent adoptions will remain high as large numbers of people remarry and assume responsibility not only for a new spouse but his/her siblings.

However, there are provisions in the Adoption Act 1976 which are designed to discourage step-parent adoption. Section 14(3) states that where an application is made by a married couple consisting of a parent and step-parent, the court 'shall dismiss the application if it considers the matter would be *better dealt with* under section 42 (orders for custody etc.) of the Matrimonial Causes Act 1973' (emphasis added).

You must ask yourself the question: In what circumstances will the application *be better dealt* with under the 1973 Act? The purpose of the provision was to recognise that if adoption took place in such circumstances then an existing relationship, say, between non-custodial parent and natural child would have to be ended. Equally the natural custodial parent would suddenly have her rights based upon the adoptive relationship rather than being the 'natural' guardian of the child. The first authoritative construction was given to the section in *Re S* [1977] 3 All ER 671. The Court of Appeal was *not* disposed to limit the effect of the section to all cases except where it was proved there were *exceptional* circumstances. Instead the court must consider whether it was in the best interests of the child's welfare to deal with the case under s. 42 of the Matrimonial Causes Act 1973 by making a joint custody order or to leave the child in the parent's sole custody. The options therefore are between making an adoption order, refusing to disturb the status quo or making an order under s. 42. If a child was already living with the parent and step-parent then the applicants would have to convince the court that there were further benefits likely to accrue to the child as a result of the adoption order being granted. This could be extremely difficult and it was felt that the construction given to the section in *Re S* did not exactly encourage parents and step-parents to think that their applications would be successful. However, in an apparent volte-face the Court of Appeal in *Re D* (1980) 2 FLR 102 declared that it was not a question of showing that adoption would be better, the correct question to pose was: Can this matter be dealt with better by a custody order? Masson *et al*. conclude their research by pointing out that 'adoption was intended to create new family relationships' and therefore an order under s. 14 would appear appropriate if, for example, the non-custodial parent has shown little or no interest in the child, and the step-parent had in the child's eyes taken over the parental role.

Custodianship and adoption

Section 37 of the Children Act 1975 makes provision for a court hearing an adoption application to proceed to make a custodianship order rather than an adoption order. Before we examine the case law on this provision, let us remind ourselves of the *purpose* behind each order. An adoption order will transfer the legal powers held by a child's parents to the applicants. As was said in *Re C (a minor) (adoption: conditions)* [1988] 1 All ER 705, in normal circumstances it is desirable that there should be a complete break on adoption. In effect the child acquires new parents. Custodianship, on the other hand, is as good as a conventional custody order to a parent but inferior to an adoption order. The custodian will be under a duty to take care of the child, have the right to make decisions about care and upbringing, to consent to medical treatment and marriage. The crucial point is that the child's *legal* relationship with his family will remain unsevered. Applications for custodianship can be made by specified persons who have been looking after the child for particular periods, ranging from three months to three years. The expectation is that step-parents, foster parents and relations, e.g., grandparents, will apply. Natural parents will be unable to apply because they can seek custody.

So custodianship can confer many benefits, not least continuity of care with some measure of legal protection preventing the parents from themselves resuming care.

However, s. 37 of the Children Act puts the court under a duty to consider whether the child's welfare would be better safeguarded and promoted by making a custodianship order rather than an adoption order, and it has to be satisfied that it would be *appropriate* to make the custodianship order. The initial application for adoption must be made by a relative of the child or step-parent and, as *Re M (a minor) (custodianship: jurisdiction)* [1987] 2 All ER 88 clearly shows, it is a prerequisite to the making of a custodianship order that the requirements of s. 16 of the Adoption Act 1976 are satisfied. So, for example, if the parents refuse their agreement to the adoption and the judge refuses to dispense with their agreement the custodianship option does not arise.

If the application for adoption is made by a person who is neither a relative or step-parent then, if the parental agreement element is satisfied and the court is of the opinion that it would be more appropriate to make a custodianship order, it *may* direct that the application be treated as one of custodianship.

It would appear that s. 37 is fraught with difficulties and all the more reason, therefore, for the topic to appear on your examination paper. In very simple terms the court when considering what the future holds for the child must choose between adoption and custodianship. But there are problems:

(i)   If custodianship can only proceed once parental agreement *to adoption* is given (or dispensed with) it would appear strange to give parents who wish to divest themselves of legal parentage a continuing legal interest in the child.

(ii)   If custodianship is deemed to be the best option then presumably it can never be unreasonable to refuse to agree to adoption. Also, what is the point in agreeing to adoption as a pre-requisite to custodianship?

(iii)   Under s. 37(1) the court has to be satisfied that 'the child's welfare would not be better safeguarded and promoted by the making of an adoption order'. This has been interpreted to mean that the court must be satisfied that custodianship will better safeguard and promote the child's welfare than adoption. The court in *Re S (a minor) (adoption or custodianship)* [1987] 2 All ER 99 went on to say that if the balance of advantage between adoption and custodianship is even, so that the court cannot decide which course is preferable, the application must be treated as one for adoption. In other words, there will always have to be some positive advantage in favour of custodianship for the provision to operate.

(iv)   There is also the further point that even if custodianship is deemed more beneficial s. 37(1) states that it must be *appropriate* to make the order. As Glidewell LJ said in *Re M* at p. 95(e):

> Therefore custodianship as a possibility is only relevant subject to the caveat that the prospective adopters may or may not decide that custodianship is an acceptable alternative.

Under s. 37(2) it is only this later test which needs to be satisfied.

In conclusion the real question is: What does the child obtain from continued links with his parents? If there are none then custodianship would appear inappropriate; if there are some then custodianship may be best subject to the prospective adopters agreeing.

The message for students must be 'watch this space!'.

Conclusion

Other information on adoption is widely available in both the standard and specialist texts. Certainly it would be worthwhile looking at who can adopt, and the s. 13 provision regarding time that the child must spend with the adopters. In some problems the examiner may bring in competing jurisdictions and ask you to advise, for instance, the natural father of an 'illegitimate' child who does not want the child adopted and who perhaps invokes wardship or makes an application for custody under the Guardianship of Minors Act 1971 or a parental rights application under s. 4 of the Family Law Reform Act 1987. The mother, often backed by the adoption agency, will be in favour of proceedings to obtain an order under the Adoption Act 1976. Such disputes are not uncommon and for an example of four separate jurisdictions coming together in an endeavour to resolve a dispute over a child see *Re C* (1981) 2 FLR 177. Roskill LJ agreed with Comyn J when he said (at p. 184):

> I am afraid the case shows that our statutory law about children, and most of our law on the subject is statutory, is in a sorry state of disarray and is not properly coordinated.

(Refer also to Ormrod LJ in *Re H* [1978] Fam 65 at p. 72.)

In *Re C* Roskill LJ thought that only in wardship proceedings could all the issues be taken account of and dealt with concurrently.

I have stated that adoption orders are seen as final orders but occasionally a court may impose terms and conditions to the order acting under s. 12(B) of the Adoption Act 1976. This provision (or at least its predecessor s. 8(7) of the Children Act 1975) was recently examined in *Re C (a minor) (adoption: conditions)* [1988] 1 All ER 705. The House of Lords decided that the section was wide enough to allow a court to impose any terms or conditions that it thought fit. In this case it approved the court's action in making provision for access to a member of the child's family where it was clearly in the child's best interest. The order allowed the female subject to continue to see her brother to whom she had become very attached.

TEN

CHILDREN II

Local authorities

The Child Care Act 1980 places local authorities under a mandatory duty to receive a child into its care in certain defined circumstances. Sections 2 and 3 of the Act seek to establish the powers and obligations of the local authorities and as a result the interpretation of these sections has caused many problems for the higher courts. The other major statute is of course the Children and Young Persons Act 1969. Section 1 empowers a local authority, if it reasonably believes that there is sufficient evidence to satisfy specific criteria, to ask a juvenile court to make a care order in its favour.

It is noticeable that there has been a marked increase in the number of questions appearing on family law examination papers which refer to local authorities, and their various rights and duties under the aforementioned legislation. Some seek to put you in the position of a social worker or advising a social worker how to respond to particular facts as they affect the child(ren) in the problem.

In the following example you would be expected to isolate areas which would be the legitimate concern of the social worker always bearing in mind that the authority has to be conscious that the child's parents must be given an opportunity to prove that they can act responsibly.

Heather is a young and inexperienced social worker. Today Mrs T, the head-mistress of the Southdown Comprehensive School, asked her to call at the school to interview Chris, a 12-year-old pupil. Chris is suffering from superficial but painful bruising to the face. It soon becomes apparent that he is suffering from like bruising to the ribs; in addition, his buttocks are marked by a number of weals. Chris tells Heather that his father, Graham, struck him around the face and body with his fist when Graham returned home drunk from a public house the previous evening. Shortly afterwards, says Chris, Graham beat him on the buttocks with a strap because he did not like the meal which Chris had prepared for him. Pat, Chris's 14-year-old sister, confirms Chris's account when Heather speaks to her shortly afterwards. Pat also says that on occasions Graham had not only strapped her also but had sometimes 'interfered with' her sexually. Heather believes that such interference may have gone as far as sexual intercourse.

Graham admits that he has strapped both children but says that Pat has been strapped only on her hands. He says that he had so punished them only because they were guilty, *inter alia,* of theft and only to an extent which he believed is reasonable in the light of his own upbringing 20 years ago in Xanadu. Graham denies strongly any sexually improper conduct on his part. His wife, a quiet and rather timid lady, supports him unequivocally: she goes on to assert that both children are deliberately being untruthful in order to 'get at' their father because he disapproves of some of their friends and has sought to discipline them accordingly.

Advise Heather as to the course of action which you believe is most appropriate.

In order to answer such a question your tutor will in all probability have placed emphasis on what has been referred to as the 'social worker's perspective'. The social worker will have to conform to certain administrative procedures as well as recognising whether or not there is sufficient evidence from which the legal department of the particular authority may take court action. In our problem there appears to be united parental opposition to the statements made by the children. One major question therefore will centre around the ability of Graham and his wife to act as responsible parents and whether or not there exists evidence which has proved them lacking in the past. Heather will therefore need to find out whether or not the children have ever been in care or if the parents were known to the social services department. Ultimately the social worker is going to pose the question whether this particular child ought to be removed from the parents and placed in the care of the local authority. That belief is likely to be strengthened if there is any evidence of non-accidental injury to the child or children of the family. In our case there is superficial bruising to the face but in addition further injury to the body. The question does not tell us that the school had on previous occasions noticed any physical ill-treatment of the boy but at the age of 12 he may only just have arrived at the comprehensive school and the school may not be aware of any problems at junior level. The social worker ought therefore to check Chris's previous school to see if the teachers had noticed any sign of injury. This would also include any signs of neglect either physical or emotional, but there is no evidence of that unless one draws that conclusion from the fact that Chris's parents were not in the habit of making meals for him. We are told that he made a meal which his father did not like. However much I, as a parent, yearn for the day my children make a contribution to the routine of the household I suspect that is mere wishful thinking on my part and that the normal 12-year-old is not likely to volunteer to prepare my dinner after I have completed a hard day at the Polytechnic! I recall one case when I was working in the Midlands of a six-year-old girl whose only topic of conversation at school was food. She was constantly asking for second helpings at lunch-time and eventually it transpired that she was kept short of food by her mother and lived in fear of complaining because her eldest brother was likely to assault her if she did. She was made the subject of a care order. This point concerning fear of parents is listed as one which ought to put social workers on their guard.

Parental history and present condition are important factors to be considered. Then there are the fairly obvious points relating to drink or drug dependence, mental illness, trouble with the police or whether the parents are 'immature'. We are given the information that the incident with Chris occurred after a drinking bout but we do not know whether this is a 'one-off' situation or whether there is evidence of alcohol dependence. Further important elements include the general home environment where the material standards of care may be low. Heather might be advised to seek comments from neighbours as to whether they are aware of fights, screams or any other signs of a hostile family environment. Are the neighbours concerned in any way? Have they ever expressed their anxiety to either social services or the NSPCC? Ultimately Heather is going to need evidence of such a degree that will satisfy the requirements of the 1969 Act if either Chris or Pat is to be made subject to a care order. Does care offer a better alternative for the children? Has the parent/child relationship reached rock bottom so that anything is likely to be preferable to staying in the home?

Since 1973 there have been over 20 public and formal inquiries into deaths from child abuse. Recently there have been the highly publicised cases of Kimberley Carlisle, Jasmine Beckford and Tyra Henry and in the latter two cases convictions for manslaughter and murder respectively against their fathers. From the inquiries the same factor seem to emerge time and again in the failures that lead to the children's deaths – communication breakdowns between social workers or other departments and agencies, failures to review cases regularly and comprehensively and misunderstandings of the jobs of other professionals. A point so vividly and tragically illustrated in the Report of the *Inquiry into Child Abuse in Cleveland 1987* (Cm 412, July 1988).

These Reports are always going to be worth looking at as they contain many recommendations for reform, not just of practice and procedure but also for legislative reform.

It is therefore apparent that there are two major facets to answering problems dealing with child abuse. The first may be termed the 'practical dimension' relating to internal procedures and administrative action. From this process will emerge the decision as to what ought to be done and this will require the second element to be introduced – the legal process.

In cases of suspected non-accidental injury action under the 1969 Act will be contemplated. If the child is in imminent danger then he can be removed under a place of safety order under powers contained in s. 28 of the 1969 Act. Section 28 permits any person to apply to a magistrate for permission to detain a child under 17 in a place of safety for a period of up to 28 days. In order to obtain a place of safety order the applicant must satisfy a magistrate that he has reasonable cause to believe that any of the conditions set out in s. 1(2)(a)-(e) of the 1969 Act are satisfied. The criticism of this procedure is that it is often used for purely routine cases where there is no immediate danger to the child. A good example of this was in *Re C* [1985] FLR 846 where the child was subject to a place of safety order even though it was only hours after the birth and the child was still in hospital. The case was eventually resolved by the father instituting wardship proceedings.

Attention has been focused on this problem as a result of the *Review of Child Care Law* undertaken in 1985, with final recommendations contained in the White Paper (1987) CM 62 entitled *The Law on Child Care and Family Services*, and the Butler-Sloss report on the *Cleveland Child Abuse Inquiry*. The White Paper clearly indicates at para 45 why the place of safety order is unsatisfactory, in particular that it does not address the emergency nature of the need to remove the child. It is proposed to replace it with an 'emergency protection order'. This new order will deal with circumstances where there is reasonable cause to believe that damage to the child's health or well being is likely unless he can immediately be removed. The responsibility for the child will be with the applicant for the order.

The order would include a specific requirement to notify the parents of the order. Also, there will be a *presumption* of reasonable access to the child unless a magistrate decrees otherwise. The present period of 28 days is deemed to be far too long given that this should be an emergency order. It is proposed that the new emergency protection order should last for eight days. In exceptional circumstances an extension may be applied for up to seven days.

The Cleveland Report endorses the need for a change in the law. It points out at para 16.14 (p. 228) that 'the granting of the order imposes upon the child a certain loss of liberty which should not be imposed without very good reasons'. The facts of the Cleveland cases will provide you with more than adequate information to call upon if you are seeking to justify why the law needs changing. In many cases a place of safety order was an 'automatic response' to certain sets of facts. The result, especially when the child was not in danger, was to polarise attitudes and make meaningful negotiation almost impossible.

The Report welcomes the proposals in the White Paper and raises other points at para 16.15 (p. 228). In particular is the suggestion that a magistrate should seek to ascertain, where practicable, the child's views.

Alternatively the applicant may seek to show that another child in the household has had his proper development avoidably prevented or neglected or his health impaired. As a result if it is probable that this will occur in the particular case then the magistrate may grant the order. The third condition relates to the child or young person being about to leave the UK in contravention of s. 25 of the Children and Young Persons Act 1933 which regulates the sending abroad of juvenile entertainers! Hardly relevant to our problem. This is a once-and-for-all order as determined by the Divisional Court in *R* v *Lincoln (Kesteven) Juvenile Court* [1976] 1 All ER 490. This case and the later case of *Nottinghamshire County Council* v *Q* [1982] 2 All ER 641 appear to be the major decisions relating to the construction of s. 28(1) and s. 28(6). This latter provision allows for an application for an interim care order to be made and if the court or justice refuses to make the order then it may be directed that the child be released from the care of the authority. The section does not make it clear who may apply for an interim care older. In the *Lincoln Justices* case the court held that the language of the section was not sufficiently explicit to exclude an application from a parent wishing to have his child released from local authority care into his charge.

Eastham J in the *Nottinghamshire* case left the question open, preferring (at p. 643) to let the Court of Appeal on a subsequent occasion decide the point:

> counsel . . . has submitted that, . . . when one analyses the provisions of the 1969 Act, only certain specified people can invoke the interim order procedure and those are the local authority, the National Society for the Prevention of Cruelty to Children and a constable. For my part, I would be reluctant to go into the matter as the decision of the Queen's Bench Divisional Court deserves the utmost respect from this court, and I . . . would think it more appropriate for the Court of Appeal to come to the conclusion that *Lincoln* was wrongly decided on that point.

Parliament has omitted to give parents a right of appeal against the authorisation of a place of safety order and it was thought that the s. 28(6) procedure could be used as a means of appealing against the s. 28(1) approval. The *Nottinghamshire* case has ruled this option out as it would, if allowed, 'frustrate the will of Parliament and therefore amounted to an abuse of the court's process'. As an aside if you are ever questioned on the strengths and weaknesses of the 1969 Act the following comment by Arnold P in the *Nottinghamshire* case at pp. 643-4 may prove of use to you:

> This is not a very good Act, as I suppose everybody now recognises. Indeed, it is a pity, as I think is now universally thought, that there is no right of appeal from a place of safety order under s. 28(1).

In our problem there is evidence of ill-treatment and it may be thought judicious to remove the child from the home while further investigation takes place as to whether an interim or full care order should be sought. Do remember though that the place of safety order is deemed to be an emergency procedure. As was said in the *Lincoln Justices* case the purpose of a s. 28(1) order was to enable a child in actual danger to be put speedily and effectively in a place of safety.

Note Cretney's comments, *Principles of Family Law,* 4th ed., p. 553, to the effect that:

> the power is so broad that it is clearly capable of abuse and it has been suggested that there is evidence that the procedure is indeed on occasion abused. In particular, it may well be thought that the power to grant such an order can be exercised too informally.

Care proceedings

What will the local authority have to establish in order to obtain a care order over a child? The care order, if granted, confers parental rights on the local authority and this may have a dramatic and potentially damaging effect on parental confidence. There may be no indication when, if ever, they will have their child(ren) back again. Parents may seek to have the order discharged under s. 21 of the Children and Young Persons Act 1969 by exercising their right under s. 70(2) of the Act to bring an application on behalf of the child.

The primary conditions upon which the juvenile court has to satisfy itself are listed in s. 1(2) of the 1969 Act. Some of the conditions are extremely broad, others more limited. An example of the former is s. 1(2)(a) to the effect that 'his proper development is being avoidably prevented or neglected or his health *is* being avoidably impaired or neglected *or* he *is* being ill-treated' (emphasis added). What do the words mean? In *F* v *Suffolk County Council* (1981) 2 FLR 208 it was held that 'development' was not confined to physical development and could properly be extended to mental development and, if it was different, emotional development. However, the court emphasised that a court must consider whether there is *present* avoidable neglect or prevention. The proper development of the child was a continuing process and a court had to look at the present conduct and its effect on the development of the child in the past, present and *foreseeable* future. This view was accepted by Butler-Sloss J in *M* v *Westminster City Council* [1985] FLR 325 and the two cases were subsequently applied by the House of Lords in *D (a minor)* v *Berkshire CC* [1987] 1 All ER 20. The three concepts of development, health and treatment, while recognised as alternative concepts, were still to be regarded as 'continuing' concepts. The use of the present tense 'is being' denoted a continuing, rather than an instant, situation. The correct procedure was for the juvenile court to consider whether immediately prior to the application for a care order there was a continuing situation of impairment, neglect or ill-treatment. The court could look at the past, even to events before the child was born which were having an adverse effect on his health, e.g., his mother was a drug addict. However, as was pointed out by Lords Griffiths, Mackay and Goff, past events could not *of themselves* support an application under this ground.

The White Paper (1987) points out at para 59 (p. 15) that the current grounds are largely confined to an examination of the present and past defects in the development and well being of the child. Where future harm is at issue the local authority often make application to the High Court for wardship. It is therefore recommended that there should be new grounds for a care order, and one element will be proof of harm or *likely* harm to the child. 'Likely harm' is intended to cover cases of unacceptable risk in which it may be necessary to balance the chance of the harm occurring against the magnitude of that harm if it does occur. The nature of the risk will have to be assessed by the court. This in its turn is bound to reduce the number of wardship applications, if one recommendation becomes law.

An example of the 'limited' category is s. 1(2)(c) which deals with a child being in moral danger. An aspect of this is raised in our problem on two fronts, first the alleged sexual misconduct towards the daughter and secondly the fact that the father's attitude towards the upbringing of his children is based upon beliefs generated 20 years ago in a foreign country. It was emphasised in *Mohammed* v *Knott* [1969] 1 QB 1 that in deciding whether or not the child was in moral danger the background and way of life of the parties were factors to be taken into account, and it must be assumed that the examiner would wish you to consider the ramifications of this case in the context of the problem.

Revision note　Surprisingly perhaps there is not a great deal of case law associated with the various subsections. My advice is to make notes on each subsection with supporting case law and in addition try to view the law as the culmination of an administrative process initiated by social workers in response to some evidence of child abuse. Perhaps the most comprehensive study is that of Dingwall, Eekelaar and Murray entitled *The Protection of Children*. Do note also that once one of the primary conditions is satisfied the court must then give consideration to s. 1(2) that is, to whether it is satisfied that the child is in need of care or control which he is unlikely to receive unless the court makes the order. It is suggested that if one of the primary conditions is satisfied then it is almost inevitable that the order will be made. Nevertheless the court must treat 'care or control' as a separate matter. (See *Re DJMS* [1977] 3 All ER 582 to the effect that if a child was not being properly educated he was not being properly cared for.)

The White Paper (1987) recommends that there should be three elements to the new grounds for a care order. We have already mentioned evidence of harm or likely harm and in addition the following will have to be proved:

(i)　the harm or likely harm is attributable to the absence of a *reasonable* standard of parental care or the child is beyond parental control; and

(ii)　that the order proposed is the most effective means available to the court of safeguarding the child's welfare.

With regard to (i) the White Paper makes it clear at para 60, p. 15 that it is not intended to imply a judgment on the parent who is doing his best but still may be unable to provide a reasonable standard of care. The latter provision is aimed at directing the court to consider all the options available, e.g., a care order may not be in the child's best interests.

Orders

Five orders – parental recognisances, supervision, care, hospital order within the Mental Health Act 1983 and a guardianship order under the Mental Health Act 1983 – are available to the court but the majority tend to be either care or supervision orders. The former commits the child into local authority care and in effect the authority becomes the child's legal parent. The options available to the authority include boarding him out or keeping him within a community home. In many cases in order to keep links with the parent the child is placed under the control of a relative, friend or even the parents. This is, of course, a *de facto* arrangement and the legal powers over the child remain with the authority. The juvenile court does not have power to impose conditions when making a care order. However, such limitations do not exist if the child in care is a ward of court placed there by the High Court under s. 7(2) of the Family Law Reform Act 1969. In *M* v *Lambeth Borough Council, The Times,* 20 December 1984, Sheldon J agreed that the 'ultimate responsibility for the welfare of the ward was that of the High Court. All the major decisions affecting the ward's welfare should be taken subject to the directions of the High Court.' (See also *J* v *Devon County Council* [1986] 1 FLR 597.)

Discharge of care orders

A care order can be discharged or varied on application by the local authority or child or parents acting pursuant to powers contained in s. 21 of the Children and Young Persons Act 1969. The court has to be satisfied that it is appropriate to discharge the order and it must be convinced that the child will continue to receive the necessary care or control. As when a child is made subject to a care order, on discharge of that order the juvenile court does not have power to impose conditions. As Cumming-Bruce LJ said in *Re J* [1984] 1 All ER 29 at p. 33:

> The juvenile court has no power to impose any conditions as the conditions on which it will discharge the care order. . . .
> In my view there is a lacuna in the statutory scheme which can only be filled by the legislator in order to complete the powers available to the local authority and to the juvenile court under the statutory scheme.

When considering whether or not to discharge an order the court is not statutorily bound to put the child's interests first. However, given that in *Re J* the Court of Appeal continued the wardship order so as to give greater flexibility in controlling the child's return it could be implied that the court felt that on discharging an order the child's welfare should be the first and paramount consideration.

This view has been adopted by the White Paper (para 65 p. 17). The Government intend that the court should be satisfied that the discharge of the order would be in the best interests of the child, and in reaching that decision the court should satisfy itself that if control is needed it will be provided.

Appeals

There are serious deficiencies in the present appeal structure in care proceedings. These are:

(i)   Appeals are heard at the Crown Court thereby confusing the civil and criminal jurisdictions.

(ii)   The appeal is only against the *making* of the order *not* the refusal to make a care order.

(iii)   The right to appeal rests in the child, although *B v Gloucester County Council* [1980] 2 All ER 746 confirmed that an appeal can be made on behalf of the child. However, it was pointed out that if the parents argued the case from their own perspective the court was likely to dismiss the appeal. Nevertheless, if a separate representation order is made under s. 32 A of the 1969 Act because of a conflict of interest between parent and child then the parent cannot represent the child. In *AR and another v Avon County Council* [1985] 2 All ER 981 a guardian *ad litem* was appointed and it was held that he was the only person who could appeal on behalf of the child to the Crown Court. The child's parents cannot appeal on the child's behalf if the guardian decides not to go ahead with an appeal.

However, consistent with the recognition that parents should have greater rights to represent their children, the Children and Young Persons (Amendment) Act 1986, s. 2 reverses the current position.

(iv)   There is no appeal against the granting of an order to discharge a care order. (Although in these circumstances wardship remains an expensive option for the party opposing the granting of the order.)

The White Paper proposes radical changes in regard to appeals. First all appeals from 'care and related proceedings' would go to the same court. This would be the Family Court should one ever be created, but until such time appeals would be to the High Court *not* the Crown Court.

The Government intends to give *all* parties to the original proceedings the right to appeal against decisions of the court. The result if implemented would be that local authorities would no longer have to resort to the wardship jurisdiction if a care order is refused.

Parties to the proceedings

In care proceedings it is the child who is the respondent. The Children and Young Persons (Amendment) Act 1986, s. 3 would allow parents to be made parties if there was a conflict of interest. The section also provides for grandparents to be made parties and s. 4 provides for legal aid to be made available. The White Paper throws aside this piecemeal change and goes for a much more radical solution. The basic proposition is that *anyone* whose legal position *could* be affected by the proceedings will be entitled to party status. This would include anyone who is seeking legal responsibility for the child by way, for example, of a custody order (a new option under the proposals).

Conclusion

I have suggested that the local authority is likely to seek to take the children into care. They have evidence of direct ill treatment of the boy and some unsubstantiated testimony that the daughter has been sexually interfered with. There is also reason to believe that the father's drinking combined with his unusual (for the UK) upbringing may lead to further harm to the children. The wife, who is described as quiet and timid, is hardly likely to defend the children vigorously against their father.

If after all investigations are completed the local authority feels it has insufficient evidence to establish one of the principal conditions then wardship remains an option if the authority feels that the children are at risk. It may well be that, given the penalties for contempt of a High Court order, the father would be more likely to adhere to it and seek to change his over-rigorous approach to his children. What standards one can expect from the 'reasonable parent' in 1988 is an open question!

It will have become obvious that care proceedings are in for a massive shake up with new legislation promised for the next Parliamentary session. More immediately, the Government are likely to seek to amend the law on place of safety orders before tackling the massive task of reformulating the laws applicable to care proceedings. This topic therefore is a prime candidate for examinations, combining as it does a piece of legislation which has been controversially inadequate, much case law and recommendations for reform. When dealing with the current law do take a structured approach but, most importantly, always remember the purpose behind the legislation. Essentially this is protection for the child, but one cannot forget that parents have rights as well and that support for the family is needed in many situations. Concurrent with dealing with each matter, note in turn the deficiencies that exist and what it is that is proposed to replace the existing law. In this way you ought to have a good command of the legal position of children who have to be taken into care.

Voluntary care

The other side of the care equation relates to circumstances in which the local authority may give support to parents who are undergoing stress or difficulties with their child. The relevant legislation is the Child Care Act 1980 as amended in part by the Health and Social Services and Social Security Adjudications Act 1983. Sections 2(1) of the 1980 Act puts an authority under a duty to receive a child under 17 into its care where 'it appears to' the local authority that:

(a)   he has neither parent nor guardian or has been and remains abandoned by his parents or guardian or is lost, or

(b)   his parents or guardian are, *for the time being* or permanently, prevented by reason of mental or bodily disease or infirmity or other incapacity or *any other circumstances* from providing for his proper accommodation, maintenance and upbringing, *and*

(c)   in either case, that the intervention of the local authority under this section is necessary in the interests of the welfare of the child.

In essence the legislation is meant to provide whenever possible short-term support to the family with the aim of returning the child to the home as soon as is advisable.

In practice the legal problems have centred around two things. First that even though parental rights do not transfer to the local authority it has been difficult for parents to obtain access to their children. The 1983 Act recognised the difficulty and inserted new ss. 12A to 12G into the Child Care Act 1980. Under s. 12G a code of practice has been published by the DHSS entitled 'Access to Children in Care' with the aim that it 'will provide a sound framework for the best of social work practice and help to spread it more widely'.

The code seeks to set out basic principles on which local authorities and other agencies should operate in *promoting* and sustaining access and in handling decisions to restrict or terminate access where that becomes necessary. Questions therefore are likely to be set upon the construction to be given to the new ss. 12A to 12G. The provisions apply to any child in the care of the local authority whether by care order or parental rights resolution (for a full list see s. 12A) but not to a child who is placed in care as a result of a High Court order, for example, in wardship proceedings.

Under the section a local authority may not *terminate* access or refuse to make arrangements for access without first giving the parent etc. notice. If notice has been served the parent etc. has a right under s. 12C to apply to the juvenile court for an access order. An appeal shall lie to the High Court against *any decision* of a juvenile court under this particular part of the Act.

Note should be made of the provisions of s. 12F which makes it quite clear that the guiding principle in such cases is that of the welfare of the child being the first and paramount consideration. In *Hereford and Worcester County Council* v *JAH* [1985] FLR 530 and [1986] 1 FLR 29 it was emphasised that access to the child was not a parental right, but had to be shown to be in the child's best interests. See also *Coventry City Council* v *T* [1986] 2 FLR 301 where the parents were eventually refused access, not having seen their daughter for four years.

One of the major complaints about the new provisions is that they apply only when the authority seeks to *terminate* access. If it restricts access to an untenable level but does not foreclose altogether then the parent has no right to challenge the action in the juvenile court. In *R* v *Bolton MBC ex parte B* [1985] FLR 343 Wood J said that 'termination' implied the bringing to an end of an existing relationship. The local authority should act speedily in making its decision whether to terminate or refuse access and a sufficient period, he suggested, would be 14 days. This case also decided that to postpone an access decision until the hearing of adoption proceedings would undermine the purpose of the new s. 12. This potential for conflict has been highlighted in *Southwark LBC* v *H* [1985] 2 All ER 657. Arnold P held that if access proceedings in the juvenile court and adoption proceedings in the High Court were on foot simultaneously, the first matter to be decided was future access between parent and child. This would be especially true if in the adoption proceedings there was an application to dispense with the parents' agreement.

It raises yet again what Waite J in *R* v *Corby Juvenile Court, ex parte M* [1987] 1 All ER 992 called a 'sad paradox'. He went on to say that:

> the law of child care, though designed to cater principally for the problems that press on the least advantaged and most defenceless families in our society, has nevertheless been allowed to become one of the most complex areas within the legal system. A mass of separate enactments, all with their confusing amendments and cross references to each other, has given growth to a legislative thicket through which even the most practised members of the legal and social work professions have to struggle to find their way. (p. 993 (g)).

Note also that the provisions do not cover a child in voluntary care. As the parent still possesses all his legal rights over the child it is unnecessary to include this in s. 12. However, if the child is with the local authority it may in practice be difficult for a parent to exercise his legal right of access to his child. Note also that, as a result of the Family Law Reform Act 1987, the father of an 'illegitimate' child, who has obtained parental right under s. 4 of the Act, is to be treated as a parent, where actual custody of the child is shared. The father may then challenge a decision to refuse or terminate access.

Parental rights resolutions

Sometimes there is no alternative to reception into care on one of the grounds in s. 2 of the Child Care Act 1980. In such circumstances the local authority is required to work towards the rehabilitation of the child with his parents etc., providing always that it is consistent with the child's welfare. It follows therefore that it should be exceptional for a child to be received into care with a view to an immediate assumption of parental rights and duties under s. 3.

If a child is in care then s. 18 puts the authority under a general duty to give *first consideration* to the need to safeguard and promote the welfare of the child throughout his childhood. Usually the child's interests will be best served within his family. However, if this is not possible then the assumption of parental rights and duties is a valuable means of safeguarding and planning for a child who would otherwise have no effective parents; and of protecting a child in cases where the need for protection had emerged since reception into care.

Parental rights and duties can be assumed only in accordance with the procedures laid down in s. 3 or, if the child is in the care of a voluntary organisation, in s. 14 of the Child Care Act 1980. Local authorities must keep parents informed of the plans for their children and if, for example, the period in care is likely to exceed six months, then the 28 days' notice provision in ss. 13 and 63 of the Act should be explained to parents.

The decision to assume parental rights will usually be made by elected members of the particular authority but the decision to recommend such a course will normally come as a result of the statutory reviews of the child which take place while he is in care. It is suggested that legal advice on whether there are statutory grounds for a resolution should be obtained at an early stage. As a matter of law local authorities are required in every case to serve notice on the person whose rights and duties have been assumed (Health and Social Services and Social Security Adjudications Act 1983, s. 9 and sch. 2, para. 46, amending s. 3 of the 1980 Act).

A resolution can be passed only over a child in care and this has resulted in problems for local authorities. The basic proposition is that if the parent or guardian desires to have the child back the authority has no power under s. 2 of the Child Care Act 1980 to retain the child. It will be obvious that in some cases the authority will be genuinely concerned that the return of the child to the parent will not be in its best interests. Section 13(2) creates a criminal offence of removing a child who has been in care for the preceeding six months unless 28 days' notice is given. In these circumstances the authority, if concerned for the child's future, has time to pass a parental rights resolution or possibly commence wardship proceedings. If the child has been in care for less than six months then there would appear to be no statutory basis for keeping the child. This matter was tackled by the House of Lords in *Lewisham Borough Council* v *Lewisham Juvenile Court Justices and another* [1979] 2 All ER 297. Lord

Salmon at p. 306 (h) said that the authority would have no legal right to retain the child in their care, and would be expected to hand over the child on demand. He goes on to add:

> I think however that an authority might, if the child had been in their care for less than six months, well consider it to be their moral duty to keep the child long enough to have it made a ward of court. This is all they could do to save the child. . . .

However, if questions are asked of the Child Care Act 1980 they are likely to centre around the grounds upon which a resolution can be based as that is where most of the case law is to be found. Therefore, taking each subsection in turn, you should list the key words and then look for cases which have assisted in the construction of the provision. To take one example from the list in s. 3, that to be found in s. 3(1)(v) which deals with parents who have so *consistently* failed *without reasonable cause* to *discharge the obligations of a parent* as to be *unfit* to have the care of the child. This subsection is packed with words which need to have meaning given to them whilst at the same time it could be argued that parents have a good chance of successfully opposing the granting of the resolution. Therefore you may proceed in the following fashion.

What are the obligations of a parent?   In *M* v *Wigan Metropolitan Borough Council* [1979] 2 All ER 958 it was held that 'obligations of a parent' included the 'natural and moral duty of a parent to show affection, care and interest towards his or her child and also the common law or statutory duty of a parent to maintain the child financially' (taken from *Re P* [1962] 3 All ER 789 at p. 794).

'Consistent'   In the *Wigan* case it was said by Sheldon J that whether or not a parent had failed and had *consistently* failed to discharge his obligations are 'questions of fact and degree depending on the particular circumstances of the case'. It was held that the word 'consistently' was not to be given the same interpretation as the word 'persistently' which had first appeared in the corresponding section in the Children Act 1948. 'Consistently' in this context:

> contemplates behaviour over a period which has constantly adhered to the pattern of which complaint is made . . . in this case . . . 'a pattern of rejection', but the length of the period will be a question of fact depending on the nature of the behaviour under review.

This was adopted in *W* v *Sunderland Borough Council* [1980] 2 All ER 514 where it was said that the failure to discharge parental duties did not have to occur over a 'substantial period' but only 'over the period of time appropriate to the matters arising in a particular case'.

Without reasonable cause   In *Wigan* the court held that it had to apply an objective standard, i.e., it had to look to see whether the cause was reasonable or unreasonable according to what a reasonable parent would have done in all the circumstances.

Discharge   What type of behaviour is relevant? In *O'Dare* v *South Glamorgan County Council* (1980) 3 FLR 1 it was held that it was plain from the authorities that the behaviour of the parent had to involve some blameworthiness or some 'self-indulgent indifference to the welfare of the child'. And Sheldon J in the *Wigan* case spoke of culpability of a high degree being necessary as evidenced by some callous or self-indulgent indifference to the welfare of the child (see also *Re C* [1964] 3 All ER 483 and *Re D* [1973] 3 All ER 1001).

In *Wheatley* v *London Borough of Waltham Forest* [1979] 2 All ER 289, the court would not divest a mother of her rights and duties because her conduct 'fell short of the high degree of culpable failure to discharge the obligations of a parent such as to be unfit to have the care of the child.'

Revision note

The benefit of this approach is that when it comes to analysing a problem in the examination your eyes should move fairly quickly to the crucial words and you will be aware of how the section will be applied in practice. I would suggest a similar approach to the other elements. So, for example, when has a child been 'abandoned' or what are the 'habits or mode of life' such that a parent is unfit to have care of the child?

Wardship and local authorities

The wardship jurisdiction has until recently been closely associated with the statutory child care code. Essentially, parental dissatisfaction with the apparent lack of rights bestowed upon them by statute has meant that they have turned to the prerogative jurisdiction in an attempt to challenge the extent of those powers granted to local authorities and often as a means of appeal where no statutory right to do so existed. It has to be said that the significant case law in the 1980s leads one to the conclusion that, as Bromley, 7th ed. puts it, there is a 'general principle of non-intervention' and this is consistent with efforts to put wardship back onto a more 'traditional' footing. However, there has been the opposite effect where local authorities have sought to exploit the jurisdiction where the statutory code has proved inadequate. Courts have encouraged its use as we have in the *Lewisham Borough Council* case. In *Re B (a minor)* [1974] 3 All ER 915 at p. 921g Lane J said:

I consider that there would be no abandonment of, or derogation from, their statutory powers and duties were they to seek the guidance and assistance of the High Court in matters of difficulty, as distinct from the day-to-day arrangements with which, as the authorities show, the court will not interfere.

Although there have been passing references which could be interpreted to place some fetter on local authority discretion to use the jurisdiction, there is no indication that the judiciary have as a matter of policy sought to restrict its use by local authorities. (See Dillon LJ in *Re D (a minor)* [1987] 1 All ER 20 at p. 32 — 'It follows that where the statutory scheme applies, there is no scope for wardship'.) So local authorities would appear free to use wardship not only to supplement the statutory code but as an alternative to it. Wardship has the advantage of being a High Court jurisdiction (but see the Practice Direction [1988] 2 All ER 103), the court has virtually unlimited powers and its procedure is much less restricted than when seeking a care order in the juvenile court.

Let us return to the former point and the restrictions upon the use of the jurisdiction to challenge local authority decisions. It would seem pointless to review the cases prior to the first significant case which severely curtailed the use of wardship. All you need to understand is that parents had very few rights under the statutory child care code and were looking for some means of challenging decisions of the juvenile court or local authorities once the child was in care. Their position is now improved in some respects, e.g., with regard to access under the Child Care Act 1980, and will be much improved once new legislation is forthcoming to implement the recommendations of the White Paper (1987 Cmnd 62). In future, therefore, the loss of access to the jurisdiction will not be crucial. But, as the law stands at the moment, there would appear to be a severe imbalance between the ability of parents and local authorities to use the jurisdiction.

There are three major cases for you to analyse. The first is *A* v *Liverpool City Council* [1982] AC 363 where access by a mother to her child was severely curtailed by the local authority because it held the view that rehabilitation of mother and child was not in the child's best interests. The House of Lords held that the courts had no jurisdiction to review a local authority's discretionary powers under a care order except by judicial review. The reasoning was that Parliament had resisted from giving the courts any reviewing powers under the child care legislation. (As a result of the 1983 amendment to the Child Care Act 1980 this use of wardship has been made redundant as there is now a statutory right to challenge access decisions in the juvenile court with a further right to appeal to the High Court.)

A further attempt to use wardship was made in 1985 in *W* v *Hertfordshire County Council* [1985] 2 All ER 301. However, the House applying the *Liverpool* decision concluded that the High Court did not have jurisdiction to supervise or review the merits of a decision of the local authority acting under the child care legislation. Perhaps of more significance was the fact that the House rejected the 'exceptional category' usage for the jurisdiction as suggested by Sir George Baker in *M* v *Humberside CC* [1979] 2 All ER 744. This really does close any loophole by which applicants could try to argue that their case fitted into the 'exceptional' category.

Finally look out for the report of the House of Lords in *Re M and H (Minors)* [1988] 3 All ER 5. The heading to the report says it all – 'Court cannot intervene over child in care'. This was an attempt by the putative father of a child who was in care under s. 3(1) of the Child Care Act to gain legal custody and access. The House had been invited to say that *A* and *W* (above) were wrongly decided for two reasons:

(i)   The principles applicable to deciding cases relating to children, i.e., the welfare principle, differed significantly from that used by local authorities under s. 18 of the Child Care Act – first consideration to safeguard and promote the welfare of the children. The House denied that *in the context of s. 18* there was any significant difference.

(ii)   That the denial of a review on the merits by a court of the decisions of local authorities was a breach of the Convention for the Protection of Human Rights and Fundamental Freedoms (1953) (Cmd 8969).

The House answered that by saying that it was up to Parliament not the courts to do something about it, if in fact there was such a breach.

It followed that *A* and *W* were not wrongly decided and the father's appeal was dismissed, on the basis that the court had no power to review the merits of local authority decisions.

Significantly you ought to note that, concurrent with this development of restriction, the Court of Appeal extended the *Liverpool* decision to a situation where care proceedings were only pending and a care order not in force (*Re E (minors) (wardship: jurisdiction)* [1984] 1 All ER 21). See also *W* v *Nottinghamshire CC* [1986] 1 FLR 565 and *W* v *Shropshire CC* [1986] 1 FLR 359.

Significantly, at a time when the House has consistently denied parents access to the wardship court, the jurisdiction was used by parents to great effect. The beleaguered parents in the Cleveland child abuse controversy sought the help of the High Court in their battle with the local authority. The Butler-Sloss Report says:

The point of jurisdiction was conveniently waived by Cleveland County Council during the latter part of 1987 in a situation of crisis and the originating summonses were issued either by the Council or by the parents. (para 16.36).

The Report goes on to say (para 16.37):

There is no doubt that the wardship jurisdiction came to the rescue of an otherwise overburdened Juvenile Court. It has proved in Cleveland to be an invaluable procedure to enable extremely difficult, complex and emotive issues to be fully considered and adjudicated upon. Wardship has an ethos which is recognised by those who use and are engaged in the jurisdiction. We see wardship having a role to play in care proceedings in the future.

and later (and most significantly):

There is an injustice in the ability of a Local Authority to issue wardship proceedings and for the parents not to have that right. In our view the decision in *A* v *Liverpool City Council* [1982] AC 363 ought to be reconsidered.

One therefore awaits with interest the proposals for new legislation and to find out what role the wardship jurisdiction will have in this respect.

Sample question

The different statutes under which a child may be taken or received into care have not been examined. Given the further information on adoption, custodianship and wardship perhaps you would now like to attempt to write an answer to the following question. Read it carefully underlining any words you think may have legal consequences. Having done that make a note of what the major issues appear to be and put against those the relevant legislation and any supporting authority. Finally give thought to the structure of your answer bearing in mind that you are advising the council. If this attempt at an answer is designed as practice for the examination then you should spend no more than 40 minutes in writing it out. This question is taken from an examination paper which demanded answers to four questions in three hours.

Re Sally Smith: proposed adoption
Blanktown Metropolitan District Council has, in care under the Child Care Act 1980, s. 2, a nine-year-old girl, Sally. She has been in the same foster home for two and a half years since her putative father Mr Smith was imprisoned for a sexual offence against her elder half-sister.

Sally's mother, Mrs Brown, was living next door to Mr Smith when Sally was born. Mr Brown had left her four months earlier. When Sally was three weeks old, Mrs Brown left Sally at Mr Smith's home with a letter (which the District Council now has) saying that Mr Smith, as Sally's father, had better cope as she (Mrs Brown) was at the end of her tether, could not make ends meet, and was going back to her mother's home in the South. Mr Smith, on the strength of the letter, got a custody order, and, with the none-too-enthusiastic help of Miss White (with whom he was living), cared for Sally until she was six.

When Sally came to the notice of the Council, on Mr Smith's conviction, she was described as 'a neglected, frightened and backward' child. After three years with the foster parents, she has made considerable progress and is now in no way behind other children of her age in physical and mental development.

Blanktown Council would like to have Sally adopted by the foster parents, who are keen to do this. They have information that Mr Smith should be released on licence early next year. Mrs Brown has been traced, and has said:

(a)   that she does not want Sally to be adopted;

(b)   that Sally's real father was her husband, Mr Brown; and

(c)   that she has formed an association with a Mr Jones, whom she is hoping to marry on the completion of certain divorce proceedings.

Describe the steps Blanktown Council will need to take to enable the foster parents to adopt Sally, explaining whose consents will be needed to those steps and what can be done if any such consent is not forthcoming.

Conclusion

It goes without saying that any family law examination should include some reference to the law on child care, given that a vast amount of energy has gone into producing two reports in 1985 and 1987 upon which new laws will be based. It is also a reasonable bet that the *Cleveland Child Abuse Inquiry Report* (1988 Cm 412) will become compulsory reading. The volume runs to over 300 pages, the majority of it dealing with the role played by individual doctors, social workers and police as well as the breakdown of the system. The value of the report is that it will help you to clarify which laws need to be amended, whether new laws are needed, as well as examining the procedures adopted by the various agencies. It also gives a valuable insight into the role of the juvenile court and the wardship jurisdiction. In particular I would urge you to read chapter 16 which deals with the Courts (pp. 226-240), chapter 10 the legal processes (pp. 172-180) and, of course, the conclusions and recommendations (pp. 243-256). Pages 14-24 outline the background to the Cleveland crisis and should also be read.

I suspect it will be unlikely for there to be a question simply on Cleveland, but it forms part of a whole series of documents to which reference should be made as you seek to glean information to underpin your study of child care law reform. In addition to the Cleveland Report look at:

Children II

(i)   The White Paper: *The Law on Child Care and Family Services* (1987, Cm 62).

(ii)   *The Review of Child Care Law* (1985).

(iii)   Recent reports relating to deaths of young children, e.g., Kimberley Carlisle (1987) Jasmine Beckford and Tyra Henry (1985).

Add to these your review of current case law and changes to the main statute, e.g., the Children and Young Persons (Amendment) Act 1986, and you should be able to face any questions with confidence. Watch carefully though for the emphasis given by your tutor, because in order to examine other family law topics he may have to be selective on this one.

Parental rights

In one sense it is probably misleading to talk of rights. We have seen that in child care matters parents have had few rights. In 1985 the House of Lords had the opportunity to review the legal position of parents, to consider the extent of their rights and responsibilities, and so it will be convenient to pose the question: What authority do parents possess with regard to their children after the decision in *Gillick* v *West Norfolk and Wisbech Area Health Authority* [1958] 3 All ER 402? The crucial point would appear to be that parental influence over a child diminishes as the child gets older and is capable of making his own decisions. Any standard textbook will outline the rights that a parent is supposed to possess (see Bromley, 7th ed., pp. 270-283). The courts are occasionally asked to adjudicate on some of these, but outside the area of consenting to medical treatment the reported decisions are few and far between. As the law stands the welfare of the child per Lord MacDermott in *J* v *C* will take precedence over the wishes of the parent, assuming that the two are in some way opposed. (*Re B (a minor) (Wardship: medical treatment)* [1981] 1 WLR 1421 is a good example of this.) Also there must come a time when the child is deemed old enough to make his own decisions even though he has not reached the magical age of 18. Parents may not necessarily agree with this, especially in circumstances where their 'child' is still living at home. It is likely that the parents will want to exercise a degree of control over him. However, this must be set against the extensive discussion of parental authority in the *Gillick* case and it will be helpful if we look at the case in some detail so that all the issues are examined.

Mrs Victoria Gillick had challenged the West Norfolk Health Authority to show that a circular issued by the DHSS which stated that doctors who prescribed contraceptives to girls under 16 would not be acting unlawfully, was indeed lawful. She maintained that in so doing doctors would be accessories to the criminal offence of unlawful sexual intercourse with a girl under 16, contrary to s. 6 of the Sexual Offences Act 1956. Secondly and perhaps more importantly for family lawyers she sought a declaration that to give advice and treatment on contraception to girls under 16 without their parents' consent was unlawful as being inconsistent with parental rights. Woolf J [1984] 1 All ER 365 held that doctors would not be committing a criminal offence if they complied with the advice given in the circular and secondly that parental 'rights' were better described as responsibilities and duties and thus to give advice did not infringe any parental right.

Subsequently ([1985] 1 All ER 533) the Court of Appeal unanimously allowed the appeal by Mrs Gillick. All the judges stressed that parental authority had to be respected unless displaced by the child's welfare, or by order of the court. The DHSS appealed to the House of Lords, and were successful by a majority of three to two. There are so many pertinent issues raised by this case that it is difficult to know where to begin. However, as a law student you will need to understand the legal issues considered by their Lordships. The majority concluded that the 'central issue' (Lord Fraser of Tullybelton) was whether a doctor could ever, in *any* circumstances, lawfully give contraceptive advice or treatment to a girl under 16 without her parents' consent. This could be considered from three viewpoints:

(a)   Could a girl under 16 herself give a valid consent to contraceptive advice and treatment?

(b)   Were parental rights infringed if such advice or treatment were given without their consent?

(c)   Whether doctors who gave such advice or treatment to the under-16s were guilty of a criminal offence.

Lord Fraser could find no statutory authority which indicated that girls under 16 lacked the legal capacity to consent to contraceptive advice, examination or treatment, provided they fully understood what was involved. He went on to say that he did not agree that parents had an *absolute* right to be informed and reminded parents that whatever rights they have exist not for the benefit of the parent but for the child. It was to fly in the face of reality to say that a child remained under the *complete* control of his parents until he attained the age of majority. Wise parents apparently relax their control gradually, usually depending upon their assessment of their child's level of understanding and intelligence. His Lordship was therefore of the opinion that 'the law ought to and did in fact have regard to such changes'. In essence therefore Lord Fraser appeared to base his conclusions upon an application of the 'welfare' principle, that the child's welfare was the first and paramount consideration. It was recognised that in the majority of cases the parents were best fitted to decide what was in their child's best interests and as such it would be most unusual for a doctor to act without the knowledge and consent of the parents. However, some under-age girls, having received advice from all possible quarters would still engage in sexual intercourse and they had to be protected. As such one then moves from the arena of parental *rights* to that of the doctor's *discretion*. Lord Fraser therefore laid down the ground rules by which a doctor would be bound before that discretion could be exercised positively. The doctor would have to be satisfied:

(a)   the girl would understand his advice;

(b)   he could not persuade her to involve her parents;

(c)   she was likely to have sexual intercourse with or without contraceptive treatment;

(d)   her mental or physical health or both were likely to suffer if contraceptives were not prescribed;

(e)   her best interests required him to give her contraception.

A failure to adhere to the above guidelines would lead one to the conclusion that the doctor had failed to carry out his professional responsibilities and he could expect to be disciplined by his professional body.

As to a doctor's criminal liability, this would depend on his intentions when he supplied the contraceptives. To be an accessory he would need to intend to encourage the unlawful sexual intercourse but if he followed the 'Fraser guidelines' it would be virtually impossible to prove that this was the case. Similarly, a doctor who followed the guidelines would not commit an offence under s. 28(1) of the 1956 Act, which provides: 'It is an offence for a person to cause or encourage . . . the commission of unlawful sexual intercourse with . . . a girl under 16 for whom he is responsible'.

Lord Scarman similarly sought to emphasise certain features of today's society which were unknown to our predecessors. Those were:

(a)   contraception as a subject for medical advice and treatment;

(b)   increasing independence of young people and

(c)   changed status of women.

The law ignored these developments at its peril. Lord Scarman was prepared to recognise the *existence* of parental rights and thought that they did not disappear until the child reached majority. They related to both the person and property of the child. However, as parental rights were derived from parental duty they existed only so long as they were needed for the protection of the person and property of the child. He thought that if absolute certainty was required then that could only be achieved by Parliament after full consideration of all the factors.

The minority, Lords Brandon and Templeman appear to have based their opinions upon public policy considerations, in particular that enshrined in the criminal law that it was unlawful for a man to have sexual intercourse with a girl under 16. The statutory provision reflecting this was enacted for the purpose of protecting the girl against herself. Thus the criminal and civil law should march 'hand in hand' on all issues and to allow any inconsistency would discredit the rule of law. Lord Templeman felt that there were many things which a girl under 16 needed to practise, but sex was not one of them. Although Parliament was free to declare that view outdated, as the law stood a girl under 16 was not competent to decide whether to practise sex and contraception. As such a doctor was not entitled to decide whether a girl under 16 should be provided with contraceptives if a parent in charge of the girl was willing to make that decision.

Advice to students First you must come to grips with the legal issues. They may be summarised as follows.

The lawfulness of the DHSS circular
Remember that the circular does emphasise most strongly that parental support should always be sought by the doctor, when considering whether or not to give contraception treatment.

> There is widespread concern about counselling and treatment for children under 16. Special care is needed not to undermine parental responsibility and family stability. The Department would therefore hope . . . the doctor . . . will always seek to persuade the child to involve the parent . . . at the earliest stage of consultation and will proceed from the assumption that it would be *most unusual* to provide advice about contraception without parental consent. (Emphasis added.)

Therefore the Lords decision does not seek to create an environment where girls under 16 are free to indulge in sexual relations with ready recourse to contraceptive supplies. In upholding the validity of the circular the Law Lords stress the limited circumstances in which a doctor may proceed without parental consent. For the full text of the circular see [1985] 3 All ER 402 at pp. 405-6.

Parental rights
The Court of Appeal judgment was widely interpreted as recognising the pre-eminent position of parents to control their children under 16. Parker and Fox LJJ stated that only the court could interfere with those rights and in addition parents such as Mrs Gillick could look to the courts to have those rights enforced.

The Lords variously recognised a bundle of parental rights, especially to control children and Lord Fraser particularly agreed with the statement of Lord Denning MR in the other significant case on parental rights, *Hewer* v *Bryant* [1970] 1 QB 357 at p. 369, that parents had 'a dwindling right which the courts will hesitate to enforce against the wishes of the child, and the more so the older he is. It starts with the right of control and ends with little more than advice.'

Criminal offences
Providing doctors adhere to the guidelines detailed by Lord Fraser then it will be difficult to establish the necessary *mens rea* for the crimes under s. 28(1) of the Sexual Offences Act 1956 and being an accessory to the s. 6 offence under the same Act. However, note that Lord Brandon believed that 'for any person to *promote, encourage* or *facilitate* the commission of such an act might itself be a criminal offence'.

Welfare of the child
The majority stress that at the end of the day the child's welfare must be paramount. You may recall that earlier in the book I quoted Lord Macdermott in *J* v *C* [1970] AC 668 at pp. 710-11 to the effect that what was in the best interests of the child could only be assessed once 'all the relevant facts, relationships, claims and wishes of the parents, risks, choices and other circumstances are taken into account and weighed'. Similarly Lord Fraser has detailed the relevant facts and circumstances to be taken into account.

The decision, as it was bound to do whatever the outcome of the case, has sparked off a tremendous controversy about whether contraceptive advice should be available to girls under 16 and if so does this offend against basic principles of morality and religion. As Lord Templeman said:

It was doubtful whether a girl under 16 was capable of a balanced judgment to embark on frequent, regular or casual sexual intercourse, fortified by the illusion that medical science could protect her in mind and body, and ignoring the danger of leaping from childhood to adulthood without the difficult formative transitional experiences of adolescence.

One view, shared by the minority, appears to be that society should through its laws do its best to discourage sexual intercourse by the young, i.e., persons under 16. The majority appear to recognise that individuals mature at different ages and that while all young people should be counselled in the dangers of early sexual activity the law should allow young people to make an informed consent to the provision of contraceptive advice or treatment.

Conclusion   The expectation must be for essay questions to be set on this topic giving full rein to the issues mentioned and many others likely to surface in the future as the debate on 'under-age sex' and 'parental rights' continues unabated. Try to categorise the issues wherever possible otherwise they may only serve to confuse you. Use different major headings with appropriate subheadings.

The impact of the decision also goes beyond parental authority as it would appear to confirm new rights for the child. His wishes really could be countenanced in custody disputes for example. Although in practice the judge would listen and take account of the child's views as he thought fit, he really now ought to ask himself in each case whether he believes the child has sufficient maturity and understanding to give an informed opinion. Equally, though this may cause conflict, a court must act in the best interests of the child, which will of necessity not always be parallel with the views of the child.

As a final point remember that parental authority can now be obtained by the father of an 'illegitimate' child under s. 4 of the Family Law Reform Act 1987.

ELEVEN

CONCLUSION

In the first edition of this book I made the point that the difficulty facing any author is that at the time of writing some matters will remain outstanding. It may even be that a case is waiting to be heard by the Appeal Court or the Lords. As a result the information stated could soon become dated. In looking forward in 1985 I specifically referred to custodianship, legitimacy and human assisted reproduction as issues that would prove of interest to family law students. Custodianship is now part of the law and has attracted judicial attention, mainly in relation to adoption proceedings (see p. 196). The law on the second topic, illegitimacy, has been radically reformed. In fact it may be more accurate to say that there has been a fresh start. There have been many references during the course of this book to the Family Law Reform Act 1987. The net effect is to sweep away the old and to herald in a new order. As the Lord Chancellor said, the policy underlying the Act is that 'to the greatest extent possible the legal position of a child born to unmarried parents should be the same as that of one born to married parents' (Hansard, HL, Vol 482, col. 647). The Act does not abolish the status of illegitimacy but aims as far as possible to remove 'any avoidable discrimination, against or stigma attaching to, children born outside wedlock' (Hansard, Vol 482, col. 647). Students therefore should become familiar with the major changes brought about by this legislation which, sadly, was only partly implemented in April 1988. It is to be expected that new case law will emerge and therefore this topic is likely to appear in your family law course. Pay particular attention to the new powers potentially available to the putative father once he has gained parental rights under s. 4 of the Act. The Act has a major impact on the provisions of the Guardianship of Minors Act 1971, abolishes affiliation proceedings, introduces new scientific tests to establish parentage and deals with the status of a child conceived by A.I.D.

My third prediction related to the creation of new legislation to give effect to the Warnock Report on *Human Fertilisation and Embryology* (Cmnd 9314, 1984). It is sad to report that no new legislation has been forthcoming, other than the hurriedly passed Surrogacy Arrangements Act 1985 prohibiting commercial surrogacy agencies from operating in the United Kingdom. There has been a DHSS Consultation Paper on *Human Infertility Services and Embryo Research* (Cm 46) and one awaits with interest the outcome of what has been a tremendously long period of review and consultation. When proposals for a draft bill surface then the subject may become popular once again with examiners.

This raises the question of what predictions would I care to make about future topics. I think I am on safe ground with Child Care Law Reform. It is suggested that draft legislation would already be with us but for the Cleveland crisis. The Government was obliged to await its recommendations. It is now only a matter of time before we have new proposals.

Whether we are likely to see a Family Court is debatable. Most commentators would appear to favour its creation; only the Treasury would seem against. Lord Justice Butler-Sloss has given her support via the Cleveland Report. In suggesting a new office of Child Protection she is working on the premise that there will be one. Unfortunately no costings have been produced by the Government – but the Family Courts Campaign has predicted that it would cost £15.4m to set up and savings could be from £24-31m. It is 14 years since the Finer Report suggested a Family Court: it may well be another 14 before those aspirations become reality. This fact alone would not stop tutors from including the topic for debate in your course. It is likely to be tied in with an examination of the role of the magistrates' court in domestic cases, together with a rationalisation of jurisdictions in child care custody matters. It is predictable then divorce will resurface as a topic. The Law Commission Discussion Paper, *Facing the Future*, (No. 170 HC 479) was published in May 1988 and recommends a radical reappraisal of the ground/facts supporting divorce. The number of decrees nisi granted in 1986 was the second highest ever at 152,073, which represents 12.9 persons divorcing per thousand married people. The breakdown into the six facts is as follows:

	No. of decrees	*% of all decrees*
Adultery	45,640	30.0%
Behaviour	63,670	41.8%
Desertion	2,770	1.8%
2 years separation with consent	29,790	19.5%
5 years separation	9,100	6.0%
Other	1,090	0.7%

Note: All figures are estimates and have been rounded down to tens, see Table 4.6, 1986 Judicial Statistics, Cm 173, p. 34.

and over 70% of those divorcing do not have to wait in order to comply with the requirements of 1(2)(c)-(e) of the Matrimonial Causes Act 1973. The Paper examines the background and operation of the law of divorce in the light of its original objectives and the hope that it can help reduce bitterness and tension between the parties. It is suggested that irretrievable breakdown as a principle should be retained. The key question to be resolved is how this should be established.

The Commission reject fault as a basis for divorce as it might make matters worse. Mutual consent or immediate unilateral demand provide no safeguards against hasty applications. The two proposals to emerge are:

(a)   divorce after a period of separation;
(b)   divorce after a period of transition in which the parents are given time to reflect and make the necessary arrangements for the future.

The Commission has invited comments and it is likely to be some time before new legislation is drafted.

This is a paper which should be studied carefully, in particular when you are examining the current law on divorce, as the major cases are discussed by the Commission, together with the arguments in favour and against reform.

Finally may I suggest that some attention may be given to the rights of the unborn child. I have mentioned the *Re F (in utero)* case elsewhere in the book and pointed out that it was a unique case for the wardship court to assess. A major issue in 1987 was the reopened debate on the rights (if any exist) of a father to prevent the mother of his child from seeking a termination of the pregnancy. The case of *C* v *S* [1987] 1 All ER 1230 received a lot of media attention but in the end the outcome was the same, although for different reasons, as in the only other case to address the issue, *Paton* v *BPAS* [1978] 2 All ER 987. The father had drawn in aid The Infant Life Preservation Act 1929 which makes it an offence to destroy the life of a child capable of being born alive. The father contended that a foetus of 18-21 weeks was capable of being born alive and the termination of the pregnancy would be an offence. It was held that, as the medical evidence was that a foetus would be incapable of breathing either naturally or with a ventilator, it could not be said to be capable of being born alive. David Alton MP sponsored a Bill which sought to reduce the time limit for abortion from 28 weeks to 18. The Bill was 'talked out' but it may be that its sponsors will endeavour to bring it back before Parliament. If so this could provide the necessary impetus to have a component in your course dealing with the legal position of the unborn child.

Whether my predictions are correct or not I am sure that there will be many issues to examine and that family law will continue to prove to be a stimulating area for study.

BIBLIOGRAPHY

H. K. Bevan & M. L. Parry, *The Children Act 1975* (Butterworths 1979).

P. M. Bromley, *Family Law,* 7th ed. (Butterworths 1987).

S. M. Cretney, *Principles of Family Law,* 4th ed. (Sweet & Maxwell 1984).

R. Dingwall, J. Eekelaar and T. Murray, *The Protection of Children* (Blackwell 1983).

M. Freeman, *Matrimonial and Family Proceedings Act 1984: A Practical Guide* (CCH Editions, 1984)

M. D. A. Freeman, *The Rights and Wrongs of Children* (Frances Pinter 1983).

M. D. A. Freeman & C. M. Lyon, *Cohabitation without Marriage* (Gower 1983).

J. Goldstein, A. Freud & A. J. Solnit, *Before the Best Interests of the Child* (Burnett Books 1980).

J. Goldstein, A. Freud & A. J. Solnit, *Beyond the Best Interests of the Child* (Burnett Books 1980).

B. M. Hoggett & D. S. Pearl, *The Family, Law and Society: Cases and Materials,* 2nd ed. (Butterworths 1987).

N. V. Lowe & R. A. H. White, *Wards of Court,* 2nd ed. (Butterworths 1986).

S. Maidment, *Child Custody and Divorce* (Croom Helm 1984).

J. Masson, D. Norbury & S. G. Chatterton, *Mine, Yours or Ours?* (HMSO 1983).

J. G. Miller, *Family Property and Family Provision,* 2nd ed. (Sweet & Maxwell 1983).

M. Parry, *Cohabitation Law,* 2nd ed. (Sweet & Maxwell 1988).

L. Rosen, *Matrimonial Offences,* 3rd ed. (Oyez 1975).

P. Seago & A. Bissett-Johnson, *Cases and Materials on Family Law* (Sweet & Maxwell 1976).

R. M. Smith, *Matrimonial and Family Proceedings Act 1984: A Practical Guide* (Oyez Longman 1984).

J. S. Wallerstein & J. B. Kelly, *Surviving the Breakup* (Grant McIntyre 1980).

G. Williams, *Learning the Law,* 11th ed. (Stevens 1982).

INDEX

TITLES IN THE SERIES

SWOT Constitutional and Administrative Law
SWOT Law of Torts
SWOT Law of Evidence
SWOT Company Law
SWOT Law of Contract
SWOT Revenue Law
SWOT Land Law
SWOT Criminal Law
SWOT English Legal System
SWOT Equity and Trusts
SWOT Commercial and Consumer Law
SWOT A Level Law
SWOT Jurisprudence
SWOT Family Law
SWOT Employment Law